D0185933

CHRIS
TARRANT'S
EXTREME RAILWAY
JOURNEYS

3
3

CHRIS TARRANT'S EXTREME RAILWAY JOURNEYS

Chris Tarrant

JOHN BLAKE

Published by John Blake Publishing Limited
3 Bramber Court, 2 Bramber Road
London W14 9PB, England

www.johnblakebooks.com

www.facebook.com/johnblakebooks
twitter.com/jblakebooks

First published in hardback in 2016

ISBN 978-1-78606-220-8

British Library Cataloguing-in-Publication Data:

A catalogue record for this book is available from the British Library.

Design by www.envydesign.co.uk

Printed and Bound in the UK by Bell and Bain Ltd

Papers used by John Blake Publishing are natural, recyclable products made from wood grown in sustainable forests. The manufacturing processes conform to the environmental regulations of the country of origin.

Thanks to Bernie, Lucian and Toby for turning my ramblings into English. To all the crews: Thanks for all the sheer fun and for keeping me sane in some insane situations and thanks to Hugh for all his support and for making us all realise that money isn't everything.

CONTENTS

KAM-AVIDA
www.kam-avida.com

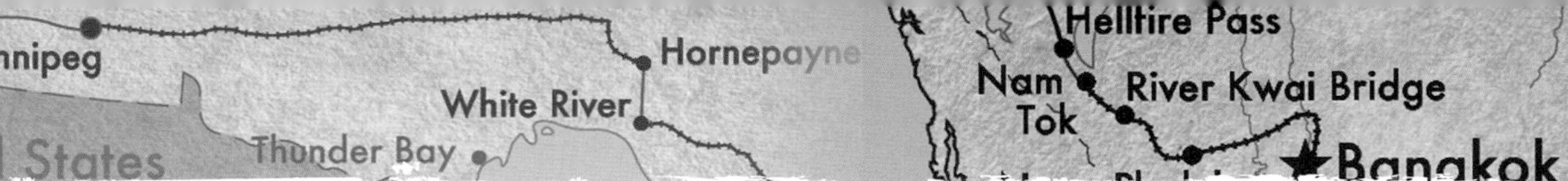

Introduction

I've always, always, loved railways – even as a little boy. My grandad, whose own father had been a railway man, bought me the *Big Book of Railways* for Christmas when I was eight and I read it from cover to cover and marvelled at its pictures for years. I loved the stories of how the old pioneers built the railways, through often seemingly impossible terrain – dense jungle, baking deserts and icy mountain ranges all around the world.

I was never a train spotter, even though we lived close to the old Great Western line in the heyday of steam. I used to see the real spotters, though, happily spotting away on the end of the platform at Reading Central, but they seemed to me to be rather a strange breed, wearing sandals and with their trouser-bottoms rolled up.

It was not the trains but the actual railways that fascinated me, particularly in remote countries with exotic-sounding names like Russia, Alaska, India and Japan. I knew that often, in wild areas of the planet where there were simply no roads, the railways were the only real link for whole populations. I just loved all the stories of the men who had the vision to build the first railways where no one thought it possible, to follow their own – often ridiculed – engineering plan and see it through, although often, tragically, with a large loss of life.

So when Channel 5 offered me an initial four programmes of *Extreme Railways* around the world, I was very excited and jumped at the chance. Outside filming was how I had started my television career, but I'd spent too many nights locked away in studios over the last two or three decades and it would be great to get out again. Little did I know what I'd really let myself in for…

CC 1101
CC 1101

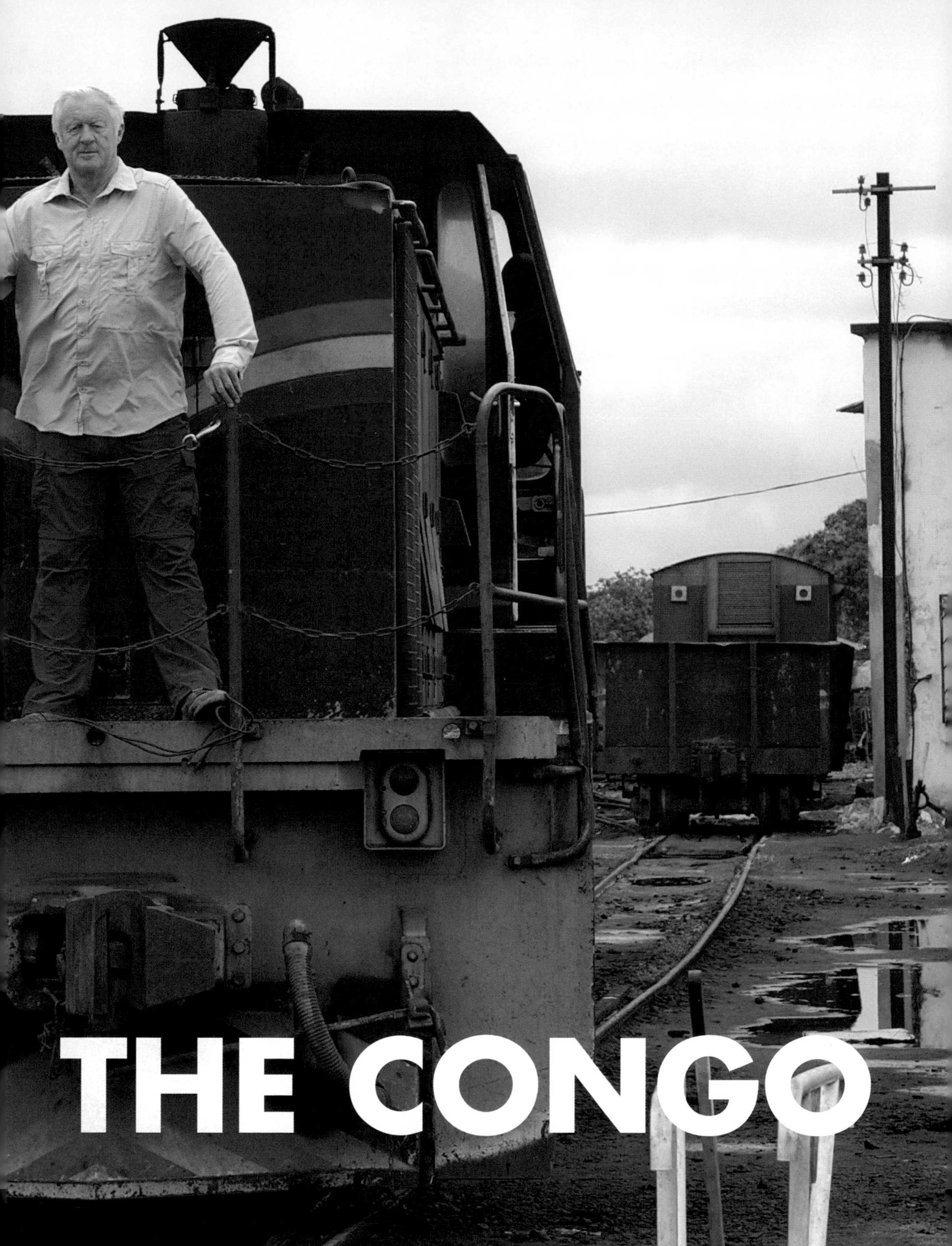

THE CONGO

Kakamoeka
Tchilounga
Bamba tunnel
Loudima
Mouyondzi
Madingou
Brazzaville
Dolisie
Madingo-Kayes
Kinkala

Central African Republic
Cameroon
Bétou
Enyellé
Bomassa
Souanké
Ngbala
Dongou
Sembé
Ouésso
Impfondo
Epéna
Republic of Congo
Mbomo
Pikounda
Ntokou
Etoumbi
Makoua
Kéllé
Orwando
Ewo
Obouya
Boundji
Oyo
Loukoléa
Mossaka
Gabon
Gamboma
N
M'Binda
Lékana
Mayoko
Ngo
Bambama
Djambala
Mpouya
Mossendou
Mossendou
N'Gabé
Komono
Kibangou
Rail
Vinza
Sibiti
Odziba
Kindamba
Mayama
Kakamoeka
Mouyondzi
Loudima
Tchilounga
Bamba tunnel
Madingou
Brazzaville
Dolisie
Kinkala
Madingo-Kayes
Boko
Pointe-Noire
0 50 100 Kilometers
0 50 100 Miles
Atlantic Ocean
Democratic Republic of Congo

The Congo

I was really looking forward to getting started on my first programme of what was a brand-new series. I have to admit that my enthusiasm was dampened when I was told that the first place we were going to visit with our film crew was the Congo.

'Isn't it one of the most dangerous places in the world?' I had the temerity to ask in our first production meeting.

'We're going to the Republic of the Congo,' I was told, 'not the Democratic Republic of Congo; DCR is the really bad one.'

'Oh, right...' I said, not reassured at all by this explanation of degrees of badness and really, *really* badness. I thought to myself, Why couldn't we go somewhere not bad at all, somewhere nice and safe? But, then again, I supposed the series was entitled *Extreme Railways* rather than *Nice and Safe Railways.*

'Actually, I was kidnapped there last time,' added Sam, our mad, Irish cameraman, 'by a load of big, scary, teenage kids with Kalashnikovs... It was really frightening actually; just me and my producer – who's a bit of a wimp. They bundled us into their car. Luckily, we got stopped at a police checkpoint so we made a run for it.' He grinned manically and continued. 'We were both expecting a bullet in the back all the time, but they were just too busy shouting at each other. Lucky. eh?'

'Yes...' I said, '*really* lucky,' thinking, What the hell have I talked myself into?

Roz, our director, said she was due to fly out the next day on a reccy. I said, 'OK, clever clogs, if you get back in one piece we'll go and film it. If you don't, we'll go somewhere else – maybe Monaco or Rome. Or even Swindon.'

I assumed I'd never ever see her again, so when she had the

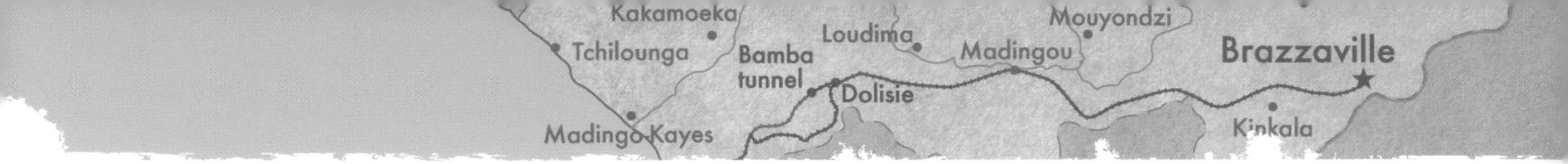

audacity to reappear beaming happily, still in one piece, about ten days later, I thought, Oh, sod it. 'OK,' I said, ' Congo – here I come…'

After a really scary Air France flight through central Africa (will somebody please tell me what the hell clear air turbulence is? Whatever it is – God, it freaks me out!), we landed bouncily but happy to be on the ground at Pointe-Noire, one of the biggest ports in West Africa, where our first extreme journey was to begin.

Passing through Passport Control to enter the country of Congo was predictably chaotic but this was to be the pattern for the next few weeks. Lots and lots of incomprehensible bureaucracy and lots of men in big hats and uniforms who did a lot of shouting, but didn't actually seem to have any idea of what was supposed to be going on.

Standing in a queue of shouting people waving passports and being sent repeatedly to the back was daunting enough, especially with a film crew and mountains of very expensive camera gear, but the queue for yellow fever documentation was even longer and much more heavily policed. Luckily, I had all my jabs and certificates up to date, but there was certainly no messing with the Congolese authorities. If you hadn't got proof of current yellow fever inoculations you would be either pointed very roughly towards the queue for the next flight out – or much much more frighteningly – you would be taken by one of three men in white coats holding up syringes into a little tent and given your yellow fever vaccination jab on the spot. Thank God they accepted my paperwork, as absolutely nothing would have induced me to risk one of their horribly blunt-looking needles.

We spent the night in a hotel, supposedly one of Pointe-Noire's finest but not so much five-star as AA-one-spanner. We found our way to the big main station – actually the only station in town, to board the 11 am Congo Ocean Railway train to Brazzaville, the country's capital. The station was unlike anywhere I had ever seen on earth, there was no departure board, nor any visible information of any sort, and seemingly nobody to ask. But there were literally thousands of men, women, children, tiny babies, dogs and a good number of bewildered looking goats, all seemingly waiting for the

Left: At the station at the start of the big wait for the only train out of town.

Below: Before I learned that it was near Bilinga station that a crash claimed the lives of many passengers.

11 am train. I had to produce my passport yet again to buy my ticket, but that seemed to guarantee that I would be on the COR express to go racing across the Congo to the capital.

However, 11 am came and went, then 11.30, 12 noon and 1 pm and still –although the station was jammed with hopeful travellers – not a single train appeared. Eventually, sometime in mid-afternoon, a single locomotive came out of nowhere, albeit pointing in the wrong direction, there were no announcements and still nothing at all on the information board.

I'd waited a very long time but I didn't want to get on the wrong train after all this. Eventually, I found myself a very nice man with gold epaulettes and a splendid hat, who was able to assure me that, yes, sir, this was indeed was my locomotive, there had been an electrical fault and it would just make a full turn-around, couple up to the carriages for the journey and off to Brazzaville we would all go. A little late with his apologies but at least we would be on our way!

I was never to see that engine or that man in the gold epaulettes and the splendid hat ever again in my life. The hours dragged on, the huge crowd began to dwindle and disperse to God-only-knows where. By 6 pm it was cold and dark, I was the only person left on the platform, I was fed up and I badly wanted a drink. There was absolutely no sign of the 11 am train to Brazzaville. The COR had failed to roll.

THE LONG WAIT

After a disturbed night, dreaming of trains going straight through stations unannounced and the lights of guards' vans disappearing into the night, leaving us and our mountains of gear on the platform, we were actually all up and out early. We assumed the train would surely be there sometime on the second morning. We hurried through our breakfast of dried bread, liver sausage and cheese and ran to the station.

It was closed. The gates were locked, there was a padlock and chain across and the great masses of hopefuls from yesterday were nowhere to be seen. There was clearly a very effective bush telegraph telling everybody for miles around when there was a train coming or, as was very clearly the case this morning, there was not. Nor this afternoon either. We got to evening without seeing a single train; we weren't panicking just yet but, particularly as it was the first programme of a brand-new series, we were certainly getting a tad worried.

The train had been scheduled for Saturday morning and it was now late on Sunday and there was still not a sign of the pride of the Congo Ocean Railway fleet. I had to be back in London in just over a week's time and we still hadn't filmed a single train – except for one going the wrong way. There was no train Monday again either, as the station again didn't open all day. We whiled away the time doing interviews with officials, drivers, guards and a man in the town's only signal box (now there's a lonely job!). We shot lots of pretty views of the station square, the platform and a few bridges; indeed, we filmed everything except for an actual train moving along an actual track.

We were assigned a Congo railway Mr Jobsworth official whose only function seemed to be chaperoning us at all times, including meals, and following us everywhere, even though we had virtually nothing to do. He was irritating, to say the least and we had one massive row with him when we tried to film me pretending to be asleep on the platform. He was enraged that we dared to suggest that their railway was anything other than punctual and, in a screaming tantrum, insisted that we give him everything we had filmed for him to tear up – even though nobody has used film for donkey's years... After much shouting, we let him have a reel of old holiday snaps that he ripped triumphantly into shreds to teach us all a lesson. It was a silly moment of light relief in yet another hopelessly frustrating day.

By Friday night, our spirits were very low. We began to think that this film and maybe even this series simply wasn't going to happen. As we ate a fairly unhappy dinner on the Wednesday evening, our young fixer guy came in excitedly from town. 'People are starting to fill the station again,' he said. 'They're all getting down to sleep there overnight, the train is definitely coming first thing tomorrow morning!' Where they all appeared from and who told them it was coming, I had no idea, but they all apparently just knew and, sure enough, early the next day – Saturday morning, just five days, one hour and 55 minutes late – there was the COR.

When the train with all its carriages came powering – well, limping actually – into the station, a huge cheer went up and people spilled all over the long passenger train. I hadn't known quite what to expect, but I've never seen anything like it. People were jammed together, some with their faces forced against the windows in each carriage, but somehow the whole mass of humanity got on the train. I say 'got on' – while most of them were inside, quite a few, perhaps those who simply couldn't afford a ticket, sat on the roof (something I'd never seen before) and even sat on the couplings between carriages. In at least two cases, while holding tiny babies. At the time, I found this absolutely terrifying although, now, three years and three series of *Extreme Railways* around the world later, I've seen a lot of it and I hardly turn a hair.

And suddenly – amazingly – we were off! With a mighty long toot of the whistle and, hopefully, just under 24 hours to go. Brazzaville, here we come. We made our way out of the densely populated centre of Pointe-Noire; there were people and children everywhere walking across the track, although somehow nobody ever actually did get run over. I'm pretty sure it must happen though and I suspect quite often.

We seemed to stop at every tiny local station. I could see right into the desperate homes around the tracks and I got a pretty quick pen portrait of how tough life is for most of the Congolese. As I have discovered, railways seem to look into a country's soul. I could also see very quickly how important this train was for lives and livelihoods. There are very few roads at all in the Congo and the railway provides an economic lifeline for the whole population, from Congo's west coast heading east through hundreds of miles of dense jungle.

It was a joyous trip; people after the long wait were in great spirits and there was even a Salvation Army band in one of the carriages. At one point, I joined in as lead tambourine!

The railway has been running since 1934, although they have had a lot of problems. It is a very dangerous and unhealthy region, prone to accidents, yet somehow the French built 610 kilometres of track, 92 bridges and ten million cubic metres of embankments.

We headed deep into the Mayombe jungle, where there was a particular point at which the train very obviously slowed down. This was where the old colonial line, snaking its way north, reached the most treacherous part of the journey. As I looked around me everybody in the carriage was making the sign of the cross. This would be what on a main road in UK we would call an accident black-spot. It's called the Mayombe escarpment; simply,

Taking a break between rides.

miles of savage mountainous terrain and virtually impenetrable jungle with rainfall and water from rivers making the ground extremely wet and unstable. It was very prone to landslides and falling rocks and trees.

DERAILMENT DEEP IN THE JUNGLE

Four major accidents have happened at this spot in the railway's history. The most catastrophic one was two years ago, when 76 people were killed and over 700 injured. Four passenger carriages came off the rails and plunged down into a ravine. This was why everybody makes the sign of the cross at that point. Gruesomely, a lot of the carriages are still down there at the bottom of the ravine, perfectly visible although covered with vines and presumably still with the bodies of the accident victims inside. It is simply too difficult and dangerous to get rescue equipment and vehicles down there.

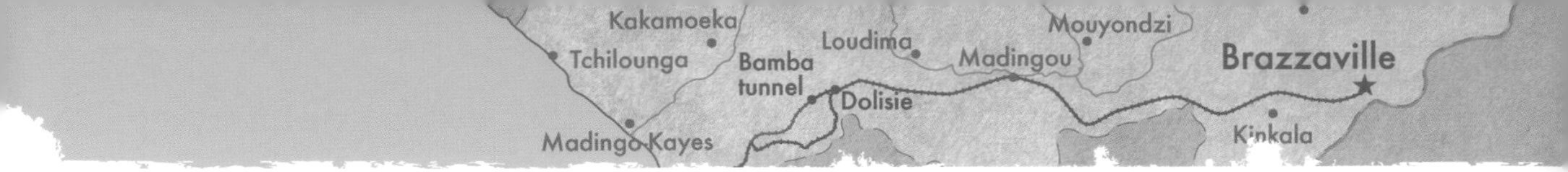

One of the big problems in the Congo, as I was to discover replicated in many other parts of the world, is that they have spent millions on all sorts of brand-new, mainly Chinese trains, but have been using the same old tracks for years. There are many many catastrophic derailments.

We made our way past a long line of sad little graves dotted along the side of the escarpment and we were very glad to be moving carefully along the rails with no sign of slipping or sliding. It had been raining during the day and the evening became very dark. Sometime around midnight, after we'd all had a couple of drinks, some bread and cheese and a bit of a doze, I was vaguely aware of the train slowing down and then stopping altogether. People were shouting from other carriages and I became quite alarmed. The train was plunged into total darkness.

This was the one time we did need some help from Mr Jobsworth from the Congo railway, but he was in a deep sleep, brought on, we discovered, by nicking our entire wine and beer ration for the next ten days and taken it to his carriage. At that moment, spark out as he was, in the corner of his cosy looking sleeper, it was tempting to wake him up and give him a smack.

However, we were genuinely frightened – we had broken down in a tunnel in the middle of the night somewhere in the Congo. Apparently, there was an electrical fault so there was no lighting and no heating. It was very cold, dark and we were unlikely to move for several hours. We decided that it was not a good plan to remain on the train, as there were a lot of very strange and quite alarming noises coming from along the carriages and the crew– two women and three blokes, plus me – decided to make a long walk towards, hopefully, the nearest village. Not that we had a clue if there even was such a thing. This was probably not a brilliant idea, but it seemed to make a lot of sense at the time. The night was absolutely pitch-black, the tunnel itself had water running down both sides of the rock, which, as we sloshed our way through it, stank of human excrement.

So here we were, in the middle of the night in the notorious Congo, on a train that was five days late and had then broken down in the middle of nowhere, splashing about in total darkness, up to our knees in shit. Would the fun ever start?

We trudged on out of the tunnel and along the main track in the darkness. We were each very silent with our own thoughts, but I for one was genuinely scared. We might have believed there was a village a couple of miles further down the line but who lived there? Would we be remotely welcome at this time of night? We had no idea.

After about half an hour, we could see lights moving towards us; it turned out to be a relief engine to come and take our stricken train on towards Brazzaville. There was every chance that this train would break down also and it was quite a long walk back, but at least we knew pretty much what we were going back to, as opposed to the mystery village option.

This was turning into the longest night of my life. When we finally got back to the train there were a lot of people standing around, aimlessly looking at the point where the two engines were being connected up. We got back into our carriage, still in total darkness, to find a lot of completely new people in our seats. Suddenly, all the lights came back on, everybody re-arranged themselves and we were back in the same seats where we had started and we were off again.

Most people did seem to be quite upset and fed up, but within another hour or so there were lights in the distance and we pulled into the station of Dolisie. It was two o'clock in the morning and we were eight hours late. We were thirsty, we were starving, but above all we were happy to be getting off without any other incident.

We had no communication from the train with anybody, and we wondered whether the hotel that we booked would even still be open, but we needn't have worried. There's a very strong bush telegraph that somehow works in the Congo and not only was our

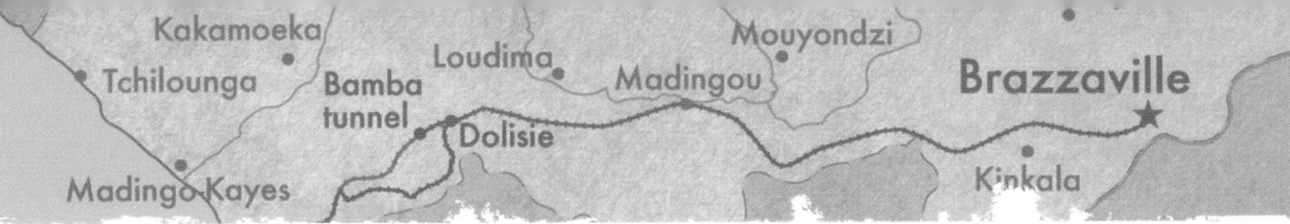

Discussing Congo's railways with a senior railway employee.

hotel open but they obviously heard the news of our disastrous night. The restaurant was still open and they'd prepared an enormous feast and lashings of wine and whisky.

Suddenly all seemed terribly well.

BEHIND THE SCENES

We had a good night's sleep and we spent the whole of the next day wandering around Dolisie. It is now the third biggest town of the Congo, behind Brazzaville and the DRC's Kinshasa and I got a chance to see a lot of the locomotives in their engine sheds. Several of them looked fairly new but even they were already in a state of disrepair. A very helpful guy called Ekondy Akala tried to explain to me what happened here.

'Many of these trains come from Germany and France,' he said. 'We also buy many from China because they are cheap, but the more expensive ones do not seem to last any longer than the

Chinese ones. We need more investment – more than anything we need investment to buy track. The government has now finally realised that only once we have new tracks can we have more locomotives; this is very important. Of the 25 locomotives that the railway owns, only 11 are operational. The boys here in the sheds do their best to make do and we do not always have the money to get spare parts from China and Germany.'

I had seen behind the scenes but not only didn't I feel more reassured, I was more frightened than ever. What was quite heartening was that some of the best engines that they had were much older and still going strong and they were British. Makes you feel proud doesn't it? But if the Congo's railway authorities can't find new tracks and put in place a system of constant monitoring along the main lines, then there are always going to be the dangers that have plagued their railways over many years.

Daniel Mayenge, a well-known Congolese historian, spent the rest of the day with me. He was a really good bloke and very helpful. He managed to get us permission to take a ride on a completely disused section of the old track. We got onto one of those hand-driven wagons that you only ever really see in cowboy films, but apparently this was the way we were going to travel on the old original colonial jungle line built by the French nearly a hundred years ago.

We travelled west from Dolisie through the Mayombe jungle heading for the infamous Bamba tunnel. This was the original line, the very first one built. It was very very bumpy and, if it didn't feel particularly safe, that's because it wasn't. At many points there was a sheer drop on either side and each time we went around a bend, I had a horrible feeling that we were going to come off the line and go straight on, it was all very precarious. It didn't help when Daniel, laughing, said, 'We will probably die!' I think this was what passes in the Congo for humour. How I laughed...

This section of line did have a really bad history. The French constructed the line in the 1920s and needed thousands of labourers. The conditions were so harsh, with heat and disease,

We took a trip down the old colonial stretch of the tracks.

that many of the locals ran away. The French then conscripted men from all over equatorial Africa. In total, 127,000 men worked on this line, more than a quarter of whom died from malaria, sleeping sickness, dysentery and sheer exhaustion. But the worst tragedy took place inside the Bamba tunnel. We travelled right into it. The tunnel had been carved from the rock by hand; it was very cold and really eerie with running water pouring down both sides. It was impossible to spot the entrance from any distance; the jungle was reclaiming it – and fast.

When the workforce at Bamba first dug through soil that had not been turned over for hundreds, possibly thousands, of years, they unwittingly let out great jets of carbon monoxide. Worker after worker died where they stood – something like 80 per cent died on the spot from gas poisoning. Horrifically, the gas was odourless, so none of them had any idea of what was happening to their workmates around them. They just all fell down in heaps and died where they had been working. For a long time there was no explanation. It was simply a mystery. There were rumours of voodoo and witchcraft.

We travelled on the next morning to Brazzaville, and this time we were in the pride of the Congo-Ocean Railway's new fleet. Daniel told me proudly it was called the *Gazelle*. 'It will leap towards Brazzaville', he told me, doing a strange animation of a gazelle leaping. 'We will be there in no time.'

I have to say I was impressed. Firstly, because I then heard the first station announcement since arriving in the Congo and, secondly, because the Gazelle leapt into our station a full five minutes early. On the Sunday morning that we boarded it, the Gazelle was only ten days old. The Congolese had paid the South Koreans £10 million for 23 new carriages and with the capital, Brazzaville, in theory now just 12 hours away, I felt the end might even be in sight.

We had to travel 200 miles eastwards to the banks of the Congo river and the Gazelle was certainly luxurious. It had air conditioning, lovely upholstery, phone points, laptop power points, buffet service and ice-cold beer. I kept expecting some dreadful catch but there wasn't one; it was a beautiful thing and people scrambled to get on board at every station. I just hoped that it had a great future, but I was very aware of the dense jungle and the extreme climate that constantly threatened to swallow up or just wash the railway line away.

DANGER OF NINJAS ON THE TRACKS

As we came into a region called the Pool department, we were warned that this area used to be famous for a militia called the Ninja. They supposedly no longer posed a threat, although I had noticed several armed guards scattered all the way along the Gazelle. It wasn't particularly reassuring though – at least two of them looked like they would bolt at the slightest sign of trouble and one looked as if he was no more than ten years old.

The Ninjas used to attack the train between Brazzaville and Pointe-Noire. They had been formed during Congo's most recent civil war – Congo is always in the middle of a civil war. They lived somewhere in the deep jungle and were extremely dangerous. They would hold the train up, get all the passengers to give them their valuables and sometimes kill the men and rape the women. On other occasions they created derailments with rocks or large piles of timber, after which they just helped themselves to anything valuable that they found on the train. Daniel told me this with a huge grin on his silly face when, after all we'd been through and with a real hope that this train would finally get us to Brazzaville in one piece, it was the last thing I wanted to hear. But maybe the Ninjas were a depleted force because we had no problems and my wallet and watch both arrived in the capital still attached to me.

It was here that Daniel announced that he was so famous in the Congo – which apparently he is – that he was being given his own chat show on the local TV station. 'Congratulations,' I said.

'Ah, yes,' he said, 'but at the moment we have no guests for my show. I would very much like you to be my first.'

I couldn't really refuse and, once we got to Brazzaville, instead of me having a large meal, a few bottles of wine and thinking, Thank God that's over, I had Daniel whisking me away to the last place where I really wanted to spend an extra minute of my life: a television studio. I have to say, though, it was a studio with a difference. I grinned happily as Daniel went about preparing for our interview because, bless him, the facilities were pretty desperate. He and I sat poles apart in the studio, with two hand microphones, which always looks a bit silly. They had three cameras but only two operators, one of whom kept grinning at me. I wasn't quite sure how it was all going to work. Instead of Daniel wearing an earpiece to hear commands, the director would emerge from a door upstairs to bellow instructions.

So, on his shouted, 'Three, two, one – go, Daniel!', I was introduced and started answering his questions... He was very nice, a little nervous, but really endearing; we chatted about what I was doing in the Congo and I glossed over the fact that the train had been

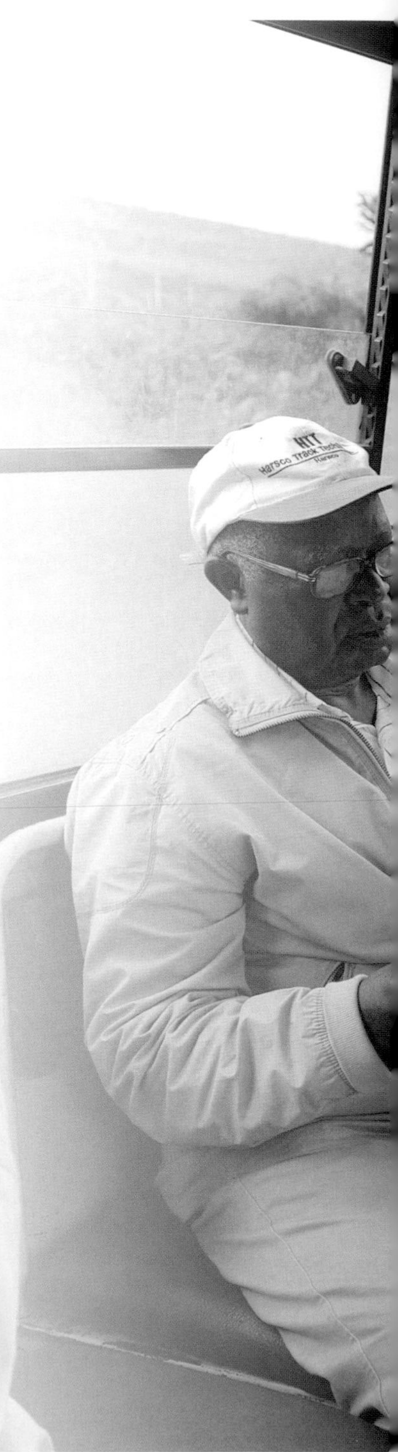

Rumours of devils and worse came along with the unexplained deaths of workers in part of the line.

five days late and said everything had gone well and I was very impressed with the facilities on the Gazelle. I urged any authorities watching to invest as much money in new tracks as they did in shiny new engines, otherwise the whole thing would be fraught with peril...

At one point, out of the corner of my eye, I caught a strange scurrying and I realised there was something going on that I had never seen before in any television studio. On some sort of cue, the nice woman on Camera Two rushed around to take over Camera Three, while the big, tall man on camera one went around to be on Camera Two. It was to give them one extra shot but any viewer would clearly hear the scampering of feet.

You couldn't make it up.

Brazzaville itself was a wonderful, lively city and I felt completely safe walking the streets at night, really enjoying the sense of having completed an extraordinary journey.

There was one place I still had to to visit before we flew back to London. I had seen pictures of it in books as a young boy and I just had to get there. We squeezed ourselves into dugout canoes – pirogues – and we wobbled precariously through a series of small streams to get ourselves onto the banks of the Congo river where it rages between the two capital cities, Kinshasa on the far shore and Brazzaville.

I have seen massive raging rivers all over the world; I've seen Victoria Falls, Niagara Falls and gone through some wild rapids in Russia, northern Canada and Alaska, but I have never ever seen anything like the maelstrom that the Congo river creates at this point. It is well over a mile wide and is the wildest stretch of water on earth. God only knows what is happening to the rock formations underneath, but it is nature at her most savage. If you fell in you would drown within seconds and it is completely impassable by boat which, of course, is why the Congo-Ocean Railway had to be built. Without this amazing railway, with all its false starts and troubles, being built through the jungle, the tremendous wealth of minerals that the Congo has beneath its soil could not possibly ever have reached the sea to be exported. This is why so many men were forced to build this railway and, tragically, this is why so many had to die.

Preparing to shoot the river sequence for the programme, on the banks of the mighty Congo, between two countries.

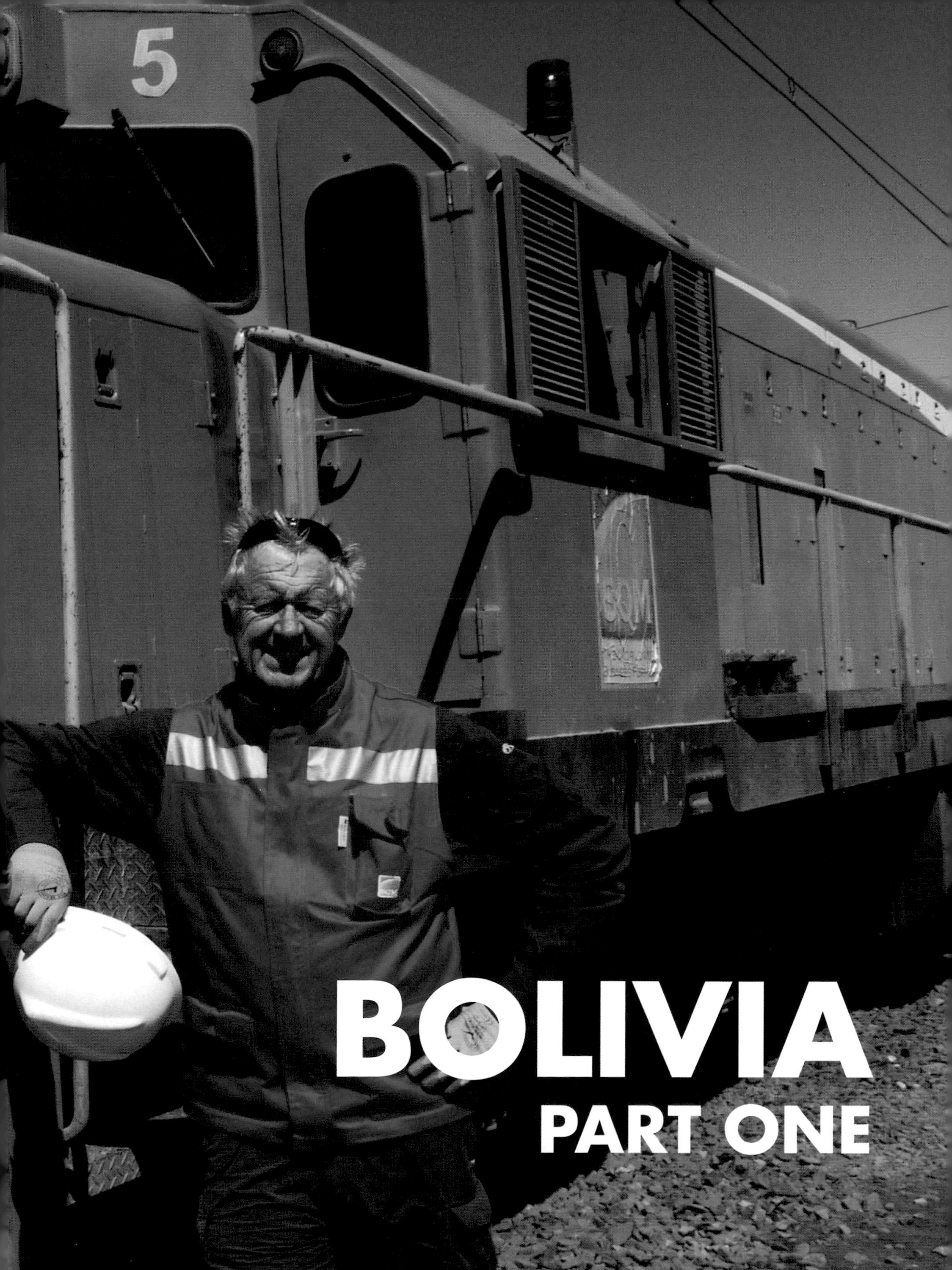

BOLIVIA
PART ONE

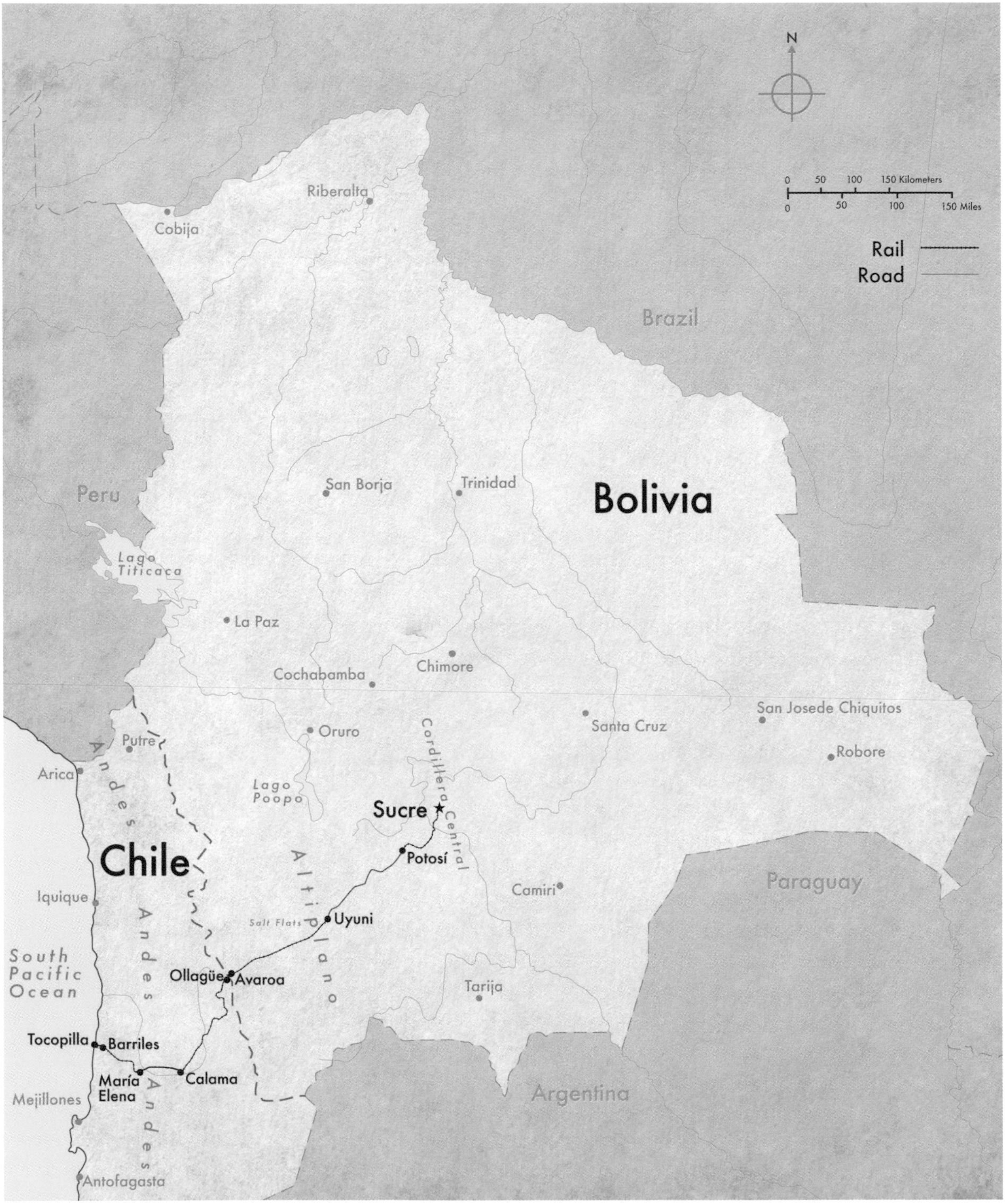

N

0 50 100 150 Kilometers
0 50 100 150 Miles

Rail
Road

Riberalta
Cobija
Brazil
Peru
San Borja
Trinidad
Bolivia
Lago Titicaca
La Paz
Cochabamba
Chimore
Oruro
Santa Cruz
San Josede Chiquitos
Robore
Putre
Arica
Andes
Lago Poopo
Cordillera Central
Sucre
Chile
Potosí
Altiplano
Paraguay
Iquique
Camiri
Salt Flats
Uyuni
South Pacific Ocean
Andes
Ollagüe
Avaroa
Tarija
Tocopilla
Barriles
María Elena
Calama
Mejillones
Andes
Argentina
Antofagasta

Bolivia
Part One

Apart from a lost week in Venezuela at some point in the 1960s, I'd never been to South America, never been to Brazil – even for the World Cup – and certainly never been to Chile or Bolivia. Little did I know then that I was going to go to both of these wild countries – twice – in the space of 12 months.

My journey started almost 6,000 miles from home, on the northern coast of Chile, at a remote mining town called Tocopilla. The place was heaving, like Blackpool on a rare sunny bank holiday. It was baking hot and everybody was jumping in and out of the sea. We assembled in a bar next to the Pacific, drank a couple of fairly savage pisco sours and looked at the map of our journey. Behind us was the ocean, looking very welcoming; immediately in front of us were the Andes, which rise straight up from the sea all along the coast. They are one of the driest, highest and most inhospitable places on Earth and – of course – instead of spending a week swimming in the warm waters of the Pacific, we were going straight up the mountains by train. Trains don't like climbing hills, let alone mountains; they don't like going up steep inclines at all. Come to think of it, nor do I...

In the nineteenth century, nitrates were discovered in this part of the world. Known locally as white gold, they were an important ingredient in the making of gunpowder and for that reason very much in demand all around the world. Our first journey would be to reach a little mining train and the only way the miners could get there was by going up the sheer face of the mountain. Our driver was a very friendly man, Alberto (every man you meet in South America is called Alberto and, if he's not called Alberto, then he's almost certainly a woman,).

Our mining marvel took us far above sea level into the Andes.

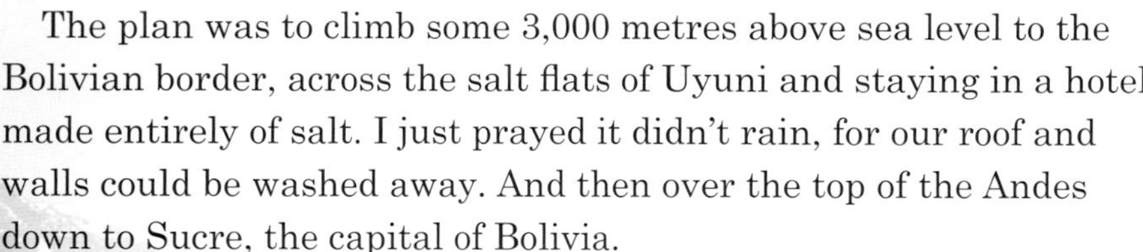

The plan was to climb some 3,000 metres above sea level to the Bolivian border, across the salt flats of Uyuni and staying in a hotel made entirely of salt. I just prayed it didn't rain, for our roof and walls could be washed away. And then over the top of the Andes down to Sucre, the capital of Bolivia.

The first time a train climbed these savage mountains was in 1888. A Chilean engineer, Ossa Manuel Ruiz, used a technique called the switchback. Instead of the train going straight up, it zig-zagged from side to side. The train gets to a certain point and the train at the front becomes the back and the train at the back becomes the front. Do you understand that? No? Neither did I, but slowly we did seem to make our way up the sheer scarp face moving erratically from side to side.

The creation of this railway was an amazing bit of engineering that took a tremendous toll on human life. Hundreds of workers died trying to lay track on these very steep rock-faces. Alberto kept smiling and pointing down to the valley, a long way below. I kept suggesting in limited Spanish that it would be better if he kept his eyes in front and concentrated on the job in hand. He said, kind of reassuringly, that going up Qa not too difficult but that coming down was far harder. Today's load was very heavy, he explained: we could be carrying more than 725 tons so they had to be extra cautious.

One weird fact about the railway is that in the early days they employed footballers to drive the trains in their spare time because of their fast reflexes. Of course, as the wages of South American footballers grew higher and higher while the wages of railwaymen stayed pretty much the same, it became a bit of a no-brainer for the likes of Pelé and Maradona to choose football as their career path rather than becoming train drivers.

There are 228 tight bends on this particular railway and Alberto laughingly said, 'I know all these bends blindfolded.' I did not find this comforting in the slightest and suggested to him, fairly forcibly, that a blindfold was really not a good idea.

The track got higher and became steeper. After a couple of hours, we were right in the middle of the famous Atacama desert; remote, wild country that was once part of Bolivia but now, like much of the land close to the coast, belongs to Chile. We arrived at Barriles – a thousand metres above sea level – quite quickly and the end of the first section of our long journey. It already seemed to me a long way up, but apparently was nothing in comparison with what lay ahead.

I went to explore Barriles only to quickly discover that there was absolutely nothing there. However, it was an important stopping point. The bigger, tougher freight trains take over from the small mining trains at this point and make their way to the María Elena nitrate mine, which is a source of tremendous wealth still to this day – but for the Chileans rather than the Bolivians. This is a sore point between the two countries; in fact, many Bolivians talk of little else.

The tremendous amount of minerals under the soil in this area would simply never have been exported without the railway. Some 700,000 tons of nitrates are excavated annually from this one mining area alone and taken to the Chilean coast. It's still very much in demand but more now for fertilizers than gunpowder.

Although the land was Bolivian at the end of the 19th century it was the British who seemed to get in everywhere and the Chileans, who worked the mines, built the railways and took most of the profits. In the 1870s Bolivia began to heavily tax the profit from the nitrate mines and Chile decided to invade. It became known as the War of the Pacific. At Calama, I met a splendid Bolivian lady, Esther Aillon, who came begrudgingly into what she clearly saw as the enemy land of Chile to talk to me at the foot of a monument to all the Bolivians who died there. She told me bitterly that the Chileans never officially declared war – they simply invaded and never went home. By 1883, thousands of men on both sides had lost their lives, but Chile had totally defeated the Bolivians. They annexed land, particularly the coastline, and have been making millions from mining the land that once belonged to Bolivia ever since. The railways have made it possible to exploit the vast wealth that lay beneath what was, for centuries, Bolivian soil. Esther became very emotional when she talked about what happened.

At the monument to the War of the Pacific with Esther Aillon.

She said, 'Our country has been mutilated and it really hurts; it hurts me at a national level. This was our land, the old province of Atacama, the coastal province. It should never have been stolen, but there is nothing we can do about it.'

CROSSING ATACAMA

We moved on to catch the next train crossing hundreds of miles of Atacama desert, going up higher towards the new border of Bolivia, now a long way from the sea. As I went further into the mountains I wondered what lay ahead. Apparently, altitude sickness could be a big problem. Even Gloria – our splendid but completely barking Bolivian guide – said she 'didn't relish travelling too high and that she often became extremely sick'. Oh, great, and she went on: 'it can have all sorts of unpleasant side effects and sometimes can be downright dangerous.' Well, that was something to look forward to, wasn't it?

At this point, we were travelling from Calama to the town of Ollagüe, where we would be somewhere over 3,500 metres above sea

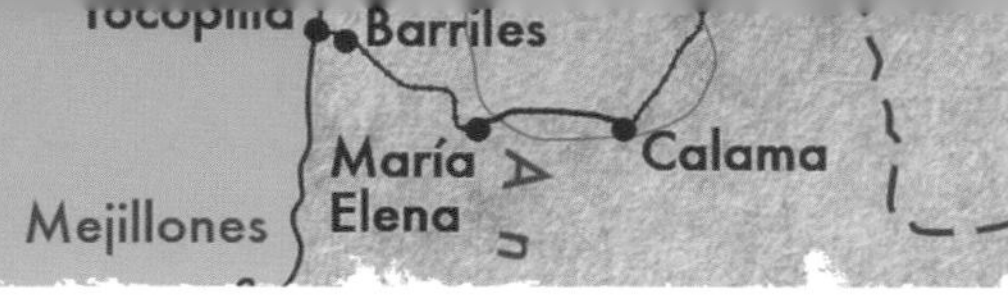

level. That was the first point when altitude sickness could become a real problem. We arrived to find Ollagüe was – and I don't mean this unkindly – a complete and utter dump. It was a one small-high-street town of the sort that you see in dozens of westerns. Usually there would be a gunfight in the street and a piano tinkling away in the one and only bar in town. The good news at Ollagüe was that there were no gunfights; the bad news is that there was no sign of a saloon either – not even an off licence. But we'd made it to the border in what is now Chile – except it used to be Bolivia and about a kilometre away was the new Bolivian border.

This meant the border between the two still very much opposed countries wasn't a particularly happy place. The Bolivians still mine a lot of valuable reserves of metal and minerals, but of course they have to pay now to get to the coast. There is an uneasy truce between the two countries and the border is very much no man's land.

It was also baking hot. We had to get off our train at the Chilean border, walk the kilometre across absolutely nothing to get to the customs and migration area of Bolivia. I had to present a lot of papers to two lots of customs staff, plus the Chilean police and the Bolivian police. We were at a station called Avaroa and, luckily, the next train was three hours late so I had plenty of time on my hands and absolutely nothing to do. There was one single train and one single track with a few sidings but, apart from that, when I actually was allowed into Bolivia by the customs and the migrations and the police, all of whom had a separate go at stamping my passport and jabbering at me incomprehensibly, there was nothing there.

I was due to catch the 1 pm to Uyuni, the only passenger train due anywhere from the Bolivian border for three days. I was an hour late by the time I got through all the bureaucracy but clearly I'd missed nothing. There did seem to be a lot of confusion about when and if the train actually would arrive. A man in a big hat pointed very excitedly to one particular train that he seemed to be assuring me was mine. However, it was pointing in the wrong direction and there was absolutely nobody on it. He disappeared for about an hour and came back smiling, and saying, 'You're right,

Bored at the Bolivian border, there was little to do but wait for the connecting train.

it is not your train. We have no record of this train, we don't know why it's here or what it's doing but it's not the one you want.'

'Great,' I said. 'Thank you so much.'

I amused myself by playing Van Morrison's 'Gloria' at full volume to our barking Bolivian, with the crew all chanting the chorus. She was highly amused and delighted and it became a daily ritual as we travelled. I sensed that she became less amused and delighted with each day that passed... and in fairness, you probably would be, too, but we all sang on, undeterred. Gloria was a wonderful woman, fiercely proud of her heritage, highly political, very intelligent and a really good laugh... which, in a place as wild and unpredictable as South America, was a tremendous asset.

Meanwhile, back at the station, a couple of freight trains shunted back and forth and they were clearly not mine either. And then we were told by the man who assured us earlier that the wrong train was the right train that the next train was definitely the right train. Surprisingly enough, I had no faith in him whatsoever and of course I was right. It turned out to be a goods train with no carriages or people, but several trucks full of coal.

And then a funny little man in a red helmet peeped out of just what might be a passenger coach and seemed to be suggesting to another man on what I laughingly called the platform – basically an area of flattened sand – that the train might link up with another seemingly abandoned locomotive that just happened to be pointing in the right direction and could actually be ours. 'This is wonderful!' I said. 'Can I get on it?'

'Yes, of course,' he said, mystified as to why I even dared to doubt him.

A bit of a 'toot-toot' came from inside the cab and, four hours later than planned, I was on my way. Almost punctual. This was a beautiful train with lovely, real leather seats, magnificent oak-panelled interiors and absolutely nobody else on the train, just me.

For 140 miles across Bolivia to the great salt flats of Uyuni – this was the high plateau of the Andes they call the Altiplano; it was the most breathtaking journey. The scenery was like nothing on this planet. Thick, red sand and high peaks, all along the horizon, typical of the terrain chosen for many classic western films. And it is no coincidence that one of the greatest westerns of them all, *Butch Cassidy and the Sundance Kid*, was made here in this part of Bolivia.

GETTING HIGH

We were now over 3,900 metres, a long way up, and we were starting to experience the first effects of altitude sickness. I had been getting headaches for several hours but I thought that was just the brightness of the sun, the heat and the dust. Gloria and a couple of the lads on the crew were feeling distinctly ill. At this point she decided to do a breakdown for us all on the effects of altitude sickness. Cerebral oedema – the brain swelling with liquid – apparently was one regular problem, although she suggested, rather unkindly, that it was unlikely to affect me. Vomiting is also common, but the real symptom to watch out for was if your lips start to turn violet. This means your body is suffering from an acute lack of oxygen.

She had a bag that was full of strange offshoots from the coca plant used to counteract the effects. I, as someone who has never taken a drug in my life, was rather wary of this, particularly as I was pretty sure we were in a part of the world where cocaine played a major part in the economy, but she went to great lengths to explain to me that cocaine has nothing to do with the coca leaf they have been using since ancient times. The Incas used the magic leaf centuries ago. It helps with altitude sickness, is a natural product and is completely harmless. To transform coca leaves into cocaine you would need a lot of kerosene, none of which, funnily enough, I was carrying in my hand luggage.

Gloria made some coca tea that was actually quite pleasant. She then offered us all some coca sweets that were actually quite disgusting. God – they were awful, but they did take my mind off my headache. We chewed coca leaves for a while which didn't make me feel much better but gave me lovely, bright green teeth.

The sun was beginning to set and, of course, being the desert,

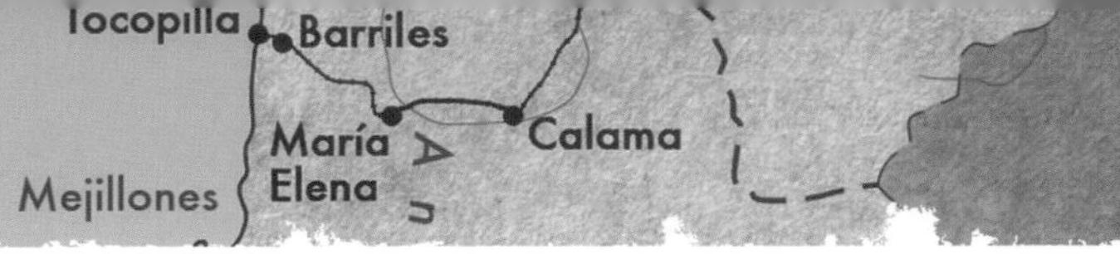

while it had been baking hot only an hour ago, it was now getting rather chilly. At this point our train broke down.

'Oh, flipping great,' I said, 'flipping wonderful.'

We were now stranded in the desert in the middle of absolutely nowhere. There was no electricity, of course, which meant there was no light or heating and we had no blankets because we didn't expect any of this to happen. All our warm clothes, food and restorative alcohol were in the crew car and that was – guess where? – also broken down, somewhere 20 miles behind us, bogged down to the axles in wet sand. A second rescue car went to dig them out of the sand and that too got stuck.

So here we were, sitting on an immobile train, freezing cold, 3,900 metres above sea level in the middle of the Atacama desert at night, our crew car and the rescue car somewhere a long way behind us; we had no light, no warm clothing and, of course, there was no bar. Things couldn't get worse, could they? Of course they could – because at this point, it started to rain.

We finally were rescued by yet another vehicle that appeared out of nowhere about three hours after dark. We were very, very pleased to see it and after a lot of 'navigation difficulties' (ie, we got completely lost), eventually we found our way into the famous hotel made entirely of salt about two o'clock in the morning. I was delighted to get to my room after the fairly disastrous last few hours, but it was well after midnight, it was still pouring with rain and I wondered if my hotel room – in fact, the whole hotel – would still be there in the morning…

But I woke up to a stunning view of the Uyuni salt flats, the clouds had cleared and the hotel – *Luna Salada,* the 'salt hotel' – hadn't been rained away. The roof, the wall, the floor – are all made of salt and the hotel has stunning views of the vast salt flats. If you want salt with your breakfast, you can just get it off the floor and sprinkle it on your eggs which, of course, I did – to the horror of the crew.

I don't know what I expected, but Uyuni was for me a bit of a let-down. The place was crawling with backpackers, but they were the worst sort, particularly a lot of the men who were much too old to really be students. My own particular favourites among the crowd were gentlemen with bald heads and clip-on ponytails, wearing Che Guevara T-shirts, many of them carrying guitar cases which almost certainly contained no guitar. But whoever they were and wherever they came from, they were all crammed into Uyuni's finest student hostels (even though many of them were pushing 50), to see the great salt flats.

The Salar de Uyuni, the world's largest salt flat, is just stunning; it covers nearly 4,000 square miles and contains more than 10 billion tons of salt. From any distance at all it looks like snow

The Bolivian graveyard for locomotives.

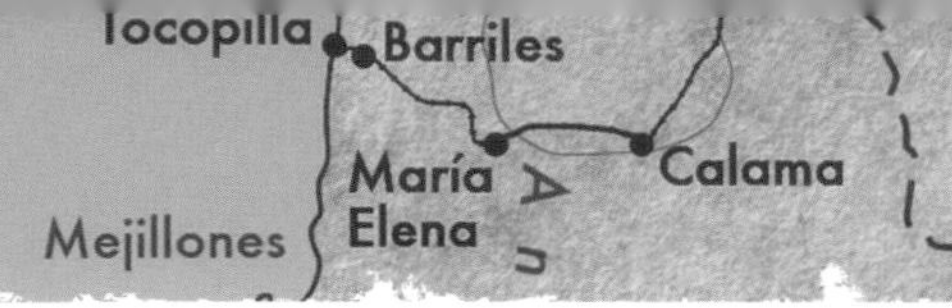

– it is a complete salt desert, a unique and incredible place. It was formed millions of years ago and, while the salt in itself is not particularly marketable, it does contain high levels of one increasingly valuable metal, lithium. This is in demand around the modern world for use in batteries for devices such as iPhones and even as a basis for antidepressants. It is increasingly valuable and it is estimated that there could be as much as US$10 trillion worth of lithium carbonate under these salt flats. That could be the saving of Bolivia.

Bolivia is determined to hold on to the wealth of their natural resources and staff of the lithium extraction plant we were allowed to visit were very tight-lipped about the product that it is producing and the amount of wealth that it generates. It could be that, with the help of the railway – which is planned to run from inside the plant itself all the way down to the coast – this could be a massive boost to the Bolivian economy and also breathe new life into the whole network of rail. But it's still only a pipe dream.

Salts of the earth: director Neil Ferguson, me and Richard Foster, the assistant producer on this programme.

THE LITTLE TRAIN THAT COULD

That meant I had to take a car to my next railway station, in Potosí, once one of the largest cities in the world. It's situated over 4,000 metres above sea level, so it's also one of the highest cities in the world. The Spanish built this city in the 16th century for one very good reason. The mountain looking down on Potosí is called Cerro Rico. This translates as 'the rich hill' and it used to contain huge amounts of silver. Over 62,000 tons was mined from the mountain, making Potosí one of the richest cities on the planet. It once had over 200,00 inhabitants, with only London and Paris having larger populations. Much of the silver, tragically, ended up elsewhere – mostly in Spain – which seems to be a sad pattern with Bolivia. The city generated so much wealth but the people are still incredibly poor. This is also because much of the money was further spent building a much grander city further down the Andes, over a thousand metres lower and only accessible by the most extraordinary type of train.

This was the final part of my journey from Potosí, the once splendid city that is now, frankly, a shambles, to Sucre, the capital of Bolivia. I had an incredible ride in a splendid but ridiculous vehicle up and over the mountain. When the train arrived, I couldn't help but laugh out loud although I was with a Bolivian railway official who didn't really take to my amusement kindly. He seemed rather proud of the vehicle in front of us, which seemed more of a bus than a locomotive. It was the most unlikely little bus/train/whatever, bearing in mind it was due to take us up and over the roof of the Andes at a serious height, on some very narrow-looking railway tracks. It looked absurdly tiny and fragile. The main plus point about it was that it was, at least, on time.

We were all struggling by now with varying degrees of altitude sickness, but Sam our cameraman was really badly hit. The previous night, he and I had a beer, chatted about the events of the day, the demise of the Bolivian economy and a waitress who Sam had taken just fifteen seconds to fall deeply in love with. As we had an early start, we went to our separate rooms, hoping for

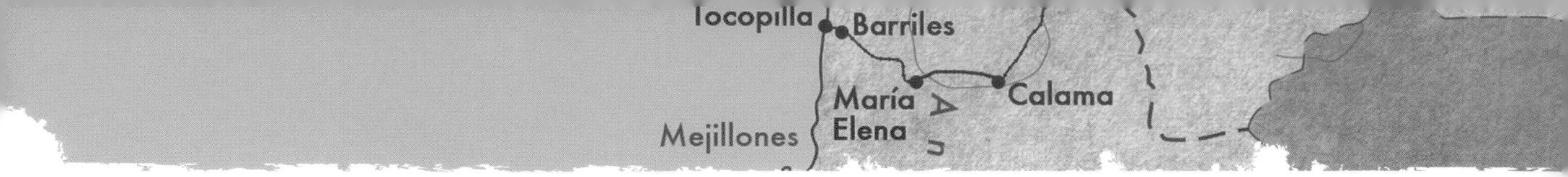

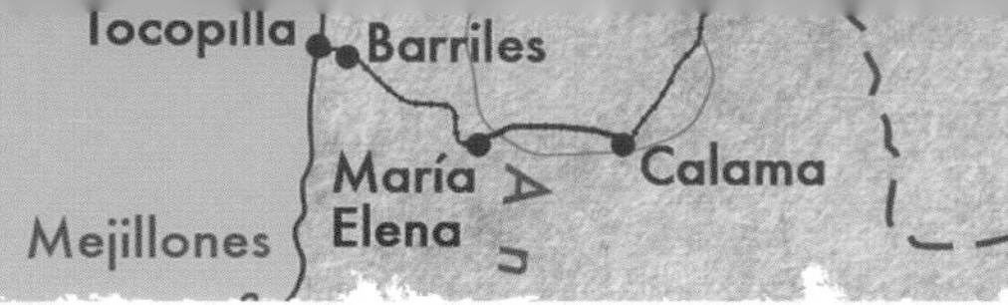

There was once a proper train serving Potosí to Sucre but now a converted Mercedes-Benz bus does the job.

a good few hours' sleep. When I came down at 5 am, I felt fine but was greeted by the sight of Sam, who's a pretty tough little Irishman, lying on the floor of the hotel foyer with a large blue oxygen tank connected to a mask on his face. He was clearly very groggy. The very fact that the hotel had such an enormous oxygen supply on hand suggested that this sort of thing is quite a regular occurrence at that altitude. Sam was in a really bad way; he had to be almost lifted to his feet and gently put onto the train but he kept complaining of an absolutely splitting headache and felt like he would be violently sick at any second. Clearly, he would be doing no filming that day. We carried on with him sitting with pillows all around his head in the corner of our train/bus/whatever and the assistant cameraman took over Sam's duties.

It was an amazing journey; it had already had the most unlikely start, but everything that happened later was more bizarre still. Ours was a request-stop service high up in the Andes and people – mainly women – would appear from absolutely nowhere. They would pop out from behind a rock and the train/bus would come to a halt and let them on board. There were women in wonderful, multi-coloured South American costumes, all with black stove hats on their heads and uniformly carrying enormous rag bundles with everything – possibly including the kitchen sink – inside. Things they certainly did carry included potatoes, knitted woollens of all sorts – presumably for market – clucking chickens and even, in one case, a very much alive and surprisingly contented baby.

Most of these women looked extremely weather-beaten and really ancient. They had beautiful but very lined faces and they grinned a lot with very bad teeth. Clearly, there would be a very good future for a dentist in that part of Bolivia, but he or she would have to be good at working at altitude. I would have put many of these women at 60 to 70 years of age, but then I slowly realised that many of them were carrying very young children. 'How old are these women?' I asked, and Gloria said many of them would be between 18 and 25.

I was lost for words for once and, trying not to be unkind or sexist, said, 'But they look so much older.'

Gloria said, 'They always do, they live in the mountains; their lives are very hard they are battered by the wind and the sun. Life expectation for them is not many years and they usually breed many babies very young.'

It is a sad life for them but they didn't seem sad at all; they kept grinning at me through the gaps in their teeth. Then they would suddenly ring the bell and get off the train, disappearing into who-knows-where. They would simply vanish behind a rock. Gloria told me many of them lived as much as six or seven miles from the drop-off point. They would just be enveloped by the mountain within seconds of leaving. It was clearly a very hard existence and without this particular railway, their life would be completely impossible.

There are lots of communities in the Andes, lots of valleys which can't be seen at all except from the air and many of the women who live there have to go to Potosí or Sucre to sell their products. There is no access road at all and this railway is one of the great examples of an essential social service for the communities of this wild remote area.

Tocopilla Barriles María Elena Calama Mejillones

We crossed yet another gorgeous mountain pass; we were now over 5,000 metres above sea level and we started to begin our careful descent. Sam was still in bad shape at the back, but slowly getting over his vicious headache and the rest of us were feeling pretty good. We got to Sucre and the journey that was supposed to take five hours had taken nearly nine – but what a fascinating trip.

A STOLEN PROGRAMME

Sucre is just magnificent. It is a UNESCO world heritage site, with whitewashed colonial buildings, tree-lined avenues and a beautifully laid out square in the centre of the city, full of flowers. It is absolutely beautiful, a magical place where our Andean adventure came to an end.

I recorded the usual sign-off to the camera after what had certainly been an epic journey. The ailing Sam, John the soundman and I began to make our way out of Bolivia towards São Paulo in Brazil for a morning flight back to Heathrow while director Neil and the second cameraman stayed on for a day or two to finish the last of the filming. We shook hands, saying, 'See you back in London.' I shared a laugh with Neil, as we put the rushes and the cans with all the films in from all of our work over the last couple of weeks into a bag. 'Isn't it bizarre that in this digital age that we all live in,' I said, 'that we still physically carry all the film home in a can.' We smiled and thought no more about our precious cargo.

The three of us then endured a truly terrifying drive down towards the Brazilian border and on to our hotel in São Paulo. We were constantly looking down at the side as we went too fast down the mountains with a sheer drop on either side. Several times we screamed out to the driver, 'Slow down! You are an idiot, slow down!' We had estimated that we should be in at approximately 8 pm for dinner, followed by a shower, a couple of drinks and an early night, rested for the flight in the morning. But we had seriously underestimated the length of this endless winding and terrifying drive, and we eventually crawled, ashen-faced, into our hotel just after 11 pm, with Sam still in a bad way. The late arrival was, frankly, the last thing we needed, but one good piece of news was that the chef was still working. The bar was open and the restaurant would not close until well after midnight. We had a magnificent meal and toasted each other. Even Sam began to get some colour back in his face.

The next morning we went to the airport, started loading the mountains of camera gear through the check-in, where a very nice lady was counting the bags and trying to keep our excess baggage payment down to the minimum. We suddenly became aware that the small bag with the rushes in was no longer hanging on the trolley where it had been as we came into the airport. There was a panic, a moment of non-belief, but then we realised the truth: it really had gone.

Some little toe-rag somewhere had stolen the bag and was probably already in his souped-up car back to the slums of São Paulo. Wherever he was, he would open the bag, realise there was absolutely nothing of use to him and probably keep the bag and throw the cans over a hedge.

We were in high panic; we raced around the airport looking frantically everywhere, even in waste bins, checking every single place we had been. I ran manically outside the airport and looked in every litter bin, over every hedge and scoured access roads and car parks, etc, but of all the work we had done over the last couple of weeks, there was absolutely no sign.

I have been filming since the early 1970s and it has always been the way that rushes get back to base. They never get stolen because they are absolutely useless to everyone else. Nothing like this had ever ever happened to me. I had never heard of it happening to anyone else either. We were absolutely devastated – gutted. Everything we'd gone through the last couple of weeks was completely pointless. Nothing was captured on film.

We told the others and all of us felt it was one of the lowest spots in our careers. It was a sick, dreadful feeling for all involved. It felt like a bereavement in the family. (To be continued in Chapter Five…)

AUSTRALIA

Indonesia
Papua New Guinea
Darwin
Wyndham
Indian Ocean
Derby
Northern Territory
Cooktown
Cairns
Coral Sea
Townsville
Cloncurry
Australia
Alice Springs
Queensland
Rockhampton
Western Australia
New Ghan
Old Ghan
Lake Eyre
Charleville
William Creek
Curdimurka
Maree
Farina
Brisbane
Geraldton
South Australia
Bourke
Coolgardie
Quorn
Port Augusta
New South Wales
Perth
Newcastle
Adelaide
Sydney
Canberra
Albany
Victoria
Indian Ocean
Melbourne
N
Tasmania
Hobart
0 200 400 600 Miles
0 200 400 600 Kilometers
Rail
Road

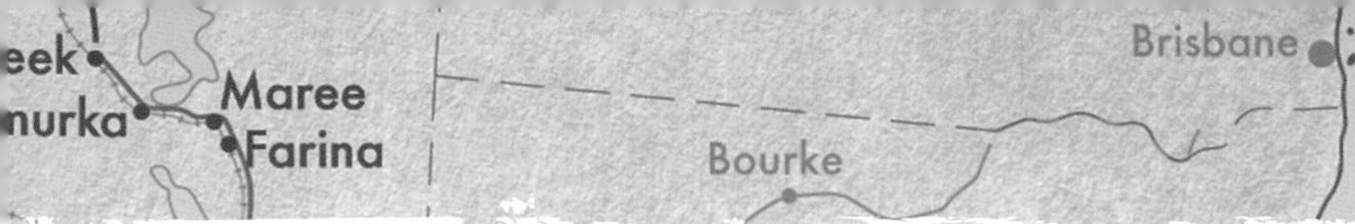

Australia

Yes, yes, I know it's very important to be refreshed and rested after a long-haul flight, particularly if you are going to appear in front of camera looking beautiful, but the reality is that sometimes, 'It just don't work out like that.'

I crawled off a long, long flight from London Heathrow via Kuala Lumpur to Sydney and then caught a middle-of-the-night connection to Adelaide, South Australia. I had no time to do anything except walk off the plane, talk to a camera and hurl myself into an Australian cab, the driver of which I felt to be a rather insensitive man. 'G'day mate,' he said. 'God, you look rough.'

We had no time to breathe, with all the flights and we had no time really to catch up with anything except a train that was imminent, so no rest, no beauty sleep, just that quick chat to camera, the mocking cab driver (in Australia, aren't they all), but a chance to get on a train that only goes once a week, the 'legendary' Ghan. This is a great Australian institution that has been taking people and goods back and forth through the very centre of Australia since 1878. The old line it used to run on has more or less disappeared in many places, but it's now been extended at a cost of over a billion Australian dollars to go right the way from Adelaide in the south to Port Augusta where it veers west a bit, then north through Alice Springs and from there all the way up to Darwin. It basically goes from the extreme south of the Australian continent to the extreme north, right up the middle, through the baking, mainly featureless, outback. The journey runs over 2,000 miles and the original construction of the railway took nearly 150 years, with massive loss of life.

Our plan was to do the whole journey, but, of course, this being *Extreme Railways*, to do it the hard way: to travel on the old Ghan line, the one they used to use a hundred years ago, or at least to follow it as best I could. Because in many places it had virtually disappeared.

We started in Adelaide, which is an absolutely beautiful city (shame I only saw it for 20 minutes), but then we were on the Ghan and away towards Port Augusta. The ticket lady was an extraordinary woman called Toula Tankosic. I don't know what her roots were but she spoke perfect English in an Australian kind of way and she did tell me that before she married Mr Tankosic she was actually Miss Van Gophelas, so I suppose, on balance, she was much better off. Certainly, the modern trend for a lady to keep her maiden name would have made her Mrs Toula Van Gophelas Tankosic, which surely would have just too much. Anyway, she was very nice and sorted me out my ticket for $98.

As I wandered alongside the very long, very busy and beautiful-looking train, I couldn't help noticing that the Ghan logo features a camel. The old camel trains used to drive people through the outback in the days before there was a railway and the camel drivers almost all came from Afghanistan. So there are now millions of camels of Afghan extraction running loose around parts of Australia and the express train that replaced the camels was originally called the Afghan Express. Aussies – predictably – abbreviated that to the Ghan. I suppose it's the Australian equivalent of the Orient-Express, a very classy train and people come from all over the world to travel on it. Some make the very long journey from Adelaide all the way up to Darwin and then come back again but, frankly, that would be over 4,000 miles of relentless and probably very similar-looking outback scenery and for me that would be much too much.

There were different classes of seating and for the absurdly wealthy or lotto winners or people with just more money than sense there was the platinum class. That was really quite, quite splendid and, I think, unlike anything in terms of sheer luxury that I've seen on any train anywhere in the world. The accommodation was on a par with any five-star hotel in London or New York and even had

The modern-day Ghan runs the length of the continent.

a really big bathroom. The food looked magnificent – a superb fillet steak was being lovingly prepared in the Platinum Class dining room which we passed, but I stress we only passed. The director, a brutal man, reminded me that I was supposed to be filming amongst the riff-raff as they sat eating their sandwiches and drinking out of their Thermos flasks in Red Class. Thanks a bunch.

But it was an amazing train, and when we had to leave it three hours later it was a real wrench. That was as much luxury as we saw. From then on it got rougher and rougher – and so did I.

GHAN BUT NOT FORGOTTEN

The old Ghan railway line was begun at Port Augusta in 1878 and, for the next hundred years, trains from here went to a string of really dusty remote towns in the Australian outback.

What is always great about Australia is that in the middle of absolutely nowhere you meet truly wonderful people. When we got to the first small boarding place along the old Ghan line at Port Augusta there was a beautiful old steam locomotive belching smoke out of its chimney and being kissed and cuddled by an extraordinary group called the Pichi Richi Railway Preservation Society. They run a railway through the Pichi Richi pass and, they insisted, 'just call us the Pichi Richi' (pronounced '*pitchee-ritchee*' – I just loved saying it: 'Pitchee-ritchee', 'pitchee-ritchee', 'pitchee-ritchee'. I wonder if Shane Pitchee-Ritchee or Guy Pitchee-Ritchee had any Australian roots? Probably not; sorry, I digress).

Thanks to these guys I became the envy or hate object of every train spotter in the world as I was allowed to travel in an old steam engine driver's cab. The locomotive was an old W-class, built in Manchester around 1951 and still going very strong to this day thanks to the pitchee-ritchee boys.

Outside Port Augusta, the old line splits from the new. The modern track carries paying passengers on the Ghan and huge amounts of freight right across Australia, while the old line had all sorts of problems. The biggest problem seemed to be that it

The Pichi Richi Rail Preservation Society keep the old Ghan route going.

was built really badly and the punctuality of the old original Ghan became a national joke. It was stylish and it was elegant, but it always breaking down and was never on time. We had the train to ourselves, we were pulling some of the old original carriages dating back to the 1920s and they still had style. But in their heyday they were often full of really fed-up passengers.

We got up to the town of Quorn but, sadly, that was as far as our journey took us before the old track ran out. We'd run out of train and we'd run out of track, so I had to jump in a four-by-four, which was about the only sort of vehicle that can get through these really old dirt roads. You can still follow the route of the old Ghan line easily enough. It's very distinctive and easy to spot because its outline is still clear along the burning sand, close to the road but most of the rails are long gone and there's absolutely nothing else in eyeline except desert. I still had no idea really just how tough the drive was going to be.

Just outside Quorn, I met yet another very likeable but completely potty Australian gentleman, Graham Cannard. He runs a camel farm and knew just about everything there was to know about the old Afghan camel trains. He confirmed that the animals were very much the normal form of transport in the outback before the railway came. 'Most Australians,' he said, 'didn't know how to work 'em and wouldn't know a camel from a dingo's dongler. But the camels really opened the country up. The Afghan drivers basically showed the engineers the route with their strings of camels and they laid the rails wherever the camels went. It sounds a bit hit-and-miss but the camel is an extraordinary animal and knows instinctively the very best route.'

At this point, of course (and I should have said, 'No'), Graham insisted on showing me how docile camels were. But camels aren't docile and they never were. I have tried my luck with camels several times on television over the years and they've always been a complete disaster. This was no different. Why is it that people who are interviewed on television with horses or camels or goats or even giant badgers insist on sticking some idiot presenter on the back of the blooming thing and laughing loudly at their incompetence? Well, this was just like that. I got on this creature that apparently went by the name of Talking Rex, who immediately turned around and tried to bite my leg and then ran round in circles making the most dreadful roaring noise from one end and farting from the other. It was extremely unpleasant for me, but not for Graham who was making nearly as much noise as Talking Rex, except Graham didn't appear to be farting so much as howling with laughter.

I had no idea how to control the dreadful thing. I pulled the rein one way and it immediately went the other, but perhaps that was the trick of it – I never did find out – and all this in 40 degrees Celsius of baking heat. Graham kept shouting useless advice like, 'Tell him where you want to go!'

And I kept saying, 'I want to go home!' I think there is no Afghan in my heritage; I hate camels and they hate me. I ate one once in Kenya – well, a few slices – and that was pretty damned unpleasant as well.

God, but I hate camels! (And, God, do they hate me!)

Thank God the railways arrived. The age of steam may have been a bit dirty and smelly with coal dust, but at least that was the only smell. At last we drove on, with the windows open, enjoying some fresh air and putting as much dusty road as we could between ourselves and Talking Rex, who clearly talked out of his arse...

GHOST OF A ROUTE

About 170 miles north of Quorn, we came to another railway town, Farina. This was really quite spooky, the complete ghost town. In the late 1890s, Farina was of great significance as the farthest point in land reached by the then shiny new Ghan railway. It boasted a flourishing hotel, a school, a hospital and over 300 inhabitants but as the railway moved on towards Alice Springs, Farina began to decline and, when the old Ghan line closed altogether in 1980, the town just died. It was a really sad place. It was still very much intact and seemed as if it was being somehow lovingly maintained. Many of the houses were still there, as was the school, but there was not a single human being.

By the time we got to the next town, a place called Marree, we were getting used to these scenes of emptiness. The whole of central Australia seems to be full of places where virtually nobody lives anymore. Marree was interesting in that just a few people are desperately trying to hang on to its old importance but, to be honest, I didn't rate their chances too highly. Marree too had been an important junction right up to the mid-1970s, although now the station was silent and deserted except for one lady who seemed to be sitting there quietly waiting for a train. I didn't like to break it to her, but there hasn't been one through there for 25 years; she was obviously a very patient woman.

I met a guy called Lyle, who owned and ran the town's motel and general store; in fact, he ran everything in town because there was pretty much only him there. When we wanted a drink he was the bartender, when we wanted fuel for our car, he was the garage owner, when we wanted to buy a map he sold us one and when we needed a spokesman on the history of Marree he just happened to know a bloke that would be ideal – himself.

He talked about the town as it if closed up only yesterday. Clearly he'd grown up there and it had been absolutely thriving, with lots of pretty houses either side of the railway. He talked lovingly, too, about Dino 's casino, an abandoned building just opposite the abandoned station and he talked animatedly about the wonderful parties they'd have in the casino every Sunday night. He did say – rather optimistically – that they've still got a great school there for the kids and he thought the future for Marree was bright. There were just a few inhabitants in the town and they did have a few kids. He was an incredibly nice bloke, so I didn't want to disillusion him. Perhaps it will somehow or other be OK. But how?

What was weird, even eerie, was that there were several abandoned locomotives scattered around the town that looked just

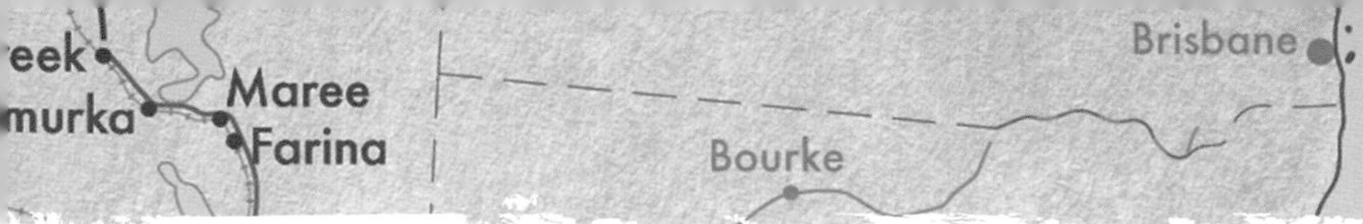

as if they just stopped where they were and the driver had just got out and gone home.

'Yes,' said Lyle, 'that's pretty much exactly what happened. The boss man just turned the railway off and everybody left their keys in the locomotive, jumped down and went home.' Very sad. But I still couldn't really work out quite what had gone wrong. Why had the Ghan railway line authorities chosen this route and why did it fail so spectacularly?

We travelled on through mile after mile of dirt road with the identical desert horizon. It was arid, it was bone dry. Luckily we'd packed gallons of water, but we were parched and finding the whole thing pretty tough. And then we came to what was unmistakeably a water tower in the middle of absolutely nowhere. Apparently, there are a lot of underground water supplies beneath this massive area and it seemed to be that it was the Afghans and their camels who found the water holes in the first place.

The Aussies call them 'bubblers' and they are an amazing natural phenomenon. In the middle of parched desert with not a tree or even a cactus to see, sometimes for hundreds of miles, these bubblers are fresh water springs scattered along the old Ghan railway line. At various points they come up through cracks in the bedrock to form beautiful springs of fresh water. The water probably fell as rain more than two million years ago and has been flowing underground ever since, through the vast system that underpins the whole of eastern Australia. And, of course, the fresh water springs made the steam railway possible. Without the water they would have been as stranded as they would have been without coal.

We even found an old salt lake called Lake Eyre. For years at a time it will be completely bone dry, but four or five times in a 50-year period there is torrential rain in Queensland, about a thousand miles away, which causes Lake Eyre to flood and wash through the whole of this valley. This, perhaps more than anything else, has caused absolute devastation to the old railway line. This was partly to do with the sheer power of the water, but also due to the fact that the railway tracks were laid really badly in the first place. When the

Steam locomotives once ran the whole of the Ghan route.

floodwaters rose, whole tracks were washed away and the railway stopped completely for weeks or sometimes even months at a time.

This next historical fact I found extraordinary. Some of the engine drivers on the original Ghan line carried rifles so that if the railway was cut off by floods and they got stranded, they could at least shoot a goat or perhaps a nice plump kangaroo or even a camel to feed themselves and the passengers. In return, the passengers were expected to try to repair the lines themselves, using picks and shovels supplied by the railway.

Suddenly, travelling on an UK railway doesn't seem quite so bad, does it?

ENGINEERING FAILS

At a place called Curdimurka Crossing there was the perfect example of the extraordinary incompetence or maybe just desperate cost-cutting on the part of the cowboys who built the

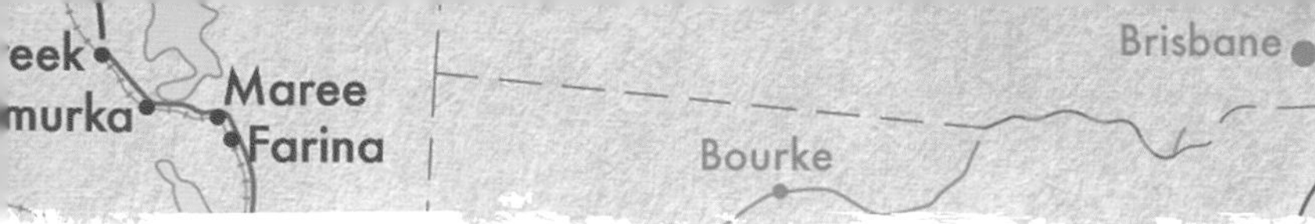

railway. They made some pretty basic mistakes, laying hundreds of miles of steel rail straight on to sand without crushed rock, gravel or ballast. The heavy trains would quickly destabilise the tracks and, to add to the problem, they made the sleepers of wood. Now one of the most common creatures in this part of Australia is the termite. Termites live on wood, so in many cases they had eaten the sleepers before the railway had officially opened. This would be laughable except that, in many cases, these stupid actions led to derailment and many deaths.

We came across one extraordinary feat of engineering,

At the crossing.

as always in the middle of absolutely nowhere, called the Algebuckina bridge, still the longest bridge in south Australia. It's an amazing construction but it stands in the middle of absolutely nowhere, no one ever uses it and there are no tracks leading to it on either side. It's a wonderful piece of Victorian architecture built in 1892 with 19 spans, each almost a hundred foot in length. The whole thing is almost 2,000 feet long. It wasn't there when the railway was officially opened. The first tracks were laid across the riverbed and they were washed away quite quickly in the first flood. Sometimes it will flood three or four times a year in this area and then you might not see any water at all for five or six years; the whole area remains completely bone dry. But when it floods, it really does flood.

Once the bridge was built, it did actually keep this section of the old Ghan running, despite the floods, for many years, but the work was exhausting and the cost in human life was high. Three-hundred-and-fifty men worked here in the most extreme desert conditions and many of them perished. What I found really deeply sad was that, in the shadows of the bridge that they'd created, which is no longer working or serving any purpose, there are the graves of all those who died working there.

In 1974, the worst floods ever all but destroyed the Algebuckina bridge and the Australian government decided enough was enough. They called time on the old railway and ordered the construction of a new line a hundred miles to the west. This was where we were headed on day four of our extraordinary journey.

With luck we could get to Alice Springs in time to re-join the luxurious modern Ghan, but I don't think we had really even begun to comprehend the sheer size of this huge country. We just seemed to be getting farther and farther behind the clock. You couldn't speed on these dirt roads and you rarely saw another human being, One whole day I drove from 8 o'clock in the morning to perhaps 7 o'clock in the evening without seeing a single car on either side of the road. The outback is just colossal.

At one point, in the middle of absolutely nowhere, we stopped in a bar that was nevertheless absolutely heaving with backpackers.

It was clearly a thriving spot, although where they'd had been all day and where they'd all come from I had absolutely no idea. I certainly hadn't seen any of them on the road and I interviewed the woman who ran the bar. 'What exactly is the population of this place?'

She looked at me, paused and said 'Five – but only three of us can vote.'

The place was called William Creek and, by chance, one of the guys in the bar, mercifully a little more sober than most of the others, turned out to have his own plane. He mainly used it for crop-spraying. Because we were so far behind our schedule we somehow talked him into flying us up to Alice Springs.

That night, as we slept in the smallest motel room, I've ever seen in my life, there was no mistaking the sound of a very strong wind blowing outside. The corrugated roof banged non-stop all night and, in the morning, we woke up to a full-scale gale. I thought Trevor, our pilot – who appeared looking a little bleary – might well call the whole thing off; in fact, I rather hoped he would. But, of course, being Australian he had that wonderful optimism.

'Oh, no,' he said, 'she'll be all right.' And up into the driving wind we went. It was a little bit bouncy to say the least and, if I thought I was being a bit of a wimp, my sentiments were reconfirmed by the unmistakable sound of our cameraman, Mike, being violently sick into a bag just behind my left ear.

It was a wild flight but Trevor seemed completely unphased by the whole thing. 'No problem, guys,' he said reassuringly. 'It's only a light breeze.'

What was unmistakable from our bouncing aircraft was that you really could see the old railway line passing right under our wings. Trevor went on: 'The coming of the Ghan was like the opening up of the west in the United States – over the Rocky Mountains and into California – that's what the Ghan did for this area.'

We were now catching up with our schedule and I almost began to enjoy the flight to our next destination. Alice Springs is one of those mystical names that everybody's heard of, presumably because of Neville Shute's *A Town Like Alice*, and I felt really optimistic about having a bit of food and maybe even a beer, before we got back on the luxurious Ghan and made our way in up to Darwin, the end of our journey. I felt we deserved a bit of comfort and, behind me, a groaning Mike clearly did.

'So, what's Alice Springs like, Trevor?' I asked, excitedly.

'Not much,' he said. 'It's a shithole full of drunks.'

And do you know what, dear reader? When we got there we found that he was absolutely right.

I DON'T LIKE A TOWN LIKE ALICE

Alice Springs really is a pretty grim place but, worse still, when we got to the station – which I had hoped was going to be the point where we got back to five-star travel, the station gates were locked and there was a large chain across them. The Ghan had gone. We were all absolutely gutted. Despite the hundreds of miles we had travelled in really tough conditions, we had actually missed the train and there wasn't another one for seven days.

There was only one option – an overnight freight train and that would get us on up to Darwin, provided we didn't mind spending 18 hours, through the night, bouncing around in a freight train, either in one of the trucks or, if we were lucky, the guard's van.

What followed was one of the best nights of my life. It didn't exactly have any of the comfort, the juicy steaks and fine wine of the 'legendary Ghan', but it was an amazing insight into just how crucial the role of the freight train driver is. We do tend to rather take them for granted all over the world. We only see big long lines of trucks, but having seen things from the driver's cab, covering a thousand miles of northern Australia, I got a whole new perspective. On the new Ghan line, the passenger service gets all the glamour and the headlines, but freight is really what it's all about, shifting hundreds of tons of just about every product you can think of across one of the biggest countries in the world. This was a seriously advanced freight train.

The first bit, the good news, was that we didn't have to travel in the guard's van. There was a lot of red tape – there always is – and we were also told that there was absolutely no chance of travelling with the driver. But of course, when you get to meet them, one-to-one, they call the shots and – if they like you – then drivers, everywhere in the world in our experience, have been as good as gold.

The driver was called Scottie, 'How many of you are there?' he asked.

'Well, just me. And maybe you would let Mike our cameraman on as well?' I asked tentatively. We had already made a contingency plan if this was not going to be possible. We would use remote-controlled GoPro cameras, but it was impossible to say what quality of pictures we'd actually get.

'What about a make-up girl?' He looked at me and said, very pointedly, 'No, you obviously don't have one.' The cheek! But then he grinned, and said, 'OK, guys, come on board.'

And we were off on a really massive train, a 4,000-horse-power, diesel electric locomotive that cost more than £4 million. Inside, the cab looked like the cockpit of a passenger plane. They were hauling 33 wagons at night across very difficult terrain. Braking would take the best part of a mile and staying awake and alert was absolute essential for the driver and his crew, but even I didn't dare nod off.

There was a strange light that came on every 30 seconds, the vigilance light. Scottie had to cancel it, by pressing a red button in front of him, to show that he was responsive. If he failed to do it the emergency brakes would be applied automatically. He and co-driver Grant were in the middle of a marathon session of driving. They'd left Adelaide 24 hours earlier, travelling virtually the whole thousand miles to Alice Springs. They would cover the same distance through the night and then tomorrow head up to Darwin.

Scottie explained they had four crew, two in the cabin and two back in the van, running eight-hour shifts, Scottie and Grant would drive for two hours at a time and, yes, he confirmed that staying awake is one of the toughest things. They really couldn't afford to drop their guard when they were thundering through the outback with a massive tonnage behind them. Sometime around dawn they had to uncouple and unload some wagons, meaning that at least we got a chance to get out, yawn and stretch. We were in the middle of nowhere, taking one carriage off that the local Aborigine community would turn into a siding before recoupling the train. If we did meet any other trains, there was a lot of bonhomie among the crews. There was a lot of mutual respect with a lot of banter.

At one point, a naked man driving an oncoming train gave us all a splendid flash. 'G'day, big boy,' came the predictable cry, and I couldn't begin to tell you what the naked man shouted back. Luckily, his flashing didn't interrupt his concentration. Although, as his carriages went past us, on one container I spotted a sign for sulphuric acid. He really would not have welcomed a splash of that on his anatomy.

The new Ghan line has modern ballast and materials and is as safe as it could possibly be for accepting these enormous tonnages. However, we did come to one spot where they'd had serious flooding and the whole line had been washed away. This was only in the last two or three years, when the sheer power of the water made it a close call for the locomotive that was crossing a bridge at the time. There had been two drivers caught in it, and we were told, 'The guys were lucky, very very lucky.' It sounded like a close call. The drivers were obviously close mates of Scottie and co.

Floods remain a serious danger and bush fires a major hazard, sometimes threatening to engulf an entire locomotive in flame. Another age-old problem and we saw a lot of this through the night, were animals on the track. The sad reality is that it's almost impossible for any train as heavy as this to stop. The train lights up the track ahead with massive floodlights but at the speed we were travelling and with the tonnage behind us we could stop for nothing. We narrowly missed several kangaroos and cows and we hit a dingo that virtually vaporised before our very eyes. It was pretty horrid as it went right under the train. Camels also are regular casualties. Grant said, 'The camels are the stupidest

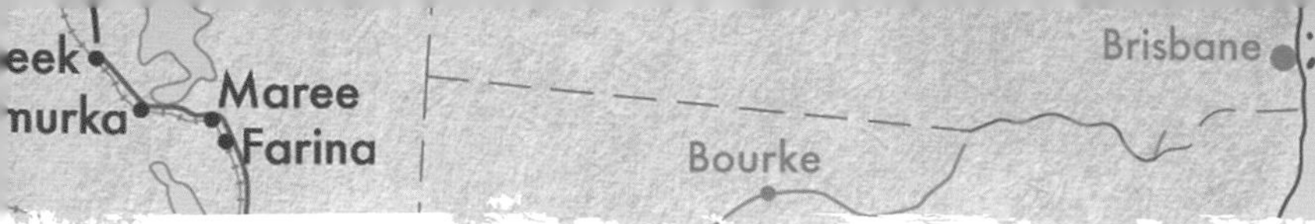

ones of all. They don't try and run; they stand there and glower at you.'

We were running a bit late. Our 18 hours had already stretched to over 20 and we still hadn't made it to Darwin. Late in the afternoon, we passed the longest train I had ever seen. It was full of iron ore and must have weighed more than 12,000 tons. I've seen trains with up to three locomotives in front, but this one had four, pulling the huge load southwards, back to Alice Springs and towards Adelaide. We had to let him through; he was clearly the boss of the line and he was just enormous.

It was nearly 7 pm as we crawled into Darwin. In all, it had taken us four days to get across the outback to Alice, but just one full 24 hours to get the final thousand miles to our final destination. I had learnt so much respect for the guys who drive these freight trains. I'd spent 22 hours with them, I was exhausted just watching, but they would get no more than a night's sleep and then, first thing tomorrow morning, pick up a brand new train and go all the way back to Adelaide. Just amazing blokes.

This new Ghan line was a modern engineering marvel and obviously a huge commercial success and it had come a very long way since the early period of construction. To begin with, the railways had been, although pioneering and exciting in their way, actually pretty disastrous. In addition, there was something really sad about the Afghan camels who started everything and showed them the way to build this amazing railway, ending up now standing dopily on the line, blinking in the headlights and getting flattened by the trains as they race northwards.

The crew, the director and I had a good old catch up on how the journey had been. Mike and I were quite eulogistic about the whole thing. In many ways we'd had a much better adventure than if we had stayed on the luxurious new Ghan, although maybe just a little bit more of that luxury wouldn't have gone amiss.

The crew went off to their hotel for a meal and a good night's sleep, and muggins here caught the evening flight to India.

INDIA

Mumbai
Dasgaon village
Pune
Maharasht

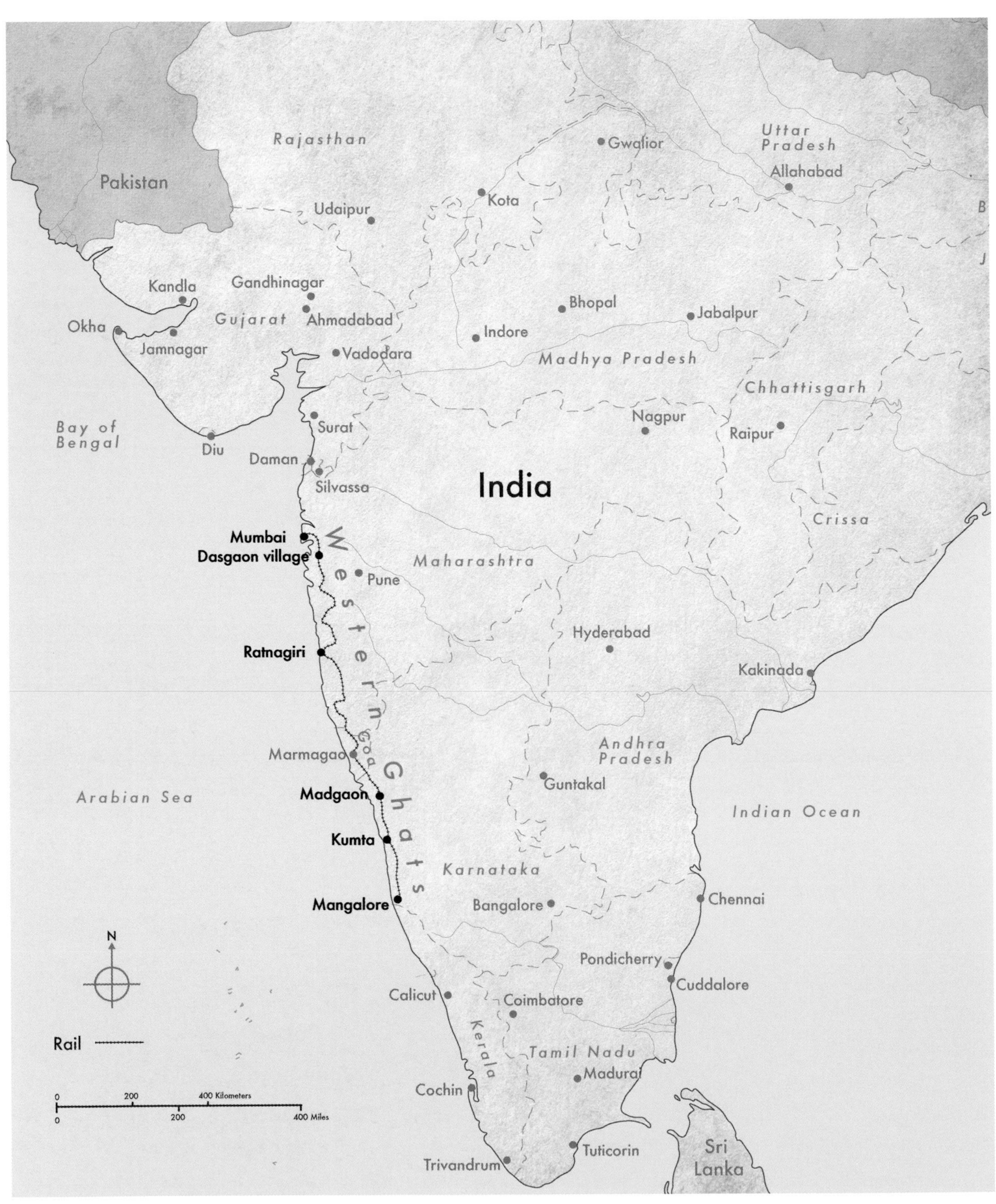

India

When you get on a train anywhere in the UK, the areas around the main stations look very busy as you travel in and out, but once you are clear and get into the countryside – whether you've left London, Manchester or Birmingham – you can go for mile after mile looking at lovely countryside with virtually not a single human being in view.

However, if you travel by train in India then, no matter where you are in this huge country, as you look out of the window, there is always somebody to be seen. Even in the wildest, most remote regions, you will always see people walking along the line, across the line or out in the fields. That's the difference between a population of 60 million and 1.2 billion. India is now the second most populous country on Earth and, within a matter of just a few years, it will certainly overtake China. India may be a vast country, but she's full to bursting point.

I'd arrived late at night from Australia, from what I thought was quite a busy city, Darwin, but, as I left my hotel to start filming, I could see that even before sunrise, Mumbai was already busy. In fact, it was manic. I had to leave Chhatrapati Shivaji terminus just after 5 am. It's one of the largest railway stations built by the rulers of the great British empire and I found it absolutely bewildering.

There were people running everywhere and the train information board was just a blur. I was looking for the Mandovi Express, which eventually I worked out was leaving in 20 minutes from Platform 16. The platform itself was extraordinary; there were people trying to sell me the most unlikely things, from dancing dolls to silk shirts to bowls of curry. I love my curry – but at 5 am from a dodgy street vendor? I don't think so...

Inexplicably, the little kiosk that sold books and newspapers on the station had a copy of Hitler's *Mein Kampf*. I had never seen a copy anywhere else in the world – certainly not anywhere in the UK – and I wasn't quite sure what sort of traveller would want to settle down to a copy during their train ride. I was intrigued, but there was no time to even glance at it because we had to hurl ourselves onto the Mandavi Express, which ran a daily service on the Konkan railway.

India's railways are the greatest legacy of the British colonial rule. They laid 40,000 miles of railway track across this huge subcontinent between 1858 and 1947. But there was one area that the British neglected and that was the western coastline – basically because we never really found a way to deal with the huge amount of water. On the western side of India are hundreds of inlets of the Arabian sea. A huge mountain range lies just a sliver of land away from the coast and draws torrential rain. It is a really treacherous area in which to contemplate building a railway, so even the enterprising British of the Raj steered well clear of it. This part of India suffered economically as a result and remained undeveloped until Konkan construction began in 1998. It was predictably very tough to build, with 95 workers losing their lives in the course of its completion.

We were hoping to travel from Mumbai to Mangalore, passing through the states of Goa, Maharashtra and Karnataka. This was a 472-mile journey, scaling difficult mountain peaks and crossing raging rivers. The trip should take 22 hours, but it rarely does. The railway issues two different timetables, one for spring and early summer and the other for the monsoon that runs from June to October. We were travelling, supposedly, at the very end of the monsoon, but this part of India has the highest rainfall in the country so a torrential downpour was never far away. Also, the monsoon doesn't have a calendar.

Our train was 18 carriages long and although pulled by a 4,000-horsepower engine, it was absolutely packed. There were 1,700 passengers – and all absolutely starving. I made my way to the kitchen, where the temperature must have been well over 40 degrees Celsius, and the guys were working at frantic speed

Hungry passengers are fed from an onboard kitchen working to full capacity.

and absolutely pouring sweat. It was pretty impressive: they serve hundreds of meals every day and everything is fresh. None of the chefs seemed at all perturbed by the fact that there were several enormous vats of boiling oil bouncing up and down as the train batted along the track at high speed. Their range included vegetable dishes, samosas, all sorts of omelettes and their 'proud speciality of the day' – which I suspected was their proud speciality every day – masala dosa.

I wasn't quite sure what masala dosa is and I'm still not, but it smelt good and fresh so I got myself a plateful and sat down to see what the morning would bring. I don't think I've ever had a curry before at six-thirty in the morning but, in India, curry is available 24 hours a day and, if it's prepared in hygienic surroundings, it's probably the safest option. The smell of curry was everywhere in India; in the most remote villages and mountain areas I could always smell curry; it was something I just got used to. It is very, very easy to get a bad tummy in India and roadside food is to be avoided. But conditions in the kitchens on the Konkan railway were almost certainly a lot cleaner and the food prepared was much fresher than it is in a lot of Indian restaurants that I use regularly back home and, of course, we had a chance to see the food being prepared.

As we headed south from Mumbai, we could see out of the window exactly what the challenges were for the men building this railway. We were travelling on a narrow piece of land through saturated rain forest, climbing up steep mountain passes with a sheer drop down to the sea on the other side. As with so many of the railways around the world we have visited, I think if the engineers had known the difficulties that lay ahead they almost certainly would never have started.

HERO OF THE KONKAN

It was undeniable that the line transformed the lives of 10 million people in one of the wettest places on earth. But its story is unusual and remarkable. The Konkan railway owes its very existence to a guy with the splendid name of Elattuvalapil Sreedharan. Born in 1932, he was an extraordinary man, a brilliant engineer but also a real hero. He promised to take on the project and complete it in just five years but wanted no interference from the railway ministry or any bureaucrats – but that meant no state funding, either. He was very much his own guy and believed in youth, enthusiasm and hard work. However much his workforce achieved every year, each time the monsoon came, it would threaten to wash it away. Most people thought he was a nutter and, in many ways he was – but he was a nutter with a vision.

There were irksome problems from the outset because there were no decent maps of the area. A proper geological survey had never been done and would have taken them years. So, Sreedharan employed a team of young graduates, gave them free motorbikes, some charts and some instruments and allocated each an area to map out in detail. Most of his staff didn't know anything about railways or anything about maps, but they were incredibly enthusiastic young men and they loved the notion that somebody was trusting them to become engineers.

Their work revealed that there was one route down the monsoon coast where it would be just possible – and only just possible – to build a railway across the whole of western India. The next problem was buying the land to lay the track. This would have been a reasonably straightforward business in most countries, but not in India, where every single acre is split into small plots owned by different families.

Sreedharan and his team had to negotiate with no less than 42,000 landowners across hundreds of small fishing and farming

The Konkan railway connected up the isolated coastline of western India.

communities. In return for the land, he promised links to the rest of India and chances for marketing their goods, for jobs and for educating their young people.

Our train stopped at Dasgaon village, a small place with hundreds of smiling children in brightly coloured clothes everywhere. The railway construction team not only had to placate all the various local landowners here, but here they had a much more difficult issue to deal with. We stopped there for tea – Indian, of course; none of your Chinese rubbish. I took tea with the village leader, Anand Minde, who had been in charge when it was suggested that a railway might come through. He said it was very difficult for the people to understand at first and that they didn't like the idea of it until they began to realise it could bring a big development to the village and real opportunities for its young people.

The extra problem in Dasgaon village was that the railway would have to run straight through a Hindu burial ground. They had used this site as a burial ground for more than 70 years and Mr Mindi became quite emotional when he explained to me that in their religion all children that die under the age of 12 were buried on this one site. All over India it is horribly common for children to die young. Special prayers had to be said before the children's bodies could be moved to a new site, constructed alongside the pyre where the adults from the village were cremated. Mr Mindi said it was a very difficult time because a lot of the villagers who had lost young members of their own families were understandably not at all happy with the idea.

In the end the graves of the children were re-consecrated and the new site was situated at the point where three rivers meet, making it a very holy place. The ashes of the children would then be scattered on the water.

As I interviewed Mr Mindi, children who were very much alive and very active seemed to come out of nowhere and swarm all over us. It was pretty much like my own house at half term.

We went to the station very early the next morning, to get back on the Konkan, and I bought my ticket for 31 rupees (about 36p) for the five-hour run to the port of Ratnagiri. The train was running at least an hour behind because of heavy overnight rain, so I took a little wander around the station. A very important-looking office in the middle belonged to the station master himself; there were signs everywhere about safety, disaster management, phone numbers to ring in an emergency and safety slogans such as the ones over his desk: 'The best safety device is a careful man. A little care makes mishap rare' and 'Always be careful is the ABC of society'. Well, they might talk a lot about safety but I have to say there was absolutely no sign of it being observed. On that very station that morning, we were nearly helpless witnesses in a major catastrophe.

If you are told, on any station in the UK, that your train is not arriving at, say, Platform Two, but is now coming in to Platform Five, you make a tutting noise and go under the underpass or over the footbridge. In India, there is none of that. They just run straight across the line, kids on their shoulders, grannies clanking along behind, dogs, cats, you name it, they all run as best they can

Welcoming villagers on the route of the railway.

across the line. It happens everywhere and it is a huge problem. Why they can't get it into their heads that this is an extremely dangerous practice, I have no idea.

In the Mumbai area alone, ten people are killed every day on the railways! That is almost inconceivable, but with such a huge population perhaps they just don't take mortality seriously. More than 30,000 people a year in India die from snake bites; that is a huge problem, but the deaths on the railways are surely completely avoidable.

Our train that morning did seem to come in on the wrong platform and everybody duly jumped on to the line and started running across. At this point an express train hurtled through on the middle track and people scattered everywhere, screaming; one stupid woman actually left her child behind her and started wailing and beating the platform. It was absolute madness; I felt sick to my stomach and very angry at their behaviour. I'll just drop in a direct quote from my rantings to camera at the time: 'No! Don't jump on the line because there is a train coming! This is ridiculous – look at everybody… Oh, my God, just watch everybody running! Oh, God, this is madness. Look at these stupid people! No wonder they get killed. What's the matter with you? Pick up your children! Stupid woman. God! Bloody dangerous!'

Hardly David Dimbleby, was it? But I was furious and convinced we were about to witness whole families being wiped out on camera... Yet, somehow, the train sped through with people panicking on both sides of the line, but nobody actually got killed – this time, anyway.

DIG FOR VICTORY

We got ourselves eventually onto a local passenger service that was also absolutely rammed and once again the train was full of vendors selling everything from food and drink to clothes, towels, toys – whatever you need and much more besides. They leap on at each station and jump off at the very last minute.

This leg of the journey was one of the toughest for Mr Sreedharan's workers. He had something like 30,000 workers building the lines and at this point the mountains come pretty much right down to the sea coast, so they had to dig dozens of railway tunnels, seven of which were then the longest in India. We had no lights in our carriages so each time we went through a tunnel we were plunged into total darkness for several minutes at a time and it became quite eerie.

In all on the Konkan railway there are 92 tunnels. Probably the most daunting of them to travel through is the Karbude tunnel; for a long time the longest in Asia, it is over 4 miles long and it took nearly ten minutes to travel through. I continued to talk to camera about how foreboding and disorientating it was and I thought it was a rather splendid commentary. Later, we realised that it had been far too dark and, while we had recorded something very nice, it was only for radio… On film we'd got El Zippo. It was claustrophobic in there and my chest got very tight. After a few minutes the air became really quite smoky. Each time I emerged from one of the long tunnels everybody's eyes were weeping.

The Pernem tunnel was the hardest to built. It took nearly seven years to finish, holding up the completion of the line. I met a chap called Joseph George, one of Sreedharan's young engineers. At the age of 24 he found himself the overall controlling engineer for the Pernem tunnel, which he called 'a job from hell'.

George said, 'You can't imagine how tough the building of this tunnel was. Many of us lost our youth here. I was a young man when I started and I was over 30 when I finished it. There was really hard rock at one end of the tunnel and soft soil at the other and it was constantly pouring with rain. The flooding during the monsoon led to constant collapsing of the tunnel; everything we built for months could be washed away in an hour.'

He showed me some pictures of his guys at work and they were just wallowing about in flood water. The whole valley at times seemed to be submerged; there were sandbags everywhere. It was often hopeless and several lives were lost. Nine died building the Pernem tunnel alone, and many others became extremely ill or badly injured.

Joseph George was the lead engineer on the arduous project to construct the Pernem tunnel.

'There were times then I just wanted to get away from the place, when a worker dies, it is horrific for all the other guys. They just feel there but for the grace of God go any of them and it's very hard for them to keep going, but we were young and we were determined to finish it.' he said. 'Building this tunnel taught me to face the great challenges of life. You don't succeed without failure and here we failed and then succeeded. We came in the prime of our youth and left this place as real men.' Joseph was an amazing guy and a great example of the mental strength, the bravery and the extraordinary determination of all the young men who constructed this railway.

We carried on through the mountains and yet more tunnels before we arrived eventually at Ratnagiri. This was one of the largest stations on the line and when we got there things were absolutely chaotic. A load of people got off and yet again dozens of vendors got on. For some silly reason, I bought something to eat on the train. I'd been travelling for several hours and was very hungry. My choice was a brightly coloured bun, but I had one mouthful and threw the rest out of the window for the buzzards to feed on. Buzzards and vultures follow the trains in India all the time because there is always food.

I was sitting next to a little boy who seemed incredibly unphased by our cameras. I couldn't get him to smile or communicate at all; he kept frowning. And then I thought of a brilliant wheeze that I knew would work on just about anyone on the continent. I turned to him and said, 'By the way, did I ever tell you that I once met Sachin Tendulkar?' The frown on his face vanished and it was as if the sun came out. He looked at me in a totally new light – it was almost adoration. I really have met legendary batsman Sachin Tendulkar, a god in India and this was to hold me in good stead for the rest of my journey. But why this small boy – who could have been no more than five or six – was travelling all on his own on the railway, I couldn't find out, but there are hundreds of dispossessed children like him travelling on trains and walking the busy roads all over India.

Travelling alone, this little lad was determinedly uninterested until I mentioned I'd met Sachin Tendulkar...

Twenty-five million passengers use the Konkan railway every year; it's not luxurious and it's not pretty, but it is very cheap, it makes the rest of India accessible for everybody and that's why it's known as the 'people's railway'. There is still crippling poverty all over India. The gap between rich and poor is probably as extreme as anywhere. A very small percentage are absurdly rich, but most of the rest are very poor and a lot of children are taught all sorts of tricks to bring a few pathetic pence into the family. You see them everywhere, performing in traffic jams, holding out their little plates. There was a small girl who did a little dance for us in our carriage and we handed her money. She was probably no more than eight years old and really should have been at school, but the money would be an essential part of some family's income.

PANVAL NADI

As the Konkan railway was completed only 20 years ago, a lot of the people who worked on the construction are still very much alive and proud of what they did. Sreedharan's right-hand man was a guy called Rajaram Bojji, the chief engineer on the whole project.

He was quite clearly held in great esteem and it had been very hard to get an interview with him because he is so busy. I met him on the station of Ratnagiri and he was incredibly helpful. He told me that Konkan had been the piece missing in the jigsaw of Indian railways. 'It was bizarre that as late as the 1990s there were thousands of people who had never seen a railway train, all living along the west coast.'

He took me to show me the Panval Nadi viaduct: 'When you see a train running along it,' he said, 'it just comes to life.' I went with him to look at his pride and joy. At 210 feet high it is the third-highest in Asia. I don't get at all wildly excited by engineering, but I must say this was something else; it looked fantastic.

Mr Bojji said, 'It never stops amazing me; it fills my heart with such a happiness, I'm telling you. There must be some kind of ultimately divine spirit that makes humans think and do things which look apparently impossible. It brings me the excitement of doing something that somebody has ordered and the acceptance of doing something that we never dreamed, so that one day we feel so happy and we end up having more than one beer.' A great bloke – we both laughed out loud. I think these guys deserve rather a lot of beer.

I took my leave of him in time to catch the train to Goa. I tried again my newly discovered technique of saying, 'Did I ever tell you I once met Sachin Tendulkar?' and it worked everywhere. I also tried it back home recently, in Southall, and it was equally effective in a crowded market when I was in a hurry. Everybody bowed and got out of my way. Try it for yourselves, it works a treat – but you do need an Indian population.

As I got on the train for Goa, there were cows on the platform. Mercifully, they didn't decide to share my carriage but just stood there mooing at me through the train window and leaving enormous calling cards on the platform.

One of our crew at this point – 6.30 am – in spite of all our warnings of being very careful with what you eat, came up to me grinning with the breakfast that he bought on the station. For a very intelligent man, he does do some incredibly stupid things. He happily shovelled down a huge, steaming bowl of liver dhansak with a not-very-clean-looking spoon. I don't know whose liver it had been, but they clearly hadn't been very well – it looked appalling, smelt appalling and he had an acutely bad stomach for the next 48 hours. I cannot imagine anyone with a quarter of a brain cell eating that anywhere in the world and certainly not India. Madness – sometimes I think the crews have just been away from home for too long. Sheer madness!

The next hop of our journey made it clear that the monsoon most certainly hadn't finished... it was absolutely lashing down and, as we looked at the rain water pouring down the little gullies and streams that ran onto the line everywhere, we could imagine just how difficult and frustrating it must have been to build this railway.

We came to the Zuari bridge; it flows over the longest river in Goa, which is tidal and very deep. They told Sreedharan it would take at least ten years to complete this bridge. His brilliant young team finished it in less than three.

Even when the Konkan railway was finished there were still problems caused by the hostile terrain and the savage monsoons. In June 2003, a landslide caused a derailment and 51 passengers died. A year later a train hit a boulder, throwing several carriages off a

The Zuari bridge over the river of the same name.

bridge and another 14 passengers were killed. Safety was always going to be a big problem in an area as wild as the west coast of India, and they now have a tremendous 24-hour team who constantly check the line for falling rocks, landslides, water damage etc.

Safety was just one of the problems for the new railway even once it was completed against all the odds. For the first ten years, the Konkan ran at a loss; they had been hoping to attract lucrative long-haul freight business, but the companies who had always used lorries found the idea of using the railway inhibiting. The despairing owners came up with the idea of a RORO (roll-on/roll-off) train, exclusively for lorries. We visited a yard where the lorries collect and there must have been over a hundred – it was a wonderful sight.

All the lorries were wildly colourful, with all sorts of personal mottos written on them, which could be philosophical, religious or plain daft. One we saw said, 'What was the meaning of life?' and another, on the front of the cab, proclaimed, 'My truck is my bride'. The RORO changed the whole economy of the region for both the railway and the haulage company and has been a fantastic financial success.

Some of the lorry drivers were very suspicious of us and gave us fierce looks, but once I tried the old 'Have I ever told you I once met Sachin Tendulkar?' routine, they melted like butter. One guy let me climb up into his cab and film him rolling onto the train. His load was spectacles, of all things – tens of thousands of them. He was driving from Mumbai to Mangalore and then Mangalore back to Mumbai, a journey of several thousand miles, but he was letting the trains do most of the work.

I used to drive lorries a long, long time ago; in fact, it was the best job I ever had, but these RORO trucks were enormous and the cabs were much more decorated and cosy than anything I used to drive from London to Liverpool. They really were beautiful.

The Konkan RORO was the first of its kind in India. Travelling at speed while sitting in the cab of a lorry on the top of an open-sided railway truck could be a bit daunting and initially a lot of the drivers were terrified that they were going to fall off, but their vehicles are heavily chained down and now there is a waiting list. The drivers save a fortune on fuel and don't have to sit for hours in traffic jams. It also saves a fortune on tyres.

NO SPITTING, NO MEN

Madgaon station was very different. A sign warning 'Anyone spitting on the station will be fined 200 rupees' greeted us as we got off and there were wonderful, full-size mural cartoons everywhere, mainly of men and women chasing each other round palm trees. Right in front of us there was a 'ladies-only waiting room'. It was very strange; this was supposedly strictly segregated and yet all the women kept waving us in. The last time I experienced that was at a brothel in Amsterdam and, no, I didn't go in there either. In still very traditional, male-dominated India, a ladies-only waiting room was really rather fun, but I didn't go in – I'm usually in enough trouble.

Looks like we got ourselves a convoy – the roll-on/roll-off (RORO) haulage business has turned around the fortunes of the Konkan railway.

Wrenching ourselves away, we made our way through the state of Karnataka towards our final destination, Mangalore. It was quite clear what a difference this railway had made. It brought work to the whole of western India and access to the rest of the continent. They called it, 'The railway built by the people for the people,' but, instead of that being no more than sickly marketing or PR-talk, it really was true – that's exactly what it is. Most of the railway's 4,500 jobs have been offered to local people and the result is that the railway has truly linked the communities. I was really impressed by the Konkan, the way it was built against all odds and the way it functions.

We came to the station at Kumta and by then it was absolutely lashing down. In the monsoon anything up to three inches of rain can fall every hour, although the locals take it in their stride. Lots of people carried on their work in shorts and I didn't see a single umbrella.

We stopped to film the Sharavati bridge, the longest on the whole of the Konkan railway at 1.25 miles in length. Looking down on it with the rain still beating down gave us a real glimpse of what it must have been like trying to complete amazing constructions like this in month after month of lashing monsoon. And yet it's just one of 2,000 bridges that had to be built. They opened on 26 January 1998 – it had taken seven years rather than five (mainly because of the problems posed by the Pernem tunnel), but it was still an incredible achievement.

The young team that were behind the railway were incredibly proud of their achievement. One of them left a wonderful note on the door of a hut beside the track that he had created: 'I take the vision which comes from dreams and apply the magic of science and mathematics, adding the heritage of my profession to create and design. I am an engineer, I serve mankind by making dreams come true.' It summed up everything that they had done in a nutshell. The Konkan railway is a wonderful tribute to an exceptional generation of Indian engineers.

The very last day of our journey we filmed the last leg as the train was nearing Mangalore, our final destination. After such an amazing journey, we had to do a big finish and Patrick the cameraman and I worked out with Barbie, our director, a splendid final piece to camera. I would be looking out of the open train door and saying something like, 'We're coming into Mangalore and, having seen what these young guys have done against everything that nature can throw at them – the monsoon, the landslides – I think what they did was just awesome. I found it inspirational and I've absolutely loved this whole journey.'

It was quite tricky to film as both the cameraman and I were bouncing around in the open doorway, so we went through it very carefully and made sure we did it in one take before one of us fell out of the train... We did it, it worked perfectly and we were elated. We shook hands, put the camera away and treated ourselves to well-deserved beers.

However – and this is something that directors always do – Barbie still wasn't happy, while the rest of us had mentally switched off. We were demob happy: we were going to have a night in a hotel, a splendid dinner and then all fly home the next morning.

Barbie suddenly said, in a pleading kind of voice, 'You know that piece we did at the end there?'

'Yes...' we said hesitantly, knowing something dreadful was coming.

'Well, wouldn't it be better if we actually were pulling into Mangalore station?'

'No,' I said immediately, 'that won't work because it will be dark by then.'

'Well...' she said, not giving up so easily, 'that would be lovely – if we had the lights of Mangalore in the background.'

Directors have a way of getting round you and, although we pleaded that we had already done the perfect ending, we grudgingly put down our beers, Pat picked up the camera again and prepared to do it one more time as darkness fell.

We really could only do this in one take as we pulled into Mangalore. The plan was that I would do my final piece and step off the train as it slowed right down. I would then walk along the platform to where it came to a final halt, the guys would pack up

Mumbai
Dasgaon village
Pune
Maharasht

quickly and they would bring all my luggage with them. Then we would all go for dinner.

'OK,' we said reluctantly, 'we've got a good take in the can anyway. We'll do it.'

About half an hour later, we saw the lights of Mangalore. 'Ready, everybody,' I said. 'Fingers crossed and good luck.' And I did the whole piece again, pretty much word for word, finishing off with, 'I've absolutely loved it.' I stepped off the slowing train. It was absolutely perfect, Barbie had been right, I realised and it had worked a treat. The train slowly passed me and I walked towards it to meet the guys, give everybody high-fives, pick up my luggage and start thinking about home.

But although the train slowed ahead of me, it never quite stopped and then, to my alarm and sheer horror, it picked up speed again and disappeared into the distance. I was completely gobsmacked. What I didn't realise at the time was that we'd filmed this epic finale as we came into Mangalore Junction. Mangalore Central, the main station, was another few miles down the track; I couldn't believe it. I was stuck in the middle of nowhere with no transport, no money and no telephone.

Luckily, I was able to use the line in the station master's office, having employed my Sachin Tendulkar routine one more time, and I got through to Barbie.

'Oh, Chris,' she said, 'this is dreadful. I'm really so, so sorry.' She said those words, all right, but from the howls of laughter from the rest of the crew in the background, I could tell she was actually fighting back hysterics. It was so absurd I broke into wild laughter myself. Well, it was dreadful, it was a five-star cock-up, but I couldn't help but see the funny side. It was one of those moments that keep camera crews and presenters going for years. In the end we used the first take anyway.

When we all met up that night, we had an even more splendid dinner than we'd planned and the next day we flew home to London.

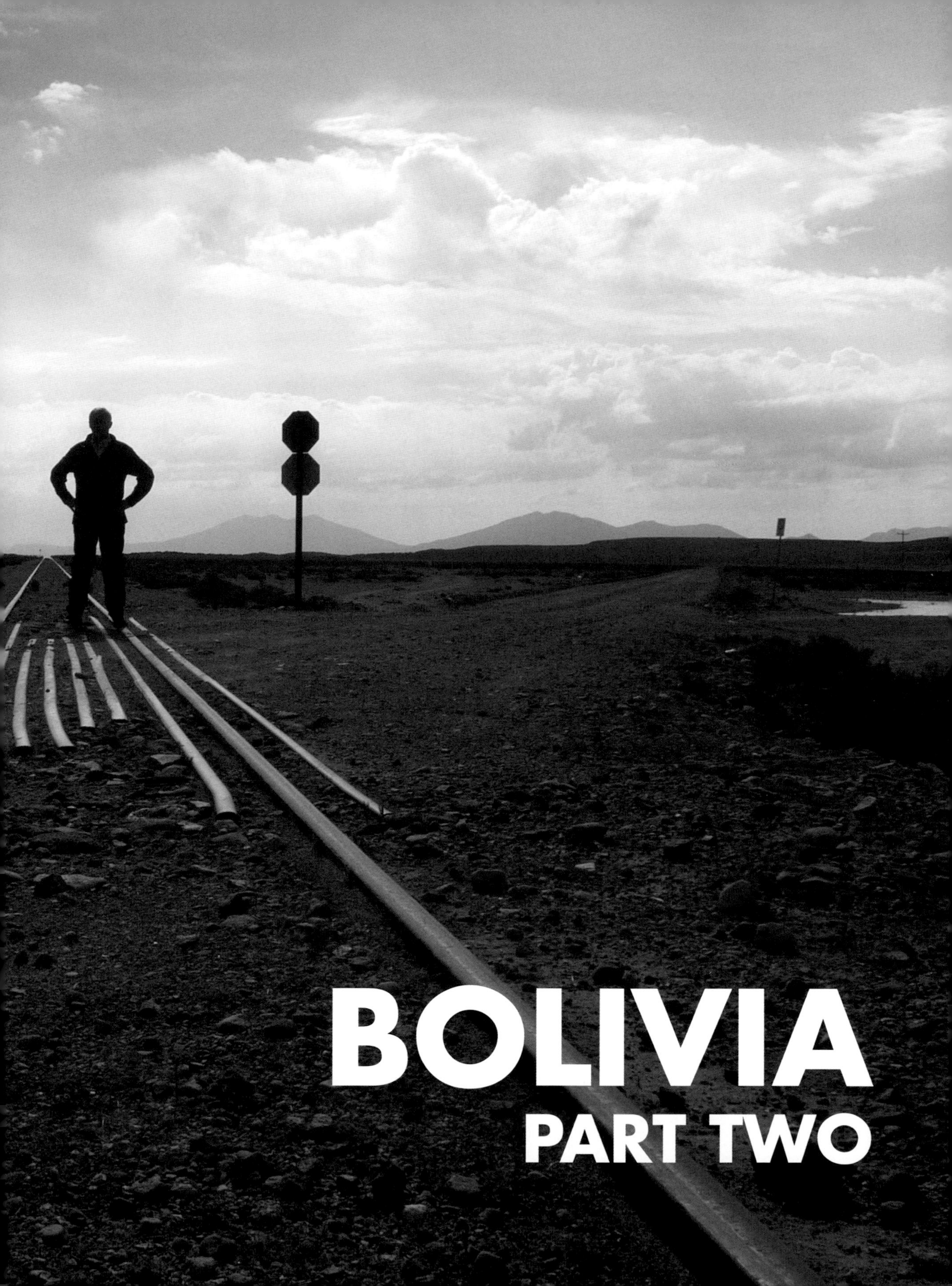

BOLIVIA
PART TWO

Barriles
María Elena
Calama
Mejillones

Following the theft of our entire film we had to return to Bolivia to make the programme all over again.

With me, from left to right: Jonathan 'JT' Thomas, Mike Harrison and Jake Martin.

Bolivia
Part Two

When we got back to Bolivia, about 18 months after our first visit (see Chapter Two), I had a sense of déjà vu. A sense of having seen it all before. But then I would because, of course, I had seen it all before, when the film had been stolen.

It had taken ages for the guys in the office to sort the insurance problems, then go through all the embarrassment of ringing people and saying, 'I'm really sorry, but the film was stolen – any chance of doing it again?' And then having to repeat the whole rigmorole of getting all the permissions and passes from the various railway authorities across two countries, Chile and Bolivia and being forced to explain why we needed permission to do exactly what we did last time. It was a logistical nightmare.

Taking all that into consideration, I was amazed at how big a welcome everybody gave us. I expected quite a few people to flatly refuse to do it again, even though it clearly wasn't our fault but the reverse was the case. The Bolivians couldn't have been nicer, made us incredibly welcome, warmly shook my hand: 'Chris, how nice to see you again...' etc.

So we started the whole trip, up and over the Andes take two. We even started at the same bar by the sea with the Andes on the other side of the road. Considering we had only been there once, we had obviously made our presence known as the barman immediately started pouring us all out pisco sours again as if we came in the pub every night. I don't remember drinking enough of them to make an impression but clearly we did and perhaps the clue is in the phrase 'I don't remember'. We got back in the little mining train and guess who was grinning at me out of the cab? Yes, Alberto. It was actually really nice to see him and he was surprisingly pleased to see me. If anything, the train ride up the sheer rockface was even more frightening than I remembered. The temperature was a lot higher than last time and our thoughts went back to brave guys who built it, back in the late 19th century, with very basic tools, in absolutely roasting heat. From Calama, we continued by train down towards Ollagüe. We were getting higher and higher and, after our experience with poor old Sam last time, we were fairly alarmed about the prospect of altitude sickness and how it might affect us.

Welcome to the hotel Atahualpa – such a lovely place. Cameraman Mike Harrison braves the 'door'.

When we got to Ollagüe, it seemed a lot smaller and less populated. We arrived in bright, sunny conditions in mid-afternoon and, although we had an address for the Hotel Atahualpa, the 'finest hotel in town', we simply couldn't find it. There was nobody around to ask, it was like the set of *High Noon*. We passed a building site two or three times that had lots of scaffolding and tarpaulin, but there was nothing else even remotely commercial. Just a row of tiny houses – not a bar, not a post office, not even a church.

As it got on towards evening and the light was beginning to fade, we began to get seriously alarmed that we might end up sleeping in the car for the night. I kept looking back at the tarpaulin-covered building site, which seemed to be in the right place but clearly wasnt a hotel. However, in desperation, I went around the back of the tarpaulin and there was a large woman with a gold tooth that glinted in the evening sunshine, sitting with two large dogs the size of horses who immediately bared their teeth and growled at me. She shouted at them in Spanish and, mercifully, they seemed to understand and put their obvious intention of eating me on ice, at least for now. She started jabbering away to me, but it was completely incomprehensible until the peso dropped and I realised that she was our host and this was indeed the Hotel Atahualpa.

I made my way back to the crew, who were sitting in the car, puzzled as to why it was taking me so long. I had a huge smile on my face. 'You're not going to believe it,' I began and, for a minute or two, they didn't. We had no choice but to accept the hospitality on offer – whatever it was. I suspected the lady propietor had had been doing some sort of renovations and had run out of money. There was certainly no sign of any builders or any sign of any work having been done for a very long time.

The front half of the hotel, with the tarpaulin, was a total bombsite and uninhabitable. There were just two rooms at the back, so we crowded into them, two to a bed. It wasn't great; in fact, it was absolutely awful, but at least there was a chance of a bit of sleep, however uncomfy, with a roof over our head (even though it could blow away at any minute if a storm came in from the Atacama desert). The upside was that the food she prepared was absolutely

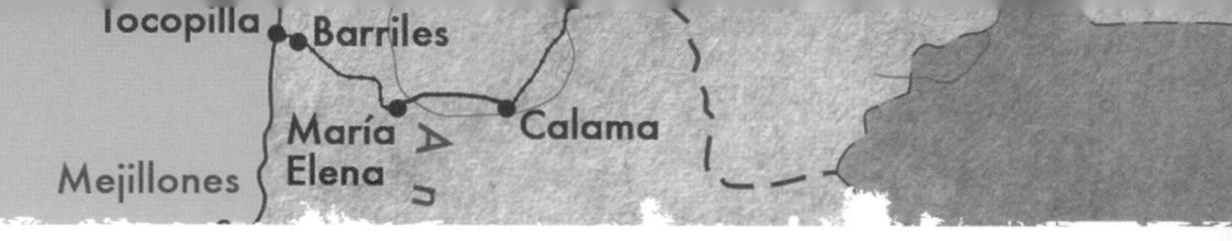

The goods trains carry valuable nitrates across Chile and Boliva.

magnificent; a huge plateful of something tasty although, to this day, when looking back on this extraordinary night, we still can't decide whether we ate lamb, pork or desert fox. We didn't care, we were starving and it tasted delicious.

I asked for a Scotch and she grinned at me and reappeared from the kitchen with a bottle of something amber in a container that could probably take about two litres. 'No, no,' I said, 'I really don't want that much,' but she wouldn't have any of it. Whatever it was, we all drank quite a lot of it between us. In fact, over the course of a hilarious evening, we gave it a damn good spanking. Whatever it was we'd been drinking, including local wines and beer and the giant bottle of amber nectar, the next morning, on the bill, it came to about ten pence.

The worst problem during the night were the enormous dogs that kept thundering up and down the corridors outside our two rooms, growling and quite clearly leaning against the doors, trying to get in our room. We ended up with a large chest of drawers across the door to keep the terrifying lurchers out. In some ways it was one of the worst nights I can ever remember, but in many ways it was so bad that we all secretly absolutely loved it. It was ridiculous and the staff couldn't have tried harder to make us welcome. Well, they could, actually – they could have put the dogs in kennels but, then again, a kennel would have been larger than any of our bedrooms.

SEARCHING FOR SALT

We awoke in high spirits because it had just been such an extreme and silly night. Anybody who ever thinks that television reporters stay in five-star hotels and are chauffered to and from location each day in stretch limos wants to have a look at the Hotel Atahualpa. I have never ever stayed anywhere like it.

The crossing of the Chilean border and then across no-man's land to the Bolivian border seemed even more senseless and pointless than ever. The Chileans were a lot tougher, going through all my documents and making annoying tutting noises, but I just did my practised gormless smile into midair and eventually they let me through. The Bolivian border patrol were even less fun but we eventually got into the country and nothing had changed. The scenery across the Altiplano was as breathtaking as ever. It really is a beautiful country and from Avaroa we took a train that got up to 4,000 metres before we started to feel ill.

We tried the various bi-products of the coca leaf again, leaving out the revolting sweets this time but doubling up on the amount of coca leaf in the tea and for most of us, that did the trick. Gloria was no more than a little queasy, most of the crew had headaches but nothing too extreme, nobody really suffered and we carried on with our ascent.

The train getting into Uyuni arrived in absolutely pouring rain and again my fears were for the salt hotel and whether it might dissolve before I got into my room. The salt roof must be reinforced somehow although, at any position in the hotel, you can wet your

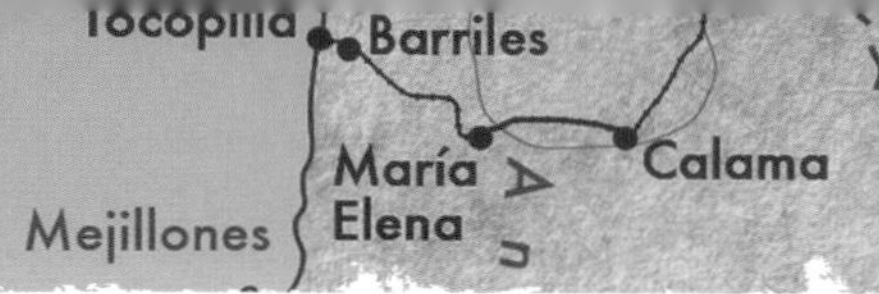

finger, touch the walls and it really does taste strongly of salt. It was, of course, a very bright hotel. Everything was white and, in the morning sunshine – the sky, luckily, had cleared overnight – it was a beautiful place to be.

However, when we got out onto the salt flats of which I had such wonderful memories, it was very different. We learnt that the rain of the previous evening had been falling for the last couple of weeks because, instead of being bright white, most of it was flooded, the water was very high and was a horrible brown colour. It was at moments like this when the anger at the theft of our film came back to haunt us because we really had shot the most beautiful scene on the salt flats that will tragically never see the light of day. Mike had taken over from Sam as our main cameraman and I had been exciting him by my description of the salt flats all the way from Heathrow. Imagine his disappointment, alongside mine, when we just found a huge, chocolate-brown flood plain. We all became completely depressed and drove on round the massive area of the flats feeling grumpy about the whole situation.

Eventually, though, we found one small area, thc land at that point a little higher. Here was a wonderful island of pure white salt, poking up through the murky water, about the size of a cricket pitch. I was so thrilled to find it, I thought nothing of wading out in my rolled-up trousers and bare feet, just to stand on a little hump of pure salt. With a bit of careful camera work and by only filming from certain angles, it looked great, although the audience will sadly never know how beautiful it was last time we called.

Even though it was in flood, it is still an amazing place. It is still the world's largest salt flat, containing more than 10 billion tonnes of salt. How absurd then that the only bit of salt that was protruding when we arrived with our cameras this time around was so small. The lithium here could be the key to Bolivia's economic future with the government planning a new railway to transport it all the way down to the coast. They would have to pay heavy duty to the deeply unpopular people of Chile.

The man whose masterplan this railway is, the new president, Evo Morales, is a staunch socialist. He is said to be a true man of

The flats were harder to capture on film the second time around.

the people and Bolivians seem to absolutely love him. So much so that every tourist shop and street stall in Uyuni sells postcards of Evo. He's a good-looking bloke with very nice hair, but I couldn't imagine there being similar demand for postcards of Theresa May, Jeremy Corbyn, Tony Blair or even Benjamin Disraeli for the cynical British market. I took a postcard of Evo around the town with me and showed it first to a man who stuck his thumb up and went, 'Yes, good man, *buena*, *buena*, *sí*, *sí*, good, super.' Quite extraordinary! And everybody else, every single man or woman that I showed it to agreed.

We drove on across the High Andes using a four-by-four to head to our next railway station. This, once again, was the centre of Potosí,

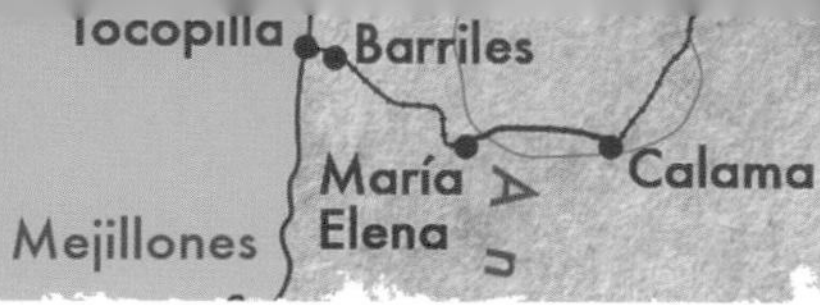

The passengers on the small train to Sucre were often dressed in traditional clothes.

formerly the capital and one of the wealthiest places on the planet. We had no big problems with altitude sickness this time around and, when we woke up, nobody was lying on the floor needing oxygen. I think we probably took more precautions on our second visit.

It was no longer a surprise what the means of conveyance was going to be from Potosí up over the mountain to the capital Sucre. It would be that funny little bus/train again that would go teetering along some very narrow-looking tracks. But what was a surprise this time was that we got a really good look at a massive old steam locomotive that was standing, looking rather unloved and abandoned, at one side of the station.

THE HIT MAN AND BOLIVIA

It turned out that this train was nearly bought years ago by record producer Pete Waterman. I see him once in a while on river banks, because Pete's a keen fisherman, but he is also an absolute train nut. So when he found this abandoned locomotive several years ago in Bolivia, he made a very large offer, which the impoverished Bolivians could barely believe. The money had been rumoured to be something around £1 million, a fantastic amount anywhere in South America and, in somewhere as poor as Bolivia, it would probably buy hundreds of houses, maybe even a whole town.

So there was tremendous excitement, communications went back and forth between Pete Waterman and the Bolivian authorities but, Bolivia being Bolivia, they simply could not get their act together. Too many bureaucrats got involved and, in the end, Waterman gave up on the whole idea, baffled and frustrated. I am afraid that this was an example of Bolivian bureaucracy at its very worst. Pete never bought the train, they never got their million and it still stands there beside the main station in Potosí, slowly rusting and falling apart.

So, shaking our heads at the story of what was nearly Pete's train, we climbed yet again onto our bus/train/whatever. The line has been running from 1916 between Sucre and Potosí. What was lovely was that Bazilio was the driver for us again; he has been driving this same train for twenty-odd years and, once again he took us up and over the mountain – this time in pouring rain.

As we looked ahead, the rails seemed to be disappearing into the mud and our train was definitely slipping. The track was extremely skiddy and the wheels didn't seem to be able to get a grip. Eventually, I jumped out with assistant driver Carlos, and we moved some fallen rocks out of the way, and literally dug around the wheels of the train like you would back home if your car got stuck in a field. Up the mountain we continued, with people getting on and off all the time.

People continued to get off, while others appeared, flagging down the train in the middle of absolutely nowhere. As we continued to climb quite steeply it became unpleasantly warm in the carriage and there was an unmistakeable smell of wee… I thought, Some of these macho-looking blokes must be more frightened than they're letting on… It was certainly a long way down. We got to the the peaks at the highest point of our journey, nearly 5,000 metres above sea level and at last we started gently going back down. We had come a very long way from the coast of Chile and right across the Atacama desert, but now we were beginning to make our descent.

From the concerned look on Bazilio's face, I could tell he wasn't at all happy. 'I hate going down in these conditions' he said. 'This is much more dangerous in the wet than going up.' At one point there was an enormous rock, a real boulder, across the line, but they got out again, smashed it with sledgehammers and moved the obstacle away from the line.

We came in over a really ancient rickety wooden bridge and the river underneath was absolutely raging. Bazilio was very quiet for this period of the journey and I was really delighted that he was concentrating so hard. Certainly, if we slipped off that bridge, I don't think any of us would have survived. Whether it was the rushing water, I'm not sure but, once we were over the bridge, seven or eight passengers got up and pressed the bell to get Bazilio to stop because they all wanted to get off to answer the call of

Rocks rather than leaves on the line are a problem for the little line in the Andes.

nature beside the track. This no longer surprised us as they'd all done exactly the same thing on our last trip. The first time, though, as I remembered, it was all men. This time around there was an equal proportion of men and women, the men turning their backs from the carriage and pointing towards the steep rocks on the side of the track. What struck me this time as unusual but also fascinating was that the ladies on the train did exactly the same. I don't know how to phrase this delicately, but they basically lifted their skirts up and pointed their bodies forwards in exactly the same direction as the men. No squatting, none of that nonsense, just stand and deliver.

All eight of them clambered back onto the train, looking relieved and very pleased with themselves, and I couldn't help noticing for the first time that all the women wore voluminous skirts and multi-layered petticoats. It could explain why the air in the carriage was so pungent – and there was me blaming the boys...

Back down at journeys end we took big gulps of fresh air and it was good to be back in Sucre again. It was a lovely city, although this time around we were taking more precautions. No film rushes were carried on the plane; we had one member of our crew, Jake, whose enthusiasm and capacity for taking on dogsbody tasks was, happily, boundless. It was his duty every night to make digital copies of each single frame of film that we'd shot each day. This time it all got home safely with dozens of spare copies of everything.

I had left Bolivia the first time around in the blackest of moods – in fact, I was sick to my gut – but we were all delighted that they'd so happily invited us all back again. Bolivians have suffered so much over the centuries and perhaps, in some ways, they have not helped themselves, but they are among the warmest people on Earth; they could not have been more helpful and friendly and the scenery was some of the most breathtaking I've seen anywhere on the planet. It was an amazing journey, a great adventure and it really did need to be captured and shared on film. OK, it took us two goes to achieve that goal, but it was well worth trekking across Bolivia a second time.

MYANMAR

Hellfire Pass
Nam Tok
River Kwai Bridge
Bangkok

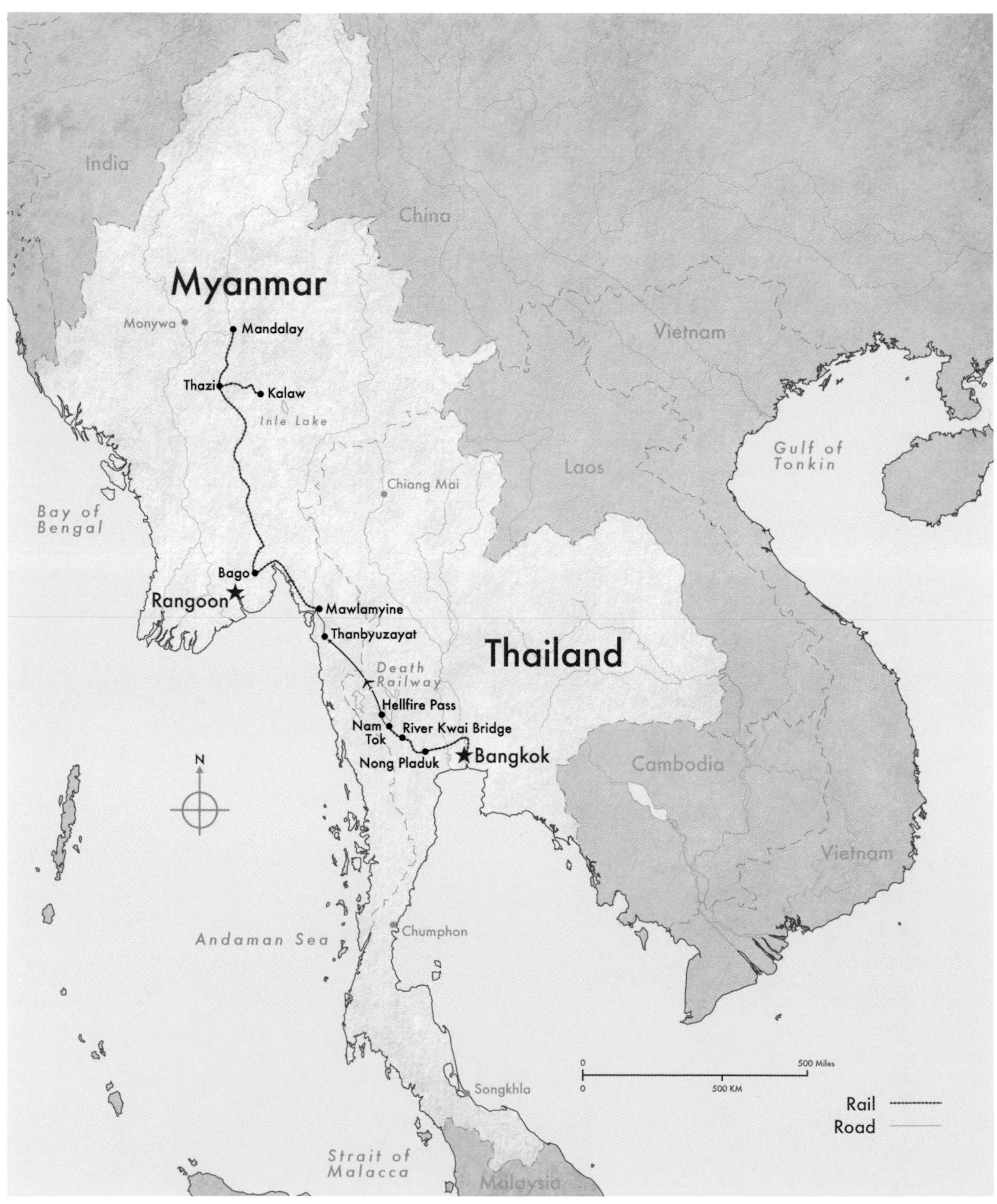

Myanmar

The last time I was in Bangkok, I ended up on stage with a Chinese girl dressed only in a bowler hat and a pair of knee-warmers, but that's not relevant to this story.

We were in Thailand on our way into the very heart of Myanmar, the former Burma. I was really excited because I had never been to Burma before. For years the military authorities had pretty much stopped any tourists from getting into the country at all. The signs were, in the years after the millennium, that at last they were beginning to relinquish their strong-arm hold, that a new more liberal government just might finally take over from the military and the doors to this beautiful ancient country might finally be starting to open, at least just a bit.

We were beginning our journey at Bangkok's Thonburi station, waiting for the 7.50 am train to Nam Tok. There was a man who looked incredibly like soul legend James Brown on the station who seemed to be in charge. He kept self-importantly looking at his watch even though there was no sign of the train coming. I regaled him with a couple of verses of 'Papa's Got a Brand New Bag' but, puzzlingly, he looked at me like I should be locked up. Funny that; it happens a lot. Eventually, our man – let's call him James – declared that the train was arriving at our platform in a few minutes' time. 'Get on up!' I exclaimed. 'You're a sex machine, shake your money-maker,' and he just wandered away, shaking his head.

The train was fairly basic to say the least and when I, rather foolishly, peeped into the toilet I decided there and then that, however urgently nature called, I would keep my knees together for the whole journey. It really was pretty grim. We bought some food on the train for the princely sum of 30 baht; I think that's about 50-60p but, once we'd taken the lid off the container we decided it didn't look too clever at all and may well have explained the state of the lavatory. Either way, we put the top back on and left it where it was. Thirty baht was 30 baht but I wasn't going to eat that.

An hour out of Bangkok, we approached the start of the first railway that we'd come to film. It's a very well-known railway line, but for all the wrong reasons. It was built at the height of WWII, when Burma and Thailand were under the control of the all-conquering Japanese army. Its official title was the Burma-Siam Railway but, for altogether horrific reasons, everybody knows it as Death Railway.

After conquering Burma in 1942, the Japanese seemed irresistible in south-east Asia, but they desperately needed to build a railway right across Thailand to bring in men, supplies and, of course, weapons. Enslaved Asian workers, plus mainly British and Australian prisoners-of-war, were put to work building the line in the most appalling conditions. It was estimated that over 100,000 labourers died building this one railway.

We were about 50 miles from Bangkok at a place called Nong Pladuk junction. This was a quiet, peaceful, pleasant little place but had been the birthplace of Death Railway. The old railway line itself fell apart and was more or less lost back into the jungle at the end of WWII after the Japanese surrendered. But in the 1950s they reconstructed parts of Death Railway, using some of the original sleepers and some of the original bits of track and this was what we were travelling along at that precise moment. Many of the prisoners who survived the appalling conditions in the camps were horrified that anyone would want to reconstruct any reminders of some of the most brutal behaviour in human history but for others, particularly the booming Thailand tourist industry – and, I have to admit, me – there is a ghoulish fascination about the whole place. It was impossible really to imagine the horrors that had occurred all along the line that we were travelling on.

They reckon that one man died for every single sleeper that was laid along the Death Railway line and that's probably an underestimation. So it was in a sombre mood that we followed the course of the Khwae Yai river, looking out of the train window, until we came to one of the most famous bridges in the world. But famous for all the wrong reasons. Notorious, really. What was fictionalised as *The Bridge Over the River Kwai* has become a tourist mecca.

I'd obviously seen the film with Alec Guinness and I was aware of the tens of thousands who died building it but what we actually found was very disturbing in a quite different way. It's now one of the biggest attractions in the whole of Asia and it even has its own railway station. Tourists flock here from all over the world, following the film and the best-selling book that it was based on, but the whole place was a giant funfair. There

The crossing later fictionalised as *The Bridge Over the River Kwai* has become something of a tourist spot.

were souvenir stalls, ridiculous hats and key rings, etc and there was blaring pop music playing across the bridge. People wandered about in 'I've crossed the bridge over the river Kwai' T-shirts, eating hot dogs and, of course, taking brainless, grinning selfies in the middle of the bridge. When I reflected on the tens of thousands that died here, I found the whole thing disgusting. Presumably, there is a new generation who have no idea of what even happened here some 70 years ago, but surely those who died should be remembered by history better than this? I found it all thoroughly sickening.

In addition, the film and the book got quite a lot of things badly wrong. For starters they picked the wrong river. Pierre Boulle, who wrote the book, made one tiny basic mistake, in getting the river wrong – it was actually on the river Mae Khlung. By the early 1960s, when the tourists started to come here in big numbers, this became a serious problem, because the bridge wasn't where they expected it to be. The enterprising Thais had a marketing brainwave and renamed the Nae Khlung the Kwae Yai ('Big Kwai'). And this is now the bridge over the river Kwai (I hope you're following this; I'm not sure that I am).

In front of the backdrop of the funfair, I met Andrew Snow, a great authority on the bridge. He was very sceptical about a lot of what was portrayed in the film. He said much of the content of the book was pretty silly and made a point of telling me that one of Boulle's other famous books was *Planet of the Apes*. He conceded that some of the details in the movie are accurate, but the basic premise of British prisoners-of-war teaching the Japanese how to build a bridge was nonsense. The Japanese were excellent engineers and knew exactly how to construct every aspect of a railway.

He said the problem with the visitors to the bridge, who come on a one-day tour, is that they probably don't even realise what they are seeing. Many of them are very ignorant and a lot of Japanese learn nothing about what happened at school at all. In fairness, he said, when they do learn the full story they are very shocked and apologetic. Whatever your misgivings about the sideshow aspect, you can't expect a generation to feel responsible for something they had never even heard about.

I was glad to have made the visit but was always aware that it was the site of one of the most sickening episodes of a horrific war that my own father and his brother were involved in. I found the armies of people with their silly hats deeply lacking in respect for all those who died.

DEATH RAILWAY VIADUCT

We boarded the train heading east and the railway started to climb. The rugged mountainous terrain must have made life for the engineers and the workers even more difficult. They had to construct 688 bridges and viaducts but, before we could get to one of the most impressive of them all, in something around 38 degrees Celsius of baking heat, our train broke down. We stopped in the middle of nowhere. We were close enough to the Wang Pho viaduct to walk along the track, which is exactly what we did. It is a massive construction that the Japanese built with forced labour and using local hardwood trees. It would be an incredible structure in any circumstances, but with the deprivation and lack of supplies in the middle of a brutal war, it was a hugely impressive achievement, although the methods used were appalling.

In 1943, the horrific regime became far more brutal than it had been even in the year before. The officers in charge introduced a new work plan known as 'Speedo'. The war-masters back in Tokyo were in a desperate hurry to get the railway finished to move the supplies they needed to take their conquering army into Burma and, presumably, from there into India and throughout Asia, but they were a long way from their supply base and nowhere near the sea.

The worst of the abuse and suffering happened at our next stop. It was a chilling and eerie place called Hellfire Pass. A very deep cutting for the railway was built while the Japanese guards stood on the top on either side, looking down on the prisoners and throwing rocks for their own amusement or firing at anyone who stopped working for even a few seconds. It has been estimated that more than 5,000 men were put to work on Hellfire Pass, from 1942 onwards. It was relentlessly harsh; many died through disease, malnutrition or sheer exhaustion, others were bayonetted or beheaded as an example to the rest of the workforce. Once Speedo began the suffering was doubly intensified.

The whole of Hellfire Pass was sheer rock and in savage heat of up to 40 or even 50 degrees Celsius, working by hand with picks, shovels and hand-drills, the labourers cut their way as best they could through the pass. But the Japanese wanted it built in half the time. They made the men work 18 hours a day. The prisoners were already pathetically under-fed and suffering from cholera, malaria and dysentery. They were forced to work all through the night, with lanterns all along the rock-face, while great chunks of flint flew everywhere and men died where they stood. One young soldier said, 'This is Dante's *Inferno*; this is a vision of hell!' Hundreds died in that short, savage summer and, by October 1943, after 16 months of appalling mistreatment and a huge loss of life, Death Railway was completed.

What I found most depressing of all was that just decades later most of it had completely disappeared and been claimed back by the jungle. There were no signs left of the old railway line on most places. Nature has reclaimed it and it is almost impossible to find any sign of the tracks or sleepers anywhere. Historically, it seems that the men who died over the course of this horrific construction mainly disappeared without trace. There were virtually no graves nor any sign of any of the men who died. Skeletons were once scattered along the way and these too have disappeared into the jungle. Some had been found with snakes slithering through their eyeholes.

There was one location where there have always been remnants of everything that happened on Death Railway. It has remained more or less intact since 1945, but because the country itself was so secretive, very few people have ever visited it.

We had to travel on by four-by-four for another couple of hundred miles to a place called Thanbyuzayat. This is where we first crossed

Myanmar had a very different atmosphere as a country to Thailand.

into Myanmar and, although we were only just over the border from Thailand, already there was a very different feel to the new country. The red-and-yellow robed monks were everywhere. They were treated with enormous respect; there were shrines or pagodas everywhere – many of them very beautiful, gleaming with gold. Everybody meditates every single day.

There were buddhas absolutely everywhere and, somehow, among all this, just on the edge of Thanbyuzayat, there was a very special place that marked the end of Death Railway. It was the war-graves cemetery, literally the real end of the line for more than 3,000 Commonwealth men who died building it. What struck me more than anything as I walked along row upon row of crosses was the age of the great majority who died – 18... 21... 22... virtually nobody over 25. I found it very hard to deal with. My own son is just 22 years old and the idea of him dying in such an horrific way is unthinkable. It was such a tragic waste of the potential of so many young lives and so many were murdered in the most evil manner – so many young promising lives just wasted. I said on film, 'You're just not supposed to see the grave of your own child in your own lifetime. I cannot imagine anything more against the rule of nature.'

And all that just to build a railway.

Away from the graveyard there was one of the original Japanese steam locomotives, a genuine survivor from WWII, one of hundreds that ran along Death Railway line. It brought supplies, men, food and arms into Burma in 1943 and 1944 and then, by the beginning of 1945, when the whole war began to change and the balance of power completely shifted, it took hundreds of defeated Japanese troops back through Thailand. Many of them were going to be executed for war crimes.

The abandoned steam locomotive was actually in a clearing in a wood, a very important place historically. It was here that Death Railway linked up with a much bigger railway system, the still busy, British-built Myanmar rail network. It remains one of the country's main lines. The British took control of Burma in the middle of the 19th century and, as they did in most places that they conquered around the world, they immediately started building railways. Almost 2,000 miles of track was laid in this area from the 1870s onwards and most of those lines still survive.

THE RAILWAY TO MANDALAY

I was really excited to be in Burma and the people were delightful. They had that lovely, gentle Buddhist quality about them, but also they were intrigued by us. Many of them had never ever seen a westerner before.

I made my way north by rustic car and distinctly unsafe motorbike to the city of Mawlamyine, once the capital of British Burma. The style of the buildings was still very white and wonderfully colonial. Most of the bigger houses date back to the days of the Raj, when British gentlemen wore pith helmets and went pig-sticking and took tiffin in the afternoons. Well, for good or bad, those days have gone but the elegant style of the architecture is still very much there.

There was a splendid pagoda in the middle of the city that was the inspiration for a young Rudyard Kipling, who was completely entranced by the beauty of a stunning young Burmese girl he saw sitting shyly on the steps. His poem 'Mandalay' was a tribute to her, although it's written through the eyes of an old cockney soldier and Kipling himself never did get to Mandalay. Still, the creator of *The Jungle Book* is surely allowed a little poetic licence and 'Come you back, you British soldier; come you back to Mawlamyine,' would somehow quite never have the same magic.

Bright and early the next day we were headed for Mandalay ourselves, back on the main line heading north. We wanted to get to the town of Bago by the end of the day, and we were warned that while the trains were regular and fairly punctual they were a bit thin on comfort.

It took a while to get my ticket because it was actually handwritten – very nice writing, very impressive but can you imagine them trying to do that in the rush hour at King's Cross?

At a Buddhist shrine in Myanmar.

Anyway, the very nice man jabbered at me in some variant of Burmese and off I was sent, into a very basic-looking carriage. There was ordinary class and upper class. We weren't too impressed by what we took to be upper class and the only way to get to standard accommodation was to jump across the open coupling. I could see the rails under my feet as I sailed over and, had I slipped, presumably I'd have been completely flattened underneath the carriages. Tourism does seem to have finally arrived in Myanmar but health and safety clearly hasn't. In any case, after my death-defying leap as we reached standard seating, it was to find it looked exactly the same as the alleged upper class.

The train itself didn't seem to be in great condition; I wouldn't like to be travelling on it in the dark, because absolutely nothing electrical seemed to work. Aside from that, it was a beautiful journey. It was early morning and the scenery outside was misty with a promise of a very hot summer's day. The sun glinted on the pagodas and we were travelling on a railway line built by British engineers well over a hundred years ago. We felt special.

Even more special, when we got to a place called Thanlwin, there was the most magnificent bridge across a large expanse of water. It's four miles long, a road and rail bridge across a gap that used to be traversable across only by a ferry that took hours and hours. Now in a car or a train you can cross it in a couple of minutes. The whole thing was created, built and paid for by the Myanmar government and neither the British nor anyone else had anything to do with its creation. This was a country that really saw its railway network as essential and was determined to keep it running. We did notice, though, that most of the railway workers were working in pretty grim conditions in stifling heat for all of the summer months. The tools they were using to repair the lines looked incredibly basic, probably the same as those used by the British in the 1890s.

There was still terrible poverty in Myanmar and the women seemed to do an awful lot of the manual work. One of the most striking sights we saw several times from our train window was gangs of very hardened-looking ladies working on the roads, with no sign of a man for miles. They resurfaced the roads a yard at a time with red-hot tar that was boiled in a bucket by the roadside and poured out very carefully and slowly for every foot of the road. This was in temperatures that were already well over 40 degrees Celsius; it must have been exhausting, arduous work and all done only by women – almost certainly for a miniscule wage. Some things in Myanmar have come a long way but clearly not everything. This work for these women looked positively medieval.

The railway workers had replaced a whole section of old wooden sleepers on our route with brand-new concrete sleepers but, apparently, they had run out of ballast. This meant, we were told, that in places the ride could become a little bumpy.

A *little* bumpy?

I had never known anything like it. The train would suddenly start to shake violently and we would find ourselves, a whole carriage at a time, being hurled up into the air, before bouncing back into our seats. At times we were propelled at least two foot into space and, for me, the finest moment of this extraordinary journey was when Mike our intrepid cameraman was thrown so violently into the air while looking through his view-finder that he actually hit the back of his head on the carriage roof and then, as he came crashing down again, had the audacity to complain.

For us, it was ridiculous, funny, painful and at times even quite scary. You got a feeling that there was something terribly wrong, but we survived and obviously the footage we got was amazing and very amusing. But the people in the rest of the carriage with us were the locals who had to suffer this same absurd journey probably twice a day, five or six times a week. When we left the carriage, they still seemed to be smiling stoically and I didn't imagine there was likely to be any improvement in the immediate future. It was just how it was and that seemed to be their approach to the trip.

BAKING IN BAGO

When we got to the station we were very, very pleased to get off and the place swarmed with food sellers. They walk all day in the baking heat with boxes piled high on their heads, loaded with a range of typical local delights. Everything seemed to be served up in banana leaves. I'm normally very careful about these sort of things when I am abroad but, presumably still concussed from the journey, I plumped for a strange-looking, dark object wrapped inside leaves with a little side cup of sticky rice. The sticky rice frankly was disgusting and whatever the dark object was it tasted like a dead donkey! I'm not an advocate of litter-louting but I have to admit my knee-jerk reaction to mine was to throw it straight out of the window.

Bago itself was a manic city, scooters tooting everywhere with

Cambodia

At four miles in length, Thanlwin bridge is the longest in Myanmar and can accommodate pedestrians as well as traffic.

tremendous hustle and bustle day and night. It is one of the busiest places I have seen in south-east Asia and, having been to Ho Chi Minh City, that's really saying something. I travelled by rickshaw to one of the most impressive sights I've ever seen anywhere in the world. It was an extraordinary discovery made in 1880 by contractors when they were sent here by the British to make some improvements on the railway lines. As they cut through a massive area of jungle they discovered what they thought was a very large boulder. They then stood back and had a better look; it was an enormous Buddha believed to have been built in the tenth century.

It is now being completely cleaned, a process which is taking years, but it still stands – or rather lies reclining – today in the place where it was rediscovered more than 130 years ago. It is worshipped by the Myanmar people and the scale of it is quite extraordinary – it's 180 feet long and over 50 feet high. Its big toe is taller than the average man and it's over a thousand years old. That something so enormous had been completely hidden in the jungle for so long was quite amazing, but the British rulers at the time showed great common sense in letting the people maintain it and protect it for the future. They built a colossal shed, like a giant aircraft hanger and that is where the people from all over the country flock to see this extraordinary statue.

The whole area is steeped in history. I was actually allowed to have a go in an ancient Victorian signal box; the very nice station-master who let me in clearly had no idea how ham-fisted I am. I started pulling a series of levers and signals outside began going up and down – I think I may have completely re-routed the Myanmar railway system for the rest of that day. But it was fun and the people there were always so polite and accommodating, however daft I was.

The next day, early in the morning (why does filming always start *so* early in the morning?), we began journeying up the mountains to a place called Kalaw. It was actually breath-taking scenery, probably the most spectacular we had seen on this trip. We were climbing into the foothills of the Shan Hills, which eventually go to the border with China. We were way above 4,000 feet and trains really don't like going uphill.

To get up one particularly steep incline and around a sharp bend, the railway builders had constructed a traditional zig-zag system that had not been changed or bettered for well over a hundred years. The Burmese version of the system works like this: a man, invariably wearing a silly hat, goes to the front of the train with a flag. Another bloke stands at the back of the train with his own flag and the driver then basically reverses uphill. At a certain point he makes a hand gesture (that's the 'zig') and will then go forward (up a 'zag') and this is repeated that all the way to the top of the mountain. They have been doing so since the 19th century.

The air at the summit was clear and sweet and the views were magnificent. Apparently, members of the British Raj used to come up here in the summer months when it got too hot for them on the plain.

There is a huge sheet of water up here, Inle Lake and there have always been many different tribes living in this area, each with its own language and traditions and virtually nothing seems to have changed since the British discovered this area. To give an idea of the scale, there were more than 70,000 people living around the shore living by selling vegetables or catching and selling fish.

The technique one tribe use for fishing is one of the oddest and silliest I have ever seen. They make a strange motion, of treading water, while slowly moving forward with long baskets held out in front of them in the water… they then leg-row slowly out into the middle of the lake, trying to attract fish into the baskets in front of them. It's incredibly hard work and, certainly when we filmed them, not particularly productive, but apparently this was a fairly typical day. Why they didn't just throw out a worm with a hook on God only knows but this technique had been used by the people of the Intha tribe for centuries so they were probably not going to change now.

The railway is the only means of access for the tribes of the rest of the world. The whole lake is one huge floating garden and they produce thousands of tons of vegetables every year. Much of that is now distributed by train right across Myanmar. It is a beautiful place with lovely welcoming people and there is a wonderful sense there of nothing having changed for hundreds of years. We liked them and they seemed to like us, but their cats didn't.

THE CAT OF THE RAILWAY TRAIN

When we grabbed some dinner in a small, back-street café, JT, our ever-so-slightly mad Welsh soundman, suddenly let out a strange, strangled squawk, jumped up holding his bare leg and whimpered. We thought it was some new Welsh folk-dance and at first found it wonderfully funny. In fact though, he'd been bitten under the table by a manky-looking moggy and, as the marks on his leg started to look very angry and swollen, we realised it might be serious.

He was jabbering and making no sense, but then he was always like that. Now, though, he was getting very hot and was in a lot of pain. We started to think it could well be rabies and we were in the middle of nowhere. Eventually, after a horrible drive through the night, JT reached a doctor and was given lots of jabs and sent home in a bad way. It was indeed an infected bite but luckily not rabies.

Another piece of luck was that we were close to the end of the film and so we muddled by without our main soundman. All was well, but it was a nasty moment, and – as far as health went – a portent of worse things to come.

On the last day, we made our way finally up to Mandalay, the city Rudyard Kipling never did get to see. We'd travelled nearly two thousand miles of railways from Thailand, following the grotesque route of Death Railway right the way through central Thailand, the line that the prisoners-of-war built, over the border into Myanmar and then we had taken a whole string of different trains (string actually being what held some of them together) to make our way up to Mandalay.

The former Burmese are extraordinary people and, rather like their railway system, they have endured and have survived. They lived under the British, they have suffered under their own, very harsh, military regime and, of course, they were treated brutally by the Japanese, but somehow they have kept their dignity and their kindness; they are amazing people.

We'd travelled something like 30,000 miles in the last month, from London to Bolivia, back to London briefly for a couple of days just to change clothes, picked up items of filming equipment and then we had travelled on to Thailand up to Mandalay. Something probably had to give and, on the way home, it did.

Lake Inle is still incredibly busy even today.

CUBA

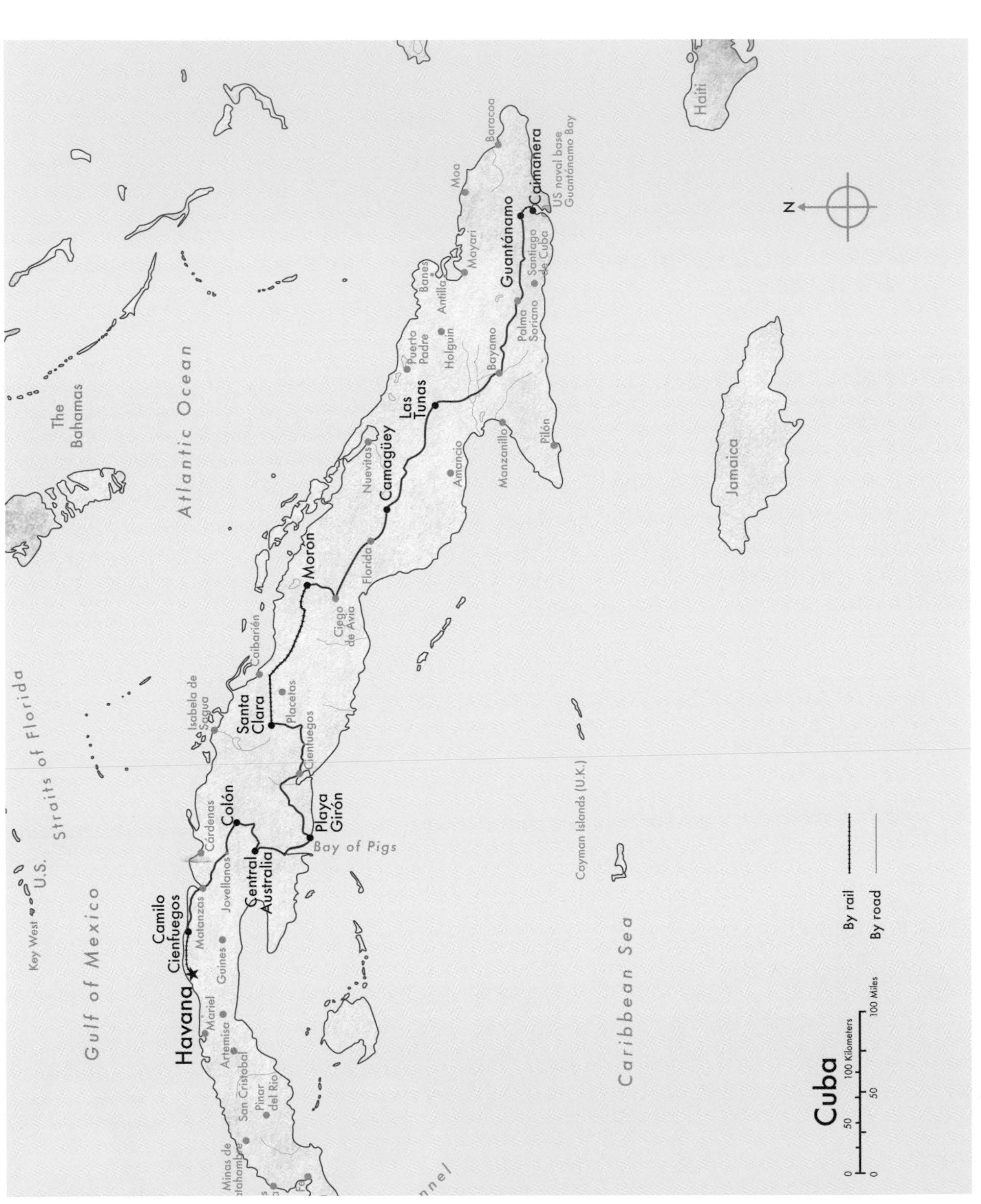

Cuba
Havana
Camilo Cienfuegos
Colón
Central Australia
Playa Girón
Bay of Pigs
Santa Clara
Morón
Camagüey
Las Tunas
Guantánamo
Caimanera
US naval base Guantánamo Bay
Key West
U.S.
Straits of Florida
Gulf of Mexico
The Bahamas
Atlantic Ocean
Caribbean Sea
Cayman Islands (U.K.)
Jamaica
Haiti
By rail
By road
N

Cuba

I got to Cuba – eventually – and, yes, I did get to the country's railway system, but first I have to retrace probably the most extreme and the most painful of any of my journeys. I was in serious danger and there wasn't a train involved yet, and, frankly, I am lucky to be here to tell you about it.

We had finished in Myanmar and it was only a short hop by plane to Bangkok for the flight home. I was looking forward to it, I hadn't really been home for weeks. I rang my girlfriend Jane from Bangkok airport, told her I loved her and that I'd be home late that night. She was coming to the airport with Jim, my driver, for the final leg of the journey home to Berkshire

I spent about an hour in the airport lounge before going down to board the plane. I was sitting quietly, waiting for the long queue of passengers to clear, when I felt a bit dizzy and – embarrassingly enough for any bloke usually in control of himself – slipped off my seat. A very nice man sitting opposite seemed to recognise me. 'Are you OK, Chris? Are you all right?' he said.

'Yes, I'm fine, sorry,' I told him. 'I've had a bit of a stint travelling and I think that was just a bit of cramp, but thanks.' I boarded the plane and looked forward to trying to get a few hours sleep. I never sleep particularly well while flying.

The rest of the blokes were still in Bangkok filming a few extra scenes and there were very few people in business class so I was pretty much on my own. After an hour in the air I felt my right leg become very numb and I realised that I'd also got a real cramp in my right arm; it came and went in a matter of minutes and I thought no more about it.

Those around me seemed to be settling in for a good night's sleep.

I tried to read, still puzzled by what had happened to my right side, but thinking it was nothing more than cramp, I dozed for a while. It was only when I went to get something out of the overhead locker that, trying to stand up, I found again my right leg just didn't seem to be working at all and I couldn't lift my right arm above my head.

At this point I became seriously worried. Again, after about ten minutes, the sensation went away and all was well. I suppose it's a typically British thing, but I didn't want to make a fuss, I just wanted to get back home. Maybe if this condition carried on coming and going much longer, I thought, I would make a point of seeing my doctor first thing Monday morning. And it did come again, about an hour later; this time it was really bad. I felt an acute pain in my leg and my arm just wouldn't lift above my waist at all. I think it was then, now it was happening for the third time that the penny began to drop – I might be having a stroke.

Absurdly, I didn't tell the stewardesses at this point. Most of them had gone to sleep and, while they were very nice, all were Thai and spoke virtually no English

In any case, I thought, if this is really bad, what could they actually do?

I had heard of situations in which people become really ill and the crew land the plane to get the emergency case hospitalised locally, but when I thought about the journey from Bangkok to London I couldn't see where on earth anybody would land. I suspected the hospital facilities in the new Myanmar still weren't great and, past there, it would be somewhere like Azerbaijan? Or Uzbekistan? Or Iraq? Iran? Syria? None of them seemed remotely like the place where anyone would want to be hospitalised for a day, let alone maybe a couple of months. Much later people would tell me, 'You must have been mad; you should have contacted the stewardesses' and, with hindsight, they are probably right, but at the time I just wanted to get home.

The numbness in my right side kept coming and going. When it went away I was absolutely fine for maybe 30–40 minutes before it returned. Each time, it seemed to be a little more severe and I began to get frightened.

It was the longest flight of my life. I desperately tried to use the in-flight satellite phone – I knew they charge something like £100 a second, but money was the least of my considerations. I wanted to ring Jane, warn her that something was seriously wrong. My plan was to try to get to the closest A&E to Heathrow as soon as we landed.

But even the satellite telephone couldn't get any sort of signal. Now I really did get very scared. A few times the thought came that I could actually die up there in that plane.

And still I stubbornly did not summon a stewardess. It must have been the longest 14 hours of my life.

Yet as we landed at Heathrow I found myself perfectly capable of standing up and getting my bag from the overhead locker. It was only as I started walking out of the plane that it finally got really bad. I walked slower and slower, everybody seemed to be going past me and giving me strange looks until, eventually, I keeled over.

I was conscious but now obviously past the point of caring. I was on the ground and completely unable to get up. The same lovely guy and his wife who'd seen me slip over at Bangkok airport spotted me again, and he said, 'You're not right, are you, Chris?' and I said, 'No, you're right, I'm really not.'

He said, 'I think it's a stroke.'

'So do I.'

At this point I have to say I have maligned Heathrow airport many times over the years for delays, long waits at passport control, absurdly long queues at the x ray machines etc. But on this night, they were fantastic. It was all a blur but, within less than a minute, a wonderful paramedic arrived, making his way through the crowds by bicycle. He was brilliant; got me settled on the floor, took all the necessary tests and confirmed, 'Yes, I'm pretty sure you've had a stroke.'

At the same time, two wonderful police officers arrived, a man and a woman and they got straight through to Jane and my driver Jim, who were waiting the other side of the barrier. They told them that I was being taken by ambulance to Charing Cross hospital. The policewoman suggested it would be best if they went straight to the hospital and meet me there. The officers couldn't have been more efficient or kinder and I was stretchered onto an ambulance in no time. With siren blaring, we raced through the Saturday night traffic to the hospital in Hammersmith.

I'd never been in an ambulance before, except when my father was very ill, and I remember lying there, listening to the siren and racing through all the traffic that pulled to one side out of the way on the Chiswick flyover, and thinking, ridiculously, Wow, this is pretty cool... There was nothing cool about it, of course; I'm an idiot but it took my mind off the real worry of my situation.

The next 24 hours passed in a haze. I was raced into the emergency ward, where a very worried Jane was waiting. She was fantastic, sitting by me and communicating with the doctors as my speech was not too good at all.

I'd completely lost the use of my right side of my body and a

Recovery from my illness took precedence over the series and it would be more than a year before I was able to get to the railways of Cuba.

quite remarkable man, Dr Sharma – clearly one of the main men in this wonderful hospital – just took over the situation. He confirmed that I'd had a stroke and told all the juniors around him exactly what drugs to start pumping into me. He got me into a private ward and was just fantastic in every way.

I was absolutely exhausted and deeply frightened but determined not to go to sleep under any circumstances. I had this wild notion that I wouldn't wake up so I kept fighting tiredness throughout the night, as different members of my family came in looking worried and shocked and took turns to hold my – working – hand.

I do remember trying to chat to my dear daughter, Jennifer, very early the next morning and desperately trying to lift my arm up but I just couldn't do it. I was so frustrated, I was sweating with effort and I just couldn't get the hand to open or the arm to lift off the bed at all. She said, 'Not to worry, Dad,' but I could tell she was frightened.

We managed a sort of slurred conversation – slurred on my part, at least – until, less than an hour later, my arm amazingly felt lighter and I was able to lift it right above my head. It was the most wonderful feeling and Jen was as delighted as I was. It wasn't to last. Later on in the day, the arm relapsed to its earlier condition, completely seizing up.

This was to be the pattern for my first 36 hours in hospital; everything would get better and then get worse again and each time it did my mood would plunge into black despair. This was the effect of the drugs kicking into my system and, by somewhere early in the morning of day two, my arms and legs were very much on the mend. I dreaded a second stroke but it never materialised, thank God and although this was a terrifying time for all of us, I could nevertheless see daily improvements.

At first I found silly things like cleaning my teeth absolutely impossible. I remember looking at myself in the mirror and saw I had a bright, white, shiny nose. But I simply couldn't master the motion we all take for granted all our lives of working a toothbrush up and down. So for a few days I used a ridiculous technique I'd developed of holding the brush still but moving my head up and down fast against it. It was pretty funny but it did give me reasonably clean teeth and I no longer had a bright white nose.

For a week or so I couldn't catch a ball, something that I'd always taken for granted. I couldn't throw a ball, either and I couldn't even run on the spot. In fact, going up and down stairs I became really wobbly, but I continued to work with my physiotherapist every day and the improvements came little and often.

After a fortnight, Dr Sharma agreed that I could go home, although I was very firmly told that I must keep taking all the medicine he prescribed and complete a full course of physiotherapy. I wanted to do the physio anyway; in fact I was looking forward to it, because I could feel that it was making me better by the day.

As I left, I shook Dr Sharma warmly by the hand and thanked him so much for everything he'd done. 'You've been very lucky, you know,' he said.

I agreed, 'Yes, I know, very lucky, I could have died,' but what he said next really shocked me.

'No, no,' he said, 'I didn't think you could have died but when you came in I did say to one of my colleagues, "I'm pretty sure this guy is going to be in a wheelchair for the rest of his life."'

That really spooked me – the prospect of living in a wheelchair just filled me with dread. I have seen a lot of very brave single minded men and women achieve amazing things after serious injury. But I am not at all sure that I could ever be that strong.

ROAD TO RECOVERY

Then followed three or four months of intensive physio – speech therapy for an hour or two every day seemed to make big strides. My voice got clearer and my diction slowly got back to somewhere near normal. This obviously was pretty important to me, partly because I talk a lot, but also because my speech is pretty essential to the way I earn my living.

A very nice lady called Sally used to come to our house and get me to do very strange shapes with my mouth and utter really weird

sounds. 'Aah, eee, ooo' was a particular favourite and she was splendidly tolerant. Slowly the speech got better. In fact, within three months or so, I would say it was back to normal.

Meanwhile, a terrifying lady called Helen used to do the physio. I'm sure she thought I was a total wimp. She had something like 'Pain equals pleasure' written on her bag. However, she was very patient with me and worked hard to help me walk properly and get the strength back in my arms.

The stroke had happened on 1 March 2014 and, by early May, I was walking well. I even did BBC's *The One Show* with Matt Baker and Alex Jones, talking about what had happened on the plane home from Bangkok. I also discussed the book about my father that I had just finished before I became ill. I was determined to do the

Cuba would be more of a challenge and chaotic than I could ever have imagined, with a railway system that defied even the most intrepid explorer.

publicity tour for the book – not for me, but because I just wanted everybody to know what a hero my dad had been.

People were wonderful. I had so many texts and cards from friends, old mates in many cases that I hadn't heard from for years and dozens and dozens from the people I work with. When Paul, my manager, told Hugh at the *Extreme Railway Journeys* production company what had happened, I always thought his response was magnificent. Instead of saying, 'Oh, my God, the rest of the series is going to have to be cancelled, all our plans for the next few programmes are off,' he said with extraordinary sympathy, 'Please wish Chris well. If there's anything we can do, don't hesitate to ask and don't even think about the rest of the series. His getting well is the only thing that matters – it's only a bit of telly!' That from a guy who was responsible for the whole series was pretty exceptional, and very rare in the media world that I live in.

I had no idea at that point whether or not I would ever go abroad again. I certainly didn't fancy ever getting on an aeroplane again. It wasn't until the end of May, when Jane and I had planned to go away to Spain, that we discussed in some depth whether I would really be up to it; not physically – that side of it didn't worry me, I seemed to be very strong again – but emotionally. The last time I was in an airport I was being carried out by stretcher to an ambulance in a pretty bad way and I wasn't at all sure how I would react. However, we jointly agreed to try it. I would take my time and be prepared to even cancel at the last minute before actually getting on the plane.

It wasn't as bad as I'd feared but I did find it very spooky. Going back through Heathrow was weird; I didn't actually have a panic attack, I just sat down quietly a couple of times and then moved on. It was only a short hop of an hour and a half to Barcelona and, once we were at cruising level, I felt OK. I suppose it's like getting back onto a horse, it was the same sort of thing – except this horse weighed 10,000 tonnes and flew at 39,000 feet. We had a great week in the sunshine, I felt really good again in myself and flew home with no problem.

After the book tour, I told Hugh that I'd be ready to record the commentaries on the films that we had made and start thinking about filming again in a matter of weeks.

In the end it wasn't until April 2015, thirteen months after the stroke, that I was really a hundred per cent fit again. I had to do all sorts of detailed medical examinations, mainly for the insurers, which was fair enough before, on 19 April, I flew out to Cuba, the biggest island in the Caribbean. The crew and I were in high spirits.

It was good to be back!

HAVANA AND HEMINGWAY

Cuba is the most extraordinary country; perhaps its turbulent history is what makes it unique but it is unlike any other Caribbean island –in fact, it is unlike any other place on Earth. In many ways, as I was to discover over the next couple of weeks, it is a complete and utter shambles but that very chaotic, frustrating feel to the place also gives it a wonderful sense of adventure.

I'd been there a couple of times for holidays, had some tremendous fishing off the north coast, enjoyed the nightlife in Havana, drank cocktails in Ernest Hemingway's bar and even sat in his chair and saw the old typewriter that the great man was supposed to have used while writing such classics as *The Old Man and the Sea* and *Death in the Afternoon*.

So I knew Cuba quite well but I'd never tried to travel by train before and I was amazed to discover that there are over 4,000 km of railway track across the island. However, that statistic doesn't say how many kilometres of the tracks are still in use, how many have closed down and how many are still running, but should be closed down. Over the next couple of weeks I was to find out.

Cubans have acquired trains from all over the world – they've had to because since the American embargo that began nearly 60 years ago. The whole island has been desperately short of spare parts and raw materials for just about everything and it is a tribute to the ingenuity of the Cuban people that anything works at all. Many of their trains are very old and break down frequently.

We were going from Havana, the bustling capital, across to Guantánamo Bay at the other side. There are, of course, faster ways to get to Guantánamo Bay but it's usually a one-way ticket and you have to wear an orange jumpsuit.

In the 1950s, Havana was the playground of Hollywood stars – Frank Sinatra was a regular – and we spent our first night in his favourite watering hole, the *Hotel Nacional de Cuba*. It had been run very profitably for years by US crime syndicates, but everything changed in 1959. Fed up with US control of just about everything, the Cuban revolutionary army, led by Fidel Castro, overthrew the corrupt dictatorship that had been controlling the country for years under US and Mafia influence and took over Cuba in his revolution.

It was a time when the USA was still obsessed with communism; there had been the witch-hunt led by Senator McCarthy for years and the communist government under Fidel Castro was obviously a real affront to the USA.

The US also feared for its safety, having a country now so politically friendly towards communist Russia being so close to the southern underbelly of the USA. They feared it would become a Russian base for attacks on America. My generation grew up in fear of the leaders of one or other of the two great powers pressing the infamous red buttons that would send nuclear missiles one way or another across the Atlantic and the ensuing retaliation that would mean the end of the world.

We believed it might happen for several decades until, eventually, we realised that the leaders of both countries, however headstrong they might be (in the cases of Khrushchev and Nixon, among others) that actually they were not completely insane. And would do everything they could never to use nuclear weapons. Terrifyingly, it can no longer be said of the leaders of many factions of the world we live in today; it is a much more frightening future for my kids' generation than it was for me. In reality, the cold war gave us all 50 years of virtual peace.

However, the Americans imposed a savage trade embargo on Fidel Castro's Cuba and everything became deep frozen in a bygone age. The cars you will see in Cuba are a wild, wonderful range of brightly coloured, old models that have all but disappeared in every other country in the world. Bright pink Cadillacs, Packards with the white-walled tyres and the running boards, Hudson Hawks and Humber Snipes – and nearly all of them in bright yellows, pinks, electric blues, hideous greens and all the colours of the rainbow. It is a car lover's paradise. It is also a train lover's paradise, although as I was to discover, getting from A to B is not easy. It's not even easy getting from A to A.

The car's the star when the US embargo resulted in vintage being the only choice. Railways were similarly starved of investment.

LEAVING THE CAPITAL

Everything about the rail system in Cuba is different, such as the timetables, for example. What's different about them is they don't have any. It was really difficult to work out where I could get my first train out of Havana central station. There was a departure board with all sorts of handwritten notes, but none seemed to make sense.

Basically, there seemed to be a train running east every three days. I'd arrived on what I'd thought was the third day but there was nothing until 12.38 the next afternoon, which was pretty useless to us. Also there was absolutely no guarantee that it would run anyway. We knew there had been no train through for 72 hours but there was one advertised in magic marker as due in about an hour, which was great, but it turned out to be scheduled to arrive at a completely different station on the other side of the capital.

I got into a wonderful taxi that you would only find in Cuba. It was what they call a 'coco cab'. It was basically a giant yellow coconut. I've no idea what make it was – I have certainly never travelled in anything like it or even seen anything like it anywhere else in the world. The driver zoomed through the streets of Havana and seemed to get me to Casablanca station for something like tuppence. No sign of Humphrey Bogart or Ingrid Bergman at Casablanca, but I was just glad to have got there in one piece through the terrifying Havana traffic.

Here's lookin' at you, setting off from Casablanca station. Comfort, style, elegance and space – all things missing from the various carriages in which I travelled across the island country.

The train we wanted did seem to be in the station as we arrived with a couple of minutes to spare and, without seeing anything of Casablanca, I hurled myself on board – after all, I would always have Paris... The train was packed, the staff got busy, trying to shut the doors and everybody shouted abuse at me as I got on. I was used to that and I was bigger than most of them, anyway.

My first Cuban train was absolutely jammed and we weren't at all sure how far it was going. It seemed to be really labouring even as we set off on a perfectly flat, straight section of railway line. The upholstery inside the carriage was non-existent. My seat seemed to have no padding whatsoever; it was like sitting on a rock. My fine, muscular buttocks were soon bruised and battered but at least we were in Cuba, we were on a train and we were on our way east. So we were even going in the right direction

We needed to travel something over a thousand kilometres from one end of the island to the other and we were hoping that this first train would get as far as a place called Camilo Cienfuegos. Our train was an old, electrically powered beast, the only one in Cuba and, in fact, one of the very oldest anywhere in the world, having been built in the 1920s. The locomotive was some Spanish creation that really didn't look too good. But it was a commuter train from Cienfuegos back and forth to Havana and, amazingly, took us the 50 or so kilometres uncomfortably but more or less punctually – in only two hours.

The town, with a very Spanish-sounding name of Camilo Cienfuegos is actually better known to the locals by its original name of Hershey – as in Hershey bars, the USA's favourite chocolate. Camilo Cienfuegos is actually named after one of the commandants of the Castro revolution, who died in a mysterious plane crash soon after Castro came to power. Whether the crash was an accident or assassination by the CIA or even Castro has never been cleared up, but in any case the town's called Hershey. By everybody.

It was built by a gentleman called William S Hershey early in the 20th century. For most of the next hundred years, Hershey was the centre of a massive sugar cane plantation, with a railway line coming right up to the main plant. The town was dominated by a massive factory producing sugar that still stands today but is completely abandoned, as is the town itself. It was one of the most famous and thriving communities in the Caribbean and even as late as WWII it still had a cinema, a golf course and a really smart hotel. It was still producing sugar until just after the millennium but the former Soviet Union, which was the main importer, had collapsed economically and the price of sugar went through the floor. The plant and, by extension, the whole town, were producing nothing that made a profit.

Hershey became a ghost town in just a few years and it was quite spooky walking through the deserted streets in the pouring rain. I hardly saw a soul. It was a sad place and I couldn't wait to move on.

We took a taxi east and I stayed overnight in a town, bizarrely called Colón, in an old hotel that dated back to 1913. I think that must have been the last year they changed the sheets and the food was grim.

ON THE SUGAR TRAIN

Next morning, we worked out that there was to be no train link-up for quite a long way, so we hired a magnificent 1950s' Chevrolet. If I drove this through the streets of London, all traffic would stop. In Cuba, cars like this are everywhere, just ten-a-peso... We were making our way to a place called Central Australia, but it was nothing to do with kangaroos or cricket. You pronounce it 'centraal', which is a Cuban word meaning sugar town and Australia literally means southern; we were on our way to a southern sugar town.

At Central Australia station, we were back on what was laughingly called the mainline. In Cuba, there was really no such thing, but it was the next link in my constantly interrupted journey across the island. We boarded a wonderful old steam locomotive that dated back at least a hundred years and was driven by a guy called Herman. Herman explained to me the train came from Germany, '...so the driver's Herman and the train is German,' he said, and howled with laughter at his joke, which I suspected he may just have told before…

This train was a vital part of the sugar exportation from the end of the 19th century. Plantation owners needed a way to move enormous quantities of sugar to the refineries around the island in places like Hershey and Colón and Central Australia and to move them from there to the ports.

Herman talked to me about the days when he used to move tons of sugar cane along this line all day every day, although now he just carries tourists. When we got to Central Australia, we said 'Goodbye' to Herman and wandered down to what is now a

This was just one of many steam trains that were once a familiar sight, transporting sugar around Cuba.

With me in Central Australia are Brian Murrell the soundman, one of the train crew, Herman – holding the camera – and cameraman Mike Harrison.

beautiful-looking beach, at Playa Girón. There was mile upon mile of lovely golden sand and palm trees.

There were a few deckchairs, but otherwise hardly anybody in sight. It's a very well-known beach in Cuba because, as you look out from the main beach at Playa Girón, you look across the *Bahía de Cochinos*, better known as the Bay of Pigs.

On 17 April 1961, what was thought to be a more than adequate small army of CIA-trained paramilitaries landed here 'to overthrow Fidel Castro and his rag-bag bunch of bearded revolutionaries'. The USA was convinced that the whole thing wouldn't take long at all and Cuba would be back in US hands by lunchtime. However, Castro proved much tougher than the US-backed mercenaries expected and they were sent packing with ridiculous ease. The whole thing was a shambles. The American mercenaries were shot down or thrown off the island and several of the ships waiting out in the bay were sunk.

I met a wonderful old soldier who'd fought with the revolution on that day, Armando Moreira Vira. He is 72 now but still became very animated and emotional as he showed me how he fired his gun at the CIA invaders. He remembered hitting the boat, which the mercenaries had to abandon before swimming to shore where Armando took them prisoner. There were 70 or more attackers and Armando talks as if he took them all prisoner single-handed. Maybe he did. He'd clearly played his part and I felt quite honoured to have spoken at length with a man who fought alongside Fidel Castro.

It was at this point that I gave up eating anything in Cuba. Since we left Havana we'd been in varying levels of hotels, motels and small B&Bs and we'd eaten everywhere from places that looked like fine restaurants right down to real cheapo cafes. The prices were uniformly good, the local booze was OK, but the food was uniformly dreadful. I started off, as I believe you should, trying various local delicacies, most of which smelt grim and tasted a lot

Armando Vira tells me how he fought off the mercenaries who invaded the Bay of Pigs.

worse. I tasted a steak that had seen better days – I suspect when it was running around Aintree racecourse – and, as we sat in a quite promising-looking restaurant late that evening, at the end of a good day's filming, I said to the guys, 'I'm not going to risk anything clever tonight. I'm going to try something that even they can't cock up – a simple bit of grilled chicken.'

I found an item listed as 'surprise chicken' on the menu, so I asked for that. The staff grinned at me happily and, quite quickly and proudly, appeared with the food. The 'surprise'? It was that the meat didn't appear to have been cooked at all. If you had just bought a raw chicken leg, still white and bleeding from the butchers and tried to put your knife and fork into it, it would feel and taste just like that. It was absolutely revolting. I took one mouthful, gasped in horror and spat it back onto my plate.

The waiter looked at me blankly as if that was a pretty normal reaction for anyone silly enough to order the surprise chicken. There was no point in complaining; apparently that's what it was supposed to look and taste like. I felt really bad, couldn't eat another thing and, in fact, didn't eat anything at all for most of the rest of the week.

Every morning before we started our long days, we used to make up a thing called the crew sandwich, which was basically two giant slices of bread full of big chunks of cheese and tomato. I had two of these wonderful, simple home creations every morning and they filled me up for the rest of the day. While some of the crew ventured into various dining rooms over the next week or so, I usually went straight to the bar. I didn't even risk the peanuts.

REVOLUTION ON THE RAILS

We moved on to Santa Clara, the final resting place of legendary revolutionary Ernesto 'Che' Guevara, whose face has launched a thousand T-shirts and teenage posters. There was a beautiful mausoleum just outside the town commemorating his life and times. He was clearly a great hero of the revolution and Santa

Does my Che look big in this? Near the Guevara mausoleum, the statue of the revolutionary behind me, featuring the inscription *'Hasta la victoria siempre'* ('Until victory, always').

Clara is where he performed what is almost certainly his best-known heroic action.

He wasn't actually Cuban at all, but Argentinean – which makes him about as Cuban as Lionel Messi – but he was devoted to Fidel Castro and it was on a level crossing in the middle of Santa Clara that he achieved the status of legend. There were carriages still in place by an old railway track and these were the carriages that, 60 years ago, were attacked by Che.

They had been full of government troops sent by Fulgencio Batista, the hated president of Cuba who wanted to throw out Castro, Che Guevara and their revolutionary army. When the troop train stopped at this level crossing, right in the middle of Santa Clara, Guevara and his guerrilla fighters threw molotov cocktails and set the train alight. The officers tried to move the train off quickly to escape, but Guevara cut off their only possible exit by ripping up the track with a bulldozer and the armoured train of soldiers crashed. It is not clear how many died, but few of the troops lived to tell the tale. To this day all the elements of this brief but historic battle are all still in place. The crashed train, the carriages and the bulldozer are all still there.

We stayed overnight, I remained on my beer-only diet, then got up at some ridiculous hour the next morning, wolfed down the crew sandwich and we made our way to the station. The information lady was fast asleep, so we were a bit thin on information – in fact, we had none, but we guessed that the only train that arrived was the one we wanted, the 5.35 am to a town called Morón (pronounced '*maw-ronn*'). Probably only a moron would get up this early to get on this train; it was absolutely disgusting. There were people literally bringing on dogs, babies and live chickens.

It was pitch-black at first, but even when the light came up it remained dark because the windows were filthy, the inside was filthy and the only place we could get a seat was next to '*el baño*' – ie, the lavatory: and it really stank. I have been in evil-smelling trains all over the world but (with the possible exception of the Congo), this one was the worst – there was a dreadful, gut-wrenching stench that made me want to vomit, even though there was very little in my stomach. We were on that train for seven hours and it was relentlessly awful. I always tell people I love my job but, some days, I lie... I was extremely uncomfortable, the seats again seemed to have been made of concrete and my head and nose were jammed against the wall of the *baño*. The distance we were to travel was only about a hundred miles, which doesn't sound much but we only seemed to be travelling at 14 miles an hour – I've no idea why. Maybe the driver, too, was overcome by the fumes from the *baño*? I dunno, but it was pretty unpleasant.

Somehow the trains keep going but their state of repair was pretty poor. They were always crowded and an endurance test not for the faint-hearted.

Having only done about 13 miles, I did something that you couldn't possibly do on an intercity to Edinburgh or Manchester. I got out of my carriage, walked along the side of the train, climbed up a little ladder and went in with the TV crew to talk to the driver. He was a lovely guy called Carlos González – well, of course he was. Could there be a more Cuban name? He told me he'd been driving trains for more than 30 years and he still loved it. One of the biggest problems for him was heavy rain that could cause rock falls and line-track slippage. There were also a lot of cows in this area that he tried not to hit as they wandered across the tracks, but he did admit that he couldn't always avoid them. I have to say that, from the manic look in his eyes, I think he quite enjoyed a squelched cow, but I may have been doing him an injustice. It did explain why we saw lots of cowboys around, with the hats, the leather chaps, the six-gun holsters and even the lariats, but we hadn't seen anybody lasso anything and, strangely enough, despite Carlos's claims about them wandering across the tracks, we'd seen no sign at all of cows. Lots of horses, yes, and the Cubans love their horses, but not one single cow.

The seat continually jarred my spine as we travelled. It took us seven hours to do what was supposedly a four-hour journey and it was certainly the hottest and smelliest of my trip so far, but we eventually arrived at Morón station. It's very odd, but while elsewhere in the world you see tourists buying T-shirts celebrating the place they're visiting, from London to New York via Paris, I didn't see anyone with Morón printed proudly on their chest – funny that.

I had to get to a place called Camagüey for our next train, just under 140 kilometres away, but the only transport available was a converted cattle truck. We were stuffed into the truck and, once again, we were on our way back to the main railway line. I once saw a movie with a truck like this in it, taking prisoners to San Quentin. In fairness though, this leg of what was now becoming a marathon was actually more comfy than the previous train journey. It was certainly much nicer-smelling.

LAST STOP BEFORE GUANTÁNAMO BAY

Camagüey was a surprisingly beautiful place. Amazing architecture, with palm trees and banana trees; it was an oasis. We were very tired and hungry by now but our next step was the big final push to Guantánamo and, good news, I found the station more or less straight away and, better, there was a train for my final destination due a few minutes after I arrived. But from the look on the faces in the waiting room, I quickly realised that the imminent train wasn't imminent at all – in fact, it just wasn't going to happen.

I'm normally fairly philosophical about these things but at this point I began to get seriously fed-up. The whole nonsense of their railway timetables was making the trip miserable – or maybe I was just suffering from malnutrition. Either way I was getting pretty cheesed off. Then again, I thought, please don't mention cheese! I had eaten rather a lot of it. Through gritted teeth I discovered there was a train to Guantánamo but it would be about a 15-hour wait, until the small hours of the morning and even then, of course, it wasn't guaranteed at all. I don't think a single train in Cuba ran on time throughout my trip, so why should this one be different? The thought of being stuck for hours in a cramped, sweaty waiting-room for a train that probably wouldn't arrive was not an option.

So, ever resourceful – or maybe plain desperate – I found myself a taxi to take me to Las Tunas, the next big town and over 100 kilometres further south-east. The taxi driver was an enormous bloke and the two of us were very cosy in his pride and joy, a tiny, white, Russian Lada. It wasn't exactly my idea of fun but then, to be honest, fun was by now but a distant memory. So was food.

Las Tunas I assumed to be named after 'tuna' and guessed it would be a pretty little fishing village with weathered old fishermen mending their nets… I was even thinking about risking a freshly caught local lobster for my tea, but then my great bear of a driver told me Las Tunas actually means 'the place of the prickly pear', although he had absolutely no idea why.

We all crashed out in a small, dingy hotel in Las Tunas then, devoid of any real hope, made our way down to the station – as always, very early the next morning, hoping to catch the promised early-morning train across the rest of the island to Guantánamo. For once there was a full information board at the station and that confirmed that, yes, the 6 am train was ON TIME and would get to Guantánamo at 1 pm. I began to recover from my bad temper of the previous day. At last a train coming on time to take me to my end destination. I even started thinking, foolishly, about some decent food on the plane home and how lovely it would be to be back in England. I should have known better by now.

When I got to the booking clerk in the station, despite the promise of the timetable and noticeboard, he shook his head and said, 'No train.'

'How do you mean, "No train"?' I asked incredulously. He shrugged his shoulders and said, 'No train, cancelled,' and walked away.

At this point, I genuinely had not a clue what to do next. There were no taxis around; there were virtually no people around. All I did manage to discover was that my train had broken down about 40 miles outside Havana and there would be no trains now for at least two days.

After much deliberation between myself, Jeff the director and Mike the cameraman, we decided the only thing for it was to do something I hadn't done for at least 40 years – hitch-hike. I used to do it all the time as a student, but we discovered that it was probably the only form of transport in Cuba that actually worked. Everybody hitch-hikes; so much so, it's organised by the government. They have men in yellow uniforms called *amarillos* (as in 'Show me the way to…'), who are official government-paid hitch-hike organisers. Amarillo is Spanish for 'yellow', by the way. So you find your man in yellow, you find clearly marked points along the main roads and the *amarillo* will flag down any vehicle with a government sticker. You must be allowed in and given a ride as far as they are actually going. What a great system… well, kind of – in a Cuban sort of way.

We found a hitching point and a grinning *amarillo*, dressed from head-to-toe in yellow like a giant banana and about as much use. He seemed to speak no English at all but waved a flag at a large car that stopped begrudgingly and my cameraman and I got in.

I spent almost as much time in taxis and hitch-hiking on my jaunt south-east as I did in trains.

Whatever the government promised, our driver, a large, sweaty man with a gold tooth, didn't seem very keen at all and to make it more unnerving, there were two other very large gentleman sitting in the front and frowning at us in the mirror. Every few kilometres he stopped put his large pudgy hand out and demanded more money. I suppose it was better than a Lada but in the end it became much more expensive. I was fairly convinced he was a gangster and Mike and I were convinced that if we ran out of dollars they'd probably shoot us both and chuck us over a hedge. OK, we might have been getting a bit carried away (but I'm still pretty confident that we were right).

Anyway, we found a stopping point of sorts, paid them off and thanked them, bowing and reversing quickly backwards out of pistol shot. The driver spat attractively and drove off. We were both just glad to be alive and a little bit further along the road. I carried on hitching for the rest of the day, pleased to see that my thumb still had the old magic that it always had. It's one of those things that, once you've got it as a kid, you never lose it and, by the end of the day, I'd covered over 180 miles in various shapes, sizes and colours of vehicles. My final drop-off was about two miles outside Guantánamo.

The last car left me in the middle of absolutely nowhere, except that it was close to a railway line, so I decided the best bet was to walk into town along the track. The one thing I could be absolutely certain of was that there was no danger from a train coming – at least, not for two days.

GUANTANAMERA

I crawled into Guantánamo and, in spite of the notoriety of the nearby US terrorist detention centre, it was a really lovely town bathed in evening sunshine, with very well-dressed men and women walking across the town square. Before the US facility was built, Guantánamo was best known as the inspiration for the song 'Guantanamera', which means 'Beautiful Girl from Guantánamo'.

I had a couple of drinks and, yet again, skipped the dinner that once again really didn't look too appetising and had an early night ready for the train the next morning, again, well before sunrise, from Guantánamo to a place called Caimanera.

It was at last to be our stopping point, the most easterly point on the island and the closest to Guantánamo Bay prison. Foreigners are not normally allowed on this train at all as it's only for workers, but we had a piece of paper signed by the government saying we had permission to get on the train and film right the way up to the prison fence. From all my experiences so far, it seemed to me highly unlikely that this piece of paper would be any use whatsoever. I thought that Neville Chamberlain would have had more chance of success with his piece of paper but, bewilderingly, when I presented it to a man at the station just after 5.00 am, he grinned at me, saluted smartly and let us through.

We got on the train in the pitch black; everybody was staring at me, nobody spoke any English and, when I said to the ticket

This was the last stop at the east of the country. This is the nearest you can travel by public transport to Guantánamo Bay.

collector something that I never thought I would find myself saying – 'Guantánamo Bay, please. One way' – I had a very uneasy feeling in the pit of my stomach. I tried to engage the bloke sitting next to me in conversation but he was having none of it. He frowned a lot and looked out the window. I kept getting this feeling that I was going to be arrested and I wondered who all these people were. They were clearly going to work but I couldn't imagine what work they did. I assumed they worked at the notorious prison but it turned out that they all worked in a salt factory right next to the boundary fence.

It was broad daylight by the time we approached the factory and a very sunny morning but it was impossible to really film the building or anything happening along the railway line, as the windows were absolutely filthy. These were probably the dirtiest I'd seen this side of the Congo.

Suddenly, I got that strange feeling of Is it something I said?, as the whole train emptied and, with just one more stop to go, I realised I was the only other person on the train. The train pulled into Caimanera and there was a very large electric fence that marked the boundary between Cuba and the tiny US outpost on the very end of the island that is Guantánamo Bay prison. I don't know where I thought Guantánamo prison was, but for some reason I never realised that the Americans actually do keep a tiny little piece of Cuba to house some of the most dangerous men on the planet. Caimanera itself was quite a nice place but the looming shadow of the world's most notorious prison camp dominated the skyline.

There was no access to the detention centre by Cuban or English film crews. This was a heavily guarded US naval base. We visited a hotel where the crew filmed from a balcony, across the bay, while I used my binoculars. Amazingly, it was fine to film over the top of the boundary fence, looking down on prison block buildings and watchtowers bristling with heavily armed sentries. The hotel itself was a beautiful sunny place, with a restaurant and a bar with a big swimming pool, but with no water in it. There wasn't a single human to be seen anywhere in the complex. This was the hotel where nobody in their right mind would want to stay or work, in case of a prison breakout. The whole set-up was very odd. As we looked down across the giant satellite dishes, the gunposts and the electrified barbed-wire, none of us spoke. It was downright eerie to be there.

The whole set-up exists through a very strange arrangement. The USA has leased this small piece of the island from Cuba since 1903, paying a considerable rent every year. However, since 1959, Fidel Castro and his brother have refused to bank 'the filthy US money', so there is a drawer in Castro's office brimming ever higher with cheques that they never cash.

Happily, there are some signs at the time of writing in 2016 that the US embargo might finally be lifted. Tourists can come once again to visit the forsaken island and Cubans may at last get parts for their cars and for their locomotives.

This was journey's end for us; it had been an exhausting trip and frequently frustrating with so many no-show locomotives or non-existent railway lines. It had been a really tough film to complete. We had done it, but I suppose we also had proved that it probably isn't possible to travel by train right across Cuba. There were too many gaps that we had to improvise filling in with cattle trucks, Russian Ladas and even my trusty hitch-hiker's thumb...

It had been an extraordinary journey but I'm not really sure that I enjoyed it much. I think it's an amazing credit to the Cubans how they have survived since the 1960s. OK, many things don't work but it's amazing that, thanks to their ingenuity, they actually get anything to work at all. In the next few years there is every chance that things will improve considerably but, in the meantime, I was pretty glad to leave the place and I was absolutely starving.

EN BOSCH
SM10
885
885

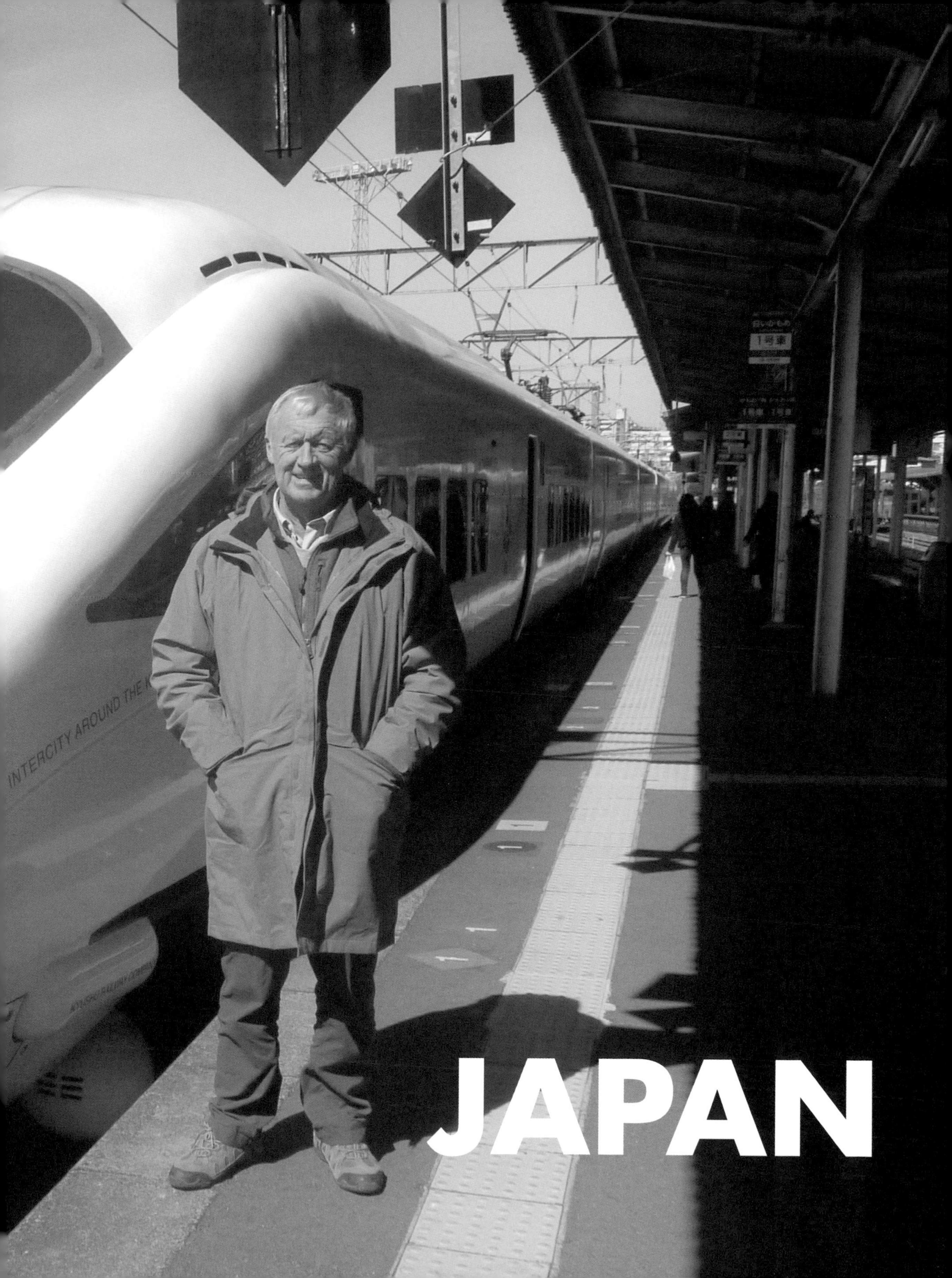

JAPAN

Hirøshima
Osaka
Wakaya
Fukuoka
Shin-Tosu

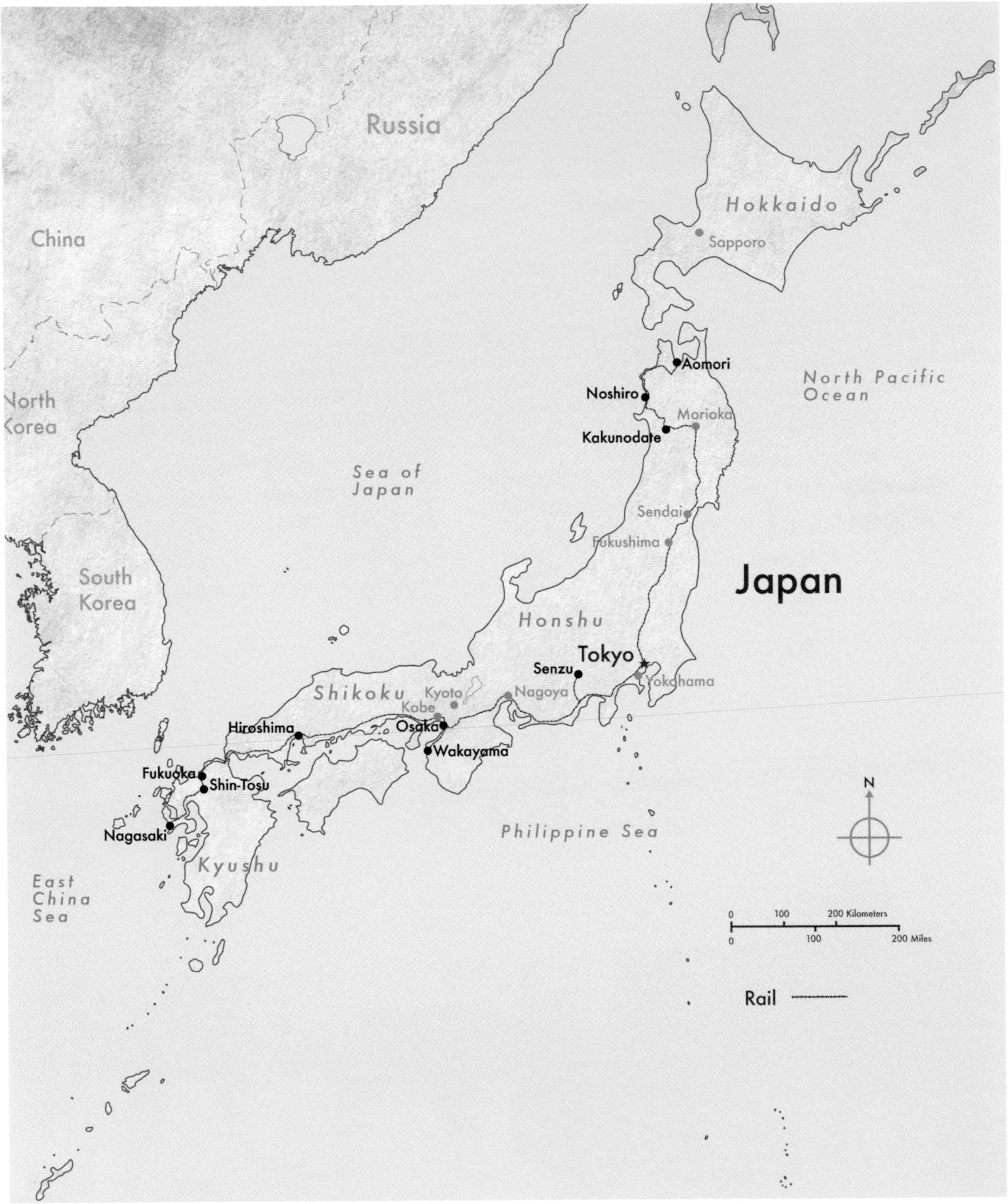

Russia
China
Hokkaido
Sapporo
Aomori
North Pacific Ocean
Noshiro
Morioka
Kakunodate
North Korea
Sea of Japan
Sendai
Fukushima
South Korea
Japan
Honshu
Tokyo
Senzu
Yokohama
Shikoku
Kyoto
Nagoya
Kobe
Hiroshima
Osaka
Wakayama
Fukuoka
Shin-Tosu
Nagasaki
N
Philippine Sea
Kyushu
East China Sea
0 100 200 Kilometers
0 100 200 Miles
Rail

Japan

Until I filmed for the series, I'd never been to Japan and nor had I had any particular wish to. I didn't have any real interest in the place and I didn't like what I'd heard about their people. My lovely uncle John, my dad's brother, had fought them in Burma during WWII and he absolutely hated them in the same way that my own father, an infantry officer who had survived Dunkirk and D-Day, had no love at all for Germans.

Inevitably, I grew up with some of their prejudices. Imagine my surprise then when I found the Japanese to be an incredibly polite, friendly, helpful people and the most organised, efficient and disciplined on Earth. Having filmed all over the world I can say there is no question that Japan's railway system is the fastest, smoothest, cleanest and most utterly punctual anywhere on the planet.

Every train we got on was exactly on time – I don't mean 'quite close', I mean to the very second. We travelled over a thousand miles from one end of the country to the other on all sorts of locomotives, from ultra-modern bullet trains to ancient steam locos from the 1920s, still working perfectly through thick snow and ice. The great British announcer's standard winge about 'Leaves on the line' would simply never be uttered in Japan. It would almost certainly lead to a public hanging. But trust me it simply wouldn't happen, ever… it just wouldn't.

We began our journey in Nagasaki, at the west of Kyushu, one of the four islands that make up Japan. This city, infamously, was one of two that were completely destroyed by the dropping of atomic bombs in 1945 to bring an end to WWII, but we made it our start point because of something else that happened there a hundred years earlier.

An enterprising Scot named Thomas Glover brought the railways to Japan in 1865. He built a short, narrow-gauge track, brought in a British steam locomotive called the Iron Duke and ran it up and down the rails in a series of demonstrations that caused tremendous excitement and interest. It was probably the first time that the Japanese had actually seen a working railway line, but 150 years later, the whole country is criss-crossed by the most advanced railway network.

The first train we boarded looked beautiful and shiny as it pulled into Nagasaki station. It was very impressive and I thought it was my first bullet train, but it turned out to be a 'limited express'. It was still just as fast as any UK high-speed trains but had nothing like the speed or the smoothness of the bullets that we were to travel on a little later. I did notice that it was incredibly quiet. In fact, across Japan, all trains are incredibly quiet; everybody talks in a hush so as not to disturb other travellers and mobile phones are only used in small, allocated areas.

The first thing that I loved was when the ticket collector came into the carriage and bowed to everybody. I became very boring and repetitive with the crew on this trip and this was the first – but not the last time – I said, 'But... can you imagine that happening on a British railway?'

It was at Shin-Tosu where we caught our first bullet train. It was due at 2.18 pm, and, of course, it arrived at exactly at 18 minutes past two. This was a Shinkansen or bullet train. Although I love railways all around the world, I've never got particularly excited about the trains themselves. However, these bullet trains are something else, absolutely breath-taking in design, beautiful and clearly built for speed. When I got inside our spotless compartment the first thing I noticed was that it actually smelt nice! I have never ever on a train in the UK said, 'Oh, this one smells nice,' but it really did. There was some sort of perfume being percolated through the air-conditioning system. I think it was lavender; it was certainly very pleasant.

The bullet trains have been running for over 50 years. The first one appeared in 1964, in time to be shown off to the world as Japan

The kingfisher bird gave engineer Eiji Nakatsu, pictured, the idea for the unique redesign of the bullet train's snout.

hosted the Tokyo Olympics. Aside from the perfume, the train was incredibly comfortable, with superb upholstery and very nice ladies, who kept bringing food and drink to us, bowing as they arrived at our seats. I remember thinking, 'This is the best train I have ever travelled on anywhere in the world' – and it was. Now, hundreds of trains later, it still is.

There are now bullet trains all over Japan and they are all in superb condition. They look great and they go like hell. If you stand on a platform when a bullet train passes through without stopping, the rush of air as the train passes is unbelievable and the noise of the train hits you seconds after it has disappeared from sight.

We stopped at a place called Fukuoka; this was a fascinating place but extremely difficult to talk about on television for an Englishman; in fact, unless you're Billy Connolly, using '*fuk*-anything' is not easy (for Fukuoka, I wimped out and went for '*Foo-koo-oh-ka*'). It was a high-security, bullet train depot, the place where the trains were brought in every couple of years for a complete overhaul and it was here that I met the man responsible for the bullet train's shape, including its pointy nose that resembles the late, lamented Concorde.

Eiji Nakatsu is an engineer but, also – and it is not irrelevant – a keen bird-watcher. He had trouble at first in eliminating the noise that the train made as it raced through narrow tunnels at high speed. 'I am a keen ornithologist,' he told me, 'and I thought about the beautiful kingfisher. When it is fishing for its food it has to enter the heavy resistance of the water from the lesser resistance of the air and this is what I wanted to simulate in my bullet train. I wanted the same shape as the kingfisher, from its beak to its head; this would solve the problem!' And it did. It was beautiful, it was simple but, of course, it was brilliant. From a fascinating conversation and realising that I was in the presence of sheer genius with Mr Nakatsu, we moved on to Hiroshima.

ATOMIC MEMORIES

Like Nagasaki, Hiroshima is known for the devastation caused by the bomb at the end of WWII and it was in that city that I met two quite extraordinary people. The second bomb hit Hiroshima on 6 August 1945, causing even more horrific devastation than the first. The whole of the city centre was completely reduced to rubble; only a few buildings remained and the loss of life was enormous. Over 80,000 people were killed immediately in the blast and tens of thousands more died from injuries and from radiation over the next 12 months.

The high-security depot for bullet trains, which, given their avian origins, might be better called the nest.

There was a memorial to those who died right in the middle of the totally rebuilt city. People come here from all over to the world to bow and pay respects to the dead. I too felt I had to bow my head. I was quite surprised – although, perhaps, I shouldn't have been – when this particular scene was broadcast and I received letters of complaint that I was honouring the Japanese warmongers of WWII. But I was not bowing to the Japanese of a different generation, but paying respect to all those innocent people who have died and are still dying in awful circumstances over which they and their families have no control all over the world.

Governments and politicians cause wars, but thousands of ordinary innocent men, women and children get killed because of someone else's madness. The two I met at Hiroshima were among the most impressive people I have ever encountered in my life But I'm jumping ahead.

Electric streetcars – better known as trams – have been operating in the city of Hiroshima for over a hundred years. At exactly 8.15 am on 6 August 1945, 123 trams were in action. Most of them were destroyed. One young conductress never forgot that day; when I met her, she was an amazing, wonderful 81-year-old woman and her name was Sachiko Masuno. She had been aged 15 in 1945, when she was working as a tram girl. These were all very young Hiroshima schoolgirls who were working because so many men and women were either away fighting in the war or had been killed. She still remembered the exact second that the bomb went off.

'It was just extraordinary; there were people running blindly,' she told me, 'bumping into each other, tangling like ghosts, their heads and their hair were on fire and their clothes were torn to pieces. There were dead and dying people everywhere, lying in the streets and all of the buildings had just vaporised – turned to ash. Of course, I did not know it was an atomic bomb. I had never heard of such a thing. I thought I was in some sort of horrific dream.'

She seemed amazingly calm, articulate, almost smiling and showing no signs of trauma. No bitterness at all, just quiet and very graceful.

Then I was introduced to a retired doctor, Tetsushi Yonezawa, another survivor. He was just 11 years old and was travelling on a busy tram when the bomb went off. He was with his mother and they were standing right in the middle of the tram. 'There was the most tremendous boom, quite, quite deafening,' he said, 'a bright flash and a roaring wind – we had no idea what had happened. My mother and I looked around; everyone else on the bus was dead, just piles of ash, it was awful. To this day, I don't understand why we were still alive. I think the mound of bodies on top of us saved us, cushioned the force somehow, we are very, very lucky.' The doctor was a lovely, gentle, polite man but almost certainly must still have nightmares. Yet we had offered to send a car to pick him up but he insisted he wanted no fuss and travelled to the interview on, of all things, a tram.

His clearest memory following the blast was that, within a matter of hours, the survivors took to the streets and started clearing out the tracks, restoring the power on the lines and salvaging burnt-out trams. Amazingly, the first tram was running again within 24 hours, as they were needed so badly to get around the devastated city...

I never thought I would meet anyone who had survived the blast of an atomic bomb: to meet two in a single morning was surreal and very humbling.

We left Hiroshima and travelled on in silence but, as is the way in Japan, it was impossible to guess what would be around the corner. We took a bullet train to Osaka and then on to a place called Wakayama, where we were told to 'follow the Poor Prince'. I had no idea what prince they meant – Prince Charles? Prince Charming? Prince Naseem Hamid? And then the penny dropped. There were strange paw marks all over the floor of the station going up the steps to the opposite platform. Paw-prints... follow the paw-prints! It was childish but we were clearly onto something...

A train came into view with a cat face on the front, rather like a feline version of Thomas the Tank Engine. This was probably the most ridiculous scenario we encountered in the whole of our visit to the Land of the Rising Sun which, at Wakayama, unmistakably turned into the Land of the Rising Cat. It was totally weird,

Feline frenzy as Tama the station master and Mitsunobu Kojima are interviewed in Kishi station among the cat's legion of fans.

but Tama was the name of a cat who is now probably the most celebrated feline in the whole of Asia. It is the station master at Kishi station, where having followed the paw-prints, our train was headed. On arrival we found total Tama-mania; there were grown-up women outside the station shouting, 'We love Tama! We love Tama!', and little girls were crying and sobbing.

There were Tama T-shirts, key-rings, postcards, mugs and 'I've seen Tama the cat' badges; it was just ridiculous. People come from all over Japan, China, India and most of Asia to take pictures of the majestic moggy and buy memorabilia

The man behind the phenomenon is a gentleman called Mitsunobu Kojima, who promoted Tama the Cat and her assorted merchandise to the tune of £6 million since the whole thing started. When he brought her out for our cameras, it was like a Beatles concert. There was a stampede of adults – men and women – who really should have known better, almost knocking each other over to get selfies standing beside the cat with its little station master's hat.

To me, it just seemed like another moggy, but I didn't dare say it out loud. I'd have been lynched. It was an extraordinary afternoon and, of course, just in case the unthinkable happened, Mitsunobu had a young Tama lookalike on standby, doing her apprenticeship at another station just along the line. She was called Nitama, presumably because she only came up to Tama's knee at that point – and was paw-marked to be the eventual successor. I didn't like to tell anyone, but when our cameras were there, Nitami actually scratched a child who got a bit too close – and rather deeply. Surely, not future station-master behaviour? Apparently, since we filmed him, Tama has been called into the great cattery in the sky, in early 2015, and Nitama – after the traditional 50 days mourning period, of course – pounced on the vacant position later that year. Hopefully, Nitama will be better behaved.

You couldn't make it up.

CROONING WITH O'HARA

Still on a high from being in the presence of Tama the cat, we caught the Ōigawa line towards Tokyo. This originated as a 1920s builders' train that took construction workers into the mountains where they were building dams for the country's water supply. It still runs today, with beautifully restored steam trains taking tourists towards the capital.

It was on this journey that I first came across the joys of the Bento Box. Now, I love Japanese food. In London, I eat sushi often twice a week, but the Japanese have some very strange, fixed ideas about their food. They believe it is vital to never be more than 80 per cent full after any meal, but they also like to have at least 30 different items in a day. In my Bento lunchbox there would typically be one or two items that were quite tasty, a maximum of about three more that, to be honest, weren't great and another 25 that were absolutely disgusting. So after most meals I was not even 8 per cent full. The service was always impeccable, though and, strangely, nowhere in Japan would they take a tip. One man in a really nice bar chased me down the road, almost in tears, beseeching me to take a few yen back.

Meanwhile, back on the train with the Bento box, there was also a Miss O'Hara. She was our train hostess with the mostest, a rather manic lady who went by the catchy full name of Hideko O'Hara and made all the train announcements. She also trebled up as the trains conductor, ticket inspector and entertainment officer, singing and playing the mouth organ to us as we travelled. Her big hit number seemed to be loosely translated as, 'Let's all sing and dance to the dance song, choo-choo, choo-choo, choo.' I tried to join in happily with the chorus but from the polite frowns and head shaking I got, I think I may have been choo-chooing in completely the wrong place.

The next morning, we fought our way manfully into the frantic centre of Tokyo's Shinjuku, simply the busiest station on Earth. Three-and-a-half million people use this station every single day; it was absolute chaos. There were so many different platforms and different lines. The Oedo line, the Keiō line, the Tokyo metro Keiō New line, the Chūō line, the Chūō-Sōbu line, the Saikyō line, the Rinkai line, the Thin Blue line, the Conga line, the Washing line… all right, I added those, but the list was absurd. And the information screens were just a blur.

Everybody seemed to be rushing somewhere in a terrible hurry – the stress levels each morning and evening must have been off the scale but, somehow, everybody got to their train, every single one of which left exactly on time. Of course, each also got to its destination bang on time. 'Sorry, sir, my train was delayed,' could never ever be used as an excuse for arriving late for work or school anywhere in Japan. In any case, no one would even dream of ever being late in the first place.

We were also given a master class in train cleaning; the trains are always spotless inside but, with never a sign of let-up in the manic schedule for each train, I did wonder how and when they ever found the time to get a dustpan and brush inside. The women who cleaned the compartments of our next bullet train showed the way and were amazing. As the long train came onto our platform, the beautifully uniformed staff bowed to each alighting passenger and then whirled into action. When were you last bowed at when you got off your train at Birmingham New Street or Manchester Piccadilly?

The train was going back where it had come from and every single seat was turned around, the space underneath each seat was cleaned and the passageway down the middle was brushed and hovered. Litter was cleared although, of course, there was hardly any; Japanese travellers just don't do litter. Then these magnificent ladies cleaned all the washrooms, the smoking areas and the dining car – phew! The whole operation took them exactly seven minutes and they finished – of course – with another elegant bow.

On my return to England, I suggested to our office cleaner that we start and end each day with a bow but she said there was no need and I'd just look silly doing it.

Is it me?

Shinjuku has 12 lines operating out of 36 platforms. There are shopping centres, amusement arcades within the centre and the station has over 200 exits and a Guinness World Record as the world's busiest station.

The next day we were allowed in to a very high-powered scientific centre, where they talked excitedly about their vision for the future – a train that was even quieter and capable of travelling at 320 kph! I've also heard that Japan is planning another train, called a Maglev (from 'magnetic levitation'). It would run on electricity and use electromagnets to enable the train to hover above the tracks while propelling it forward. Did you follow that? No, nor did I, but it means there would be no friction between train and track. All right, it seems unbelievable but this is Japan and I wouldn't bet against them.

As we boarded our next bullet train later that afternoon we decided to try an experiment of our own. We had a very basic app on one of our iPhones that was a crude speedometer. Just how fast was our bullet train actually going? We cruised along easily enough through built-up areas at 120–130 mph, but once we got into derestricted areas the driver suddenly decided he was Lewis Hamilton, only faster and without the silly earring: 150... 160... 170 mph! Then 180, even 190 – surely not – 200 mph! But, yes, and we did it easily. The crew and I jumped up and clapped but then realised we were being noisy and stared at, so we abruptly sat down again, looking sheepish. In the end, our train was cruising effortlessly at 207 mph, yet our coffee cups never spilled a drop and conversation in the train carried on exactly the same level throughout the whole journey.

It was an amazing ride and not remotely frightening, indeed there has not been a single casualty on a bullet train since they arrived in the 1960s. But our final leg of our trip to the Land of the Rising Train was a little less comfortable.

DON'T WANT TO BE A GONO GONER

We joined the Gonō line, spectacularly beautiful, but a line with a history of problems. It follows the northern sea coastline and is

Bullet trains can go from the station to over 200 mph outside urban areas without apparent effort.

Right: As we headed towards the north of the country the temperature outside plummeted.

Below: On a surprisingly small train that tackles the mountainous region and is kept financially viable by the help of local residents.

notoriously hazardous. It was regularly washed away right up to the 1960s and it didn't help that, as we boarded, we were hit by a violent storm with driving winds and snow. Filming became really difficult. We were horribly close to the cliff edge, looking down on razor sharp rocks and pounding waves. I was feeling sick and, I admit, really frightened. The train seemed to be labouring and there seemed to us to be the real possibility of an avalanche or a derailment. Of course, there wasn't; after over a thousand miles on Japanese trains we should really have known better. They have taken so many steps to make sure that the accidents of the 1960s can never happen again. And we pulled into our final destination, Aomori, exactly on time. Of course we did! I left this extraordinary country with a very revised opinion of the place and its people. They really do have the best railways in the world.

The day after I got back to the UK, I had to go up to Manchester on the Sunday evening for some filming on the Monday. If I caught the 6.50 pm out of Kings Cross St Pancras, I should be there nicely in time for dinner about half-past nine. It's a good fast service – well, it can be. This time, it was delayed leaving till about 7.30 pm. 'Oh, well,' we all said, 'not *too* bad – only about three-quarters of an hour…' Eventually, we went racing north, I had a drink and all seemed to be well until we got to just outside Manchester Piccadilly and came to a halt. Then, of course, That Voice came over the Tannoy with that world-weary, non-apologetic tone it always has: 'Ladies and gentlemen, our apologies, but we have to remain here outside the station briefly because of late running engineering work…'

In the end our 'brief' delay lasted over forty minutes – and we all shrugged and went, 'Oh, well, not *too* bad…'

… because that's what we Brits do. I'd just come back from a land where every single train was not even a minute late and my very first train back in England was late by an hour and a half. Not too bad? It's absolutely shocking! What's the matter with us? Aaaaaagggggghhhhh!

НА ЭТОМ ПАРОВОЗЕ 28 ИЮНЯ 1944г.
МАШИНИСТ ДЕПО ВОРКУТА П.П.ДЬЯЧЕНКО
ПРОВЁЛ ПЕРВЫЙ ИЗ ДЕСЯТИ ЭШЕЛОНОВ
УГЛЯ, ОТПРАВЛЕННЫХ ТРУДЯЩИМИСЯ
ВОРКУТЫ В ПОДАРОК ОСВОБОЖДЕННОМУ
ЛЕНИНГРАДУ
720

SIBERIA

Belarus
Moscow
Kotlas
Pechora
Salekhard

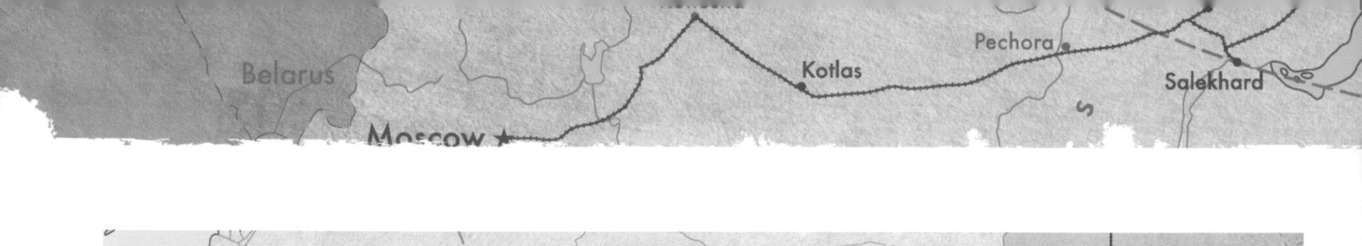

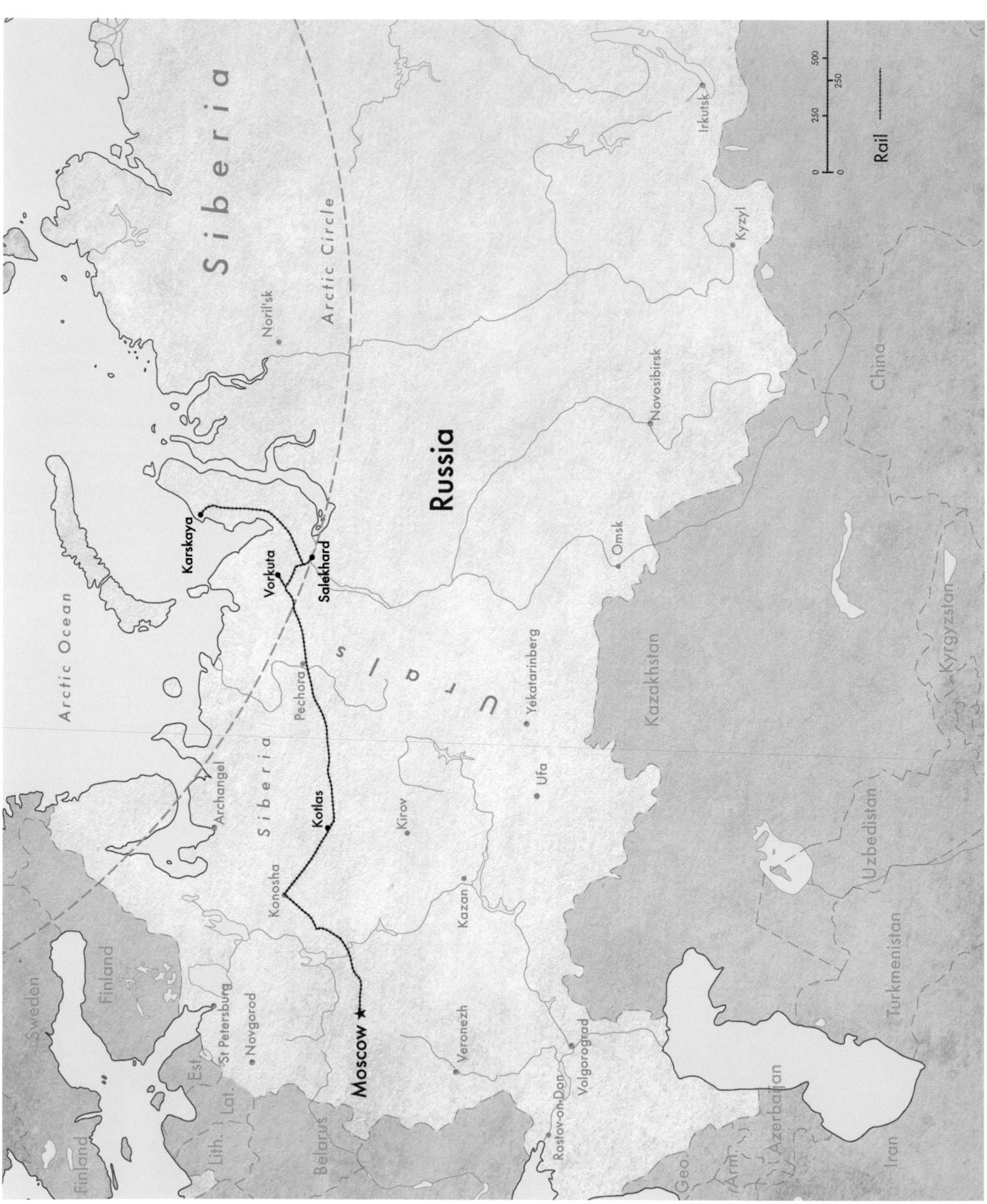

Arctic Ocean
Siberia
Arctic Circle
Noril'sk
Russia
Karskaya
Vorkuta
Salekhard
Pechora
Urals
Archangel
Siberia
Kotlas
Konosha
Kirov
Kazan
Yekaterinburg
Ufa
Omsk
Novosibirsk
Irkutsk
Kyzyl
Moscow
St Petersburg
Novgorod
Veronezh
Volgograd
Rostov-on-Don
Sweden
Finland
Finland
Est.
Lat.
Lith.
Belarus
Kazakhstan
China
Kyrgyzstan
Uzbedistan
Turkmenistan
Azerbaijan
Iran
Geo.
Arm.
0
250
500
0
250
Rail

Arctic Circle
Yatusk

Siberia

I'm not sure about Russia. I'm not sure about Russians actually, come to that, there seem to be millions of them now, all in the places where I go on holiday. But enough of that... I used to spend a lot of time each year in Murmansk and the salmon fishing in the north of Russia is still probably the finest on earth. There was one enormous salmon that I caught in Russia and is now on my wall at home. It was certainly the biggest I am ever likely to catch. It's huge; it's bigger than two London buses superglued together... and they say fishermen exaggerate.

I stopped going in recent years after a couple of really bad helicopter crashes that happened in the area and that, along with a drowning rather put me off... No fish was worth dying for. But Murmansk – my only real experience of Russia before our filming trip – was truly dreadful. It made me look forward to Stranraer – it made me look forward to Staines.

So, when I flew into Moscow for the start of our epic Siberian adventure, it was with mixed feelings. I was rather excited about going north of the Arctic Circle, but I didn't expect to be very impressed by Moscow and I expected the Russian customs officials to be the most bloody-minded on Earth... I was right on the last two counts. I really didn't think much of Moscow. It is a city steeped in history and it is extraordinary to think how much its people have changed and developed in the last few years. And where have all these beautiful girls come from and where have all the shot-putters gone?

But as for the look of this mega-wealthy city – apart from Red Square and the notorious Kremlin, which was really well-preserved, Moscow desperately needed somebody to go round and give it a coat of paint. Outside its centre, Moscow still had the same old Soviet drabness of the days of the USSR. In fact, away from Red Square, Moscow looked just like Murmansk.

Our brief was to get to the most northerly railway station on earth, a 2,000-mile journey on railways built during some of the darkest periods in Russian history and we started in Moscow on a beautiful spring morning; the first, apparently, after a long, bitterly cold winter.

The tube station in central Moscow was truly splendid, so much more ornate than the streets above. It was better looked-after, painted and loved than most parts of Moscow. It was really elegant, with a wonderful ceiling. It was built in the 1930s, under the guidance of Joseph Stalin himself. He wanted the Moscow tube to be a triumph of communism. The place was amazing, but my biggest problem was that I didn't speak a word of Russian, I didn't read any words of Russian and the Russian alphabet is Cyrillic and completely different to any other language. Also, if I wanted to ask anybody the way to somewhere, most of the names of most of the places I wanted to visit were completely unpronounceable.

For example, my first stop was Yaroslavsky. I said this several times to a couple of passers-by, who looked at me like I'd arrived from Mars. I then tried writing it down in big letters on a piece of paper and, eventually, I got a man to give me three fingers (not two fingers – I get given that a lot on my travels). The rouble dropped, eventually, that he was saying to me it was three stops from this tube station.

So off I went from Komsomolskaya to Yaroslavsky – and those were the names of only two of the stations I needed for this journey. I expect you're probably beginning to see my problem.

It's unlikely that anybody would be daft enough to try to upset Mr Putin by bombing the centre of Moscow but, just in case they are, a word to the wise. The tube station is a really good place to hide. It's the largest nuclear bunker in the world and it was deliberately strengthened by Stalin and then Khrushchev and co. during the Cold War in case of a nuclear strike by the Americans.

From Moscow station you can get on the Trans-Siberian railway, the world's longest railway, and you can go right across to Beijing, to Vladivostok or even outer Mongolia. It is a massive station and it's the starting point for some of the world's greatest railway adventures. You can even choose to go straight up to the middle of absolutely nowhere.

Surprise, surprise – that was what we chose.

All we knew was that it was 2,000 miles straight up north and it would be absolutely freezing... What could be more fun?

The first mainline train was to be a 19-hour sleeper to Kotlas. Kotlas was the first place on our journey I could actually pronounce, but my joy was short-lived as to get there I had to ask for the 1.35 pm train to Kubbledecac. Anyway, we found a train with something that looked, alphabetically, vaguely similar to *kubbledecac* and, pleasingly, it was right on time. There were very nice ladies with very nice red hats all the way along the train and when you said 'Kotlas' to them they all nodded their red heads happily, so I felt we were in the right place. I got into carriage

The train staff with their distinctive outfits, who nodded encouragingly when I asked if this was the train to Kotlas.

number seven, sleeper number eight and settled in for a nice, gentle 678-mile journey.

Even when we eventually did get up to Kotlas, we were still less than halfway to the Arctic Circle and it was still about the same again to get to our eventual destiny, in the very far north. Everything about Russia was enormous – everything about its railway system was colossal. It's the third-largest railway system in the world. They have 20,000 locomotives, they go through 11 different time zones and there are over 50,000 miles of track.

The railways in Russia date back to the 1800s. They were the pride of Imperial Russia many years before the Revolution. Most of the thousands of miles of track were built by prisoners and its main purpose in those days was getting timber from the massive forests of the north down to the port of Archangel for export.

Our train wasn't exactly luxurious, but then I don't think you really expect luxury in most parts of Russia. Yet it was also very expensive. A very strange woman kept grinning at me but then I realised she was grinning because she'd just charged me £10 for a cup of tea and, basically, I had to make it myself. She just gave me a cup and a teabag and pointed to the boiling samovar in the corner... Oh, and there was no milk, either. They don't seem to do much milk in Russia but, as I was to find out, boy do they do cabbage.

My sleeper was reasonably comfy for a night's rest, during which, sometime in the small hours, we moved across from the Archangel line to a railway built by Stalin. With daylight we realised there had been a lot of snow overnight and there was a very strong, bitter cold wind blowing. We'd already travelled more than 600 miles and the temperature had clearly plunged, but I suppose I didn't expect it to drop quite so much so fast.

ICE-COLD IN KOTLAS

Kotlas was also very, very cold. The only thing that really cheered us up was knowing that, by the time we finished, we would be

Soundman Jon 'JT' Thomas, me, director Ed Venner and cameraman Mike Harrison with a huge great train on display in Vorkuta.

much colder. We had been supplied back at base with a fantastic range of thermal clothes and all sorts of quite alarming survival gear, including each of us being supplied with a one-man tent. I didn't really anticipate splitting up from the crew but our specialist cold weather expert, who kitted us out back in the UK, had said, 'If you are cut off and you're stuck on a station overnight with no sign of any trains, you will definitely thank me for this tent.'

'OK,' I said – but, secretly, I hoped I didn't have to thank him.

I was beginning to wonder what the hell I'd let myself in for. As we came into Kotlas station, we saw a truly enormous locomotive right by the side of the track. It was a massive old iron horse that would have been used in the Arctic, probably 150 years ago. Some of these, amazingly, are still running to this day.

From Kotlas, our next journey was going to be almost 800 miles, heading still further north and slightly east, over the Urals and into Siberia. It would be a 22-hour overnight sleeper and outside it was still very cold. Thick snow lay everywhere with hardly any trees and we were still nowhere near the Arctic Circle.

We were on our way to a remote town called Vorkuta. The line was constructed to bring coal down from the extreme north that Stalin urgently needed for his bitter war against Germany. They started building in 1940 and conditions were absolutely appalling. Hundreds of thousands of prisoners were used, including criminals, political prisoners and, basically, anybody who had upset Stalin. They were housed in a series of brutal, forced-labour camps all along the line.

It was difficult to consider how horrific life would have been here at any time, but particularly in the depths of an Arctic winter. Any little shelter you had, you would have had to create yourself from frozen local timber – the shed you slept in and the sleepers that were laid on the tracks. We were told quite unemotionally by one of the officials on our train that we would be travelling over the graves of thousands of men who'd died building this railway.

At first light the next morning, there was a lovely clear dawn with a sunny day on its way. There was a lot of snow and, noticeably now, no trees. It was much colder and it was beginning

Much of the line that I travelled on at first was ordered by Stalin as part of the fight against Nazi Germany.

to look bleaker and bleaker. It seemed to just go on for mile after mile with no change in the landscape. With my breakfast mainly cabbage I was served a nice cup of tea with a mug that had a picture of Joseph Stalin on the outside. I suppose it would be the same as drinking a cup of coffee with Adolf Hitler grinning at you. Very, very strange.

There was one guy I watched fascinated all through the long day. He seemed to drink vodka pretty much non-stop from first thing in the morning until late at night, but once in a while he'd put on a grey coat, stand upright – perhaps just to prove that he still could

– and start stoking the fire. Yes – a fire. I think it was the first time I'd seen a live fire inside a railway compartment; Health & Safety clearly haven't arrived yet in modern Russia but it was wonderful. We could pour ourselves non-stop quantities of tea from the boiling kettle that was always on the flames. And it kept the inside of our carriage lovely and warm.

Around midday, we finally crossed the Arctic Circle. There was no sign; no announcements. We found out from our compasses, otherwise we wouldn't have had a clue... just snow and more snow... snow, snow, snow. After about 20 hours staring at nothing, I began to hallucinate, seeing lamp-posts, post offices and pubs. I kept shaking my head to clear it but eventually, some time towards the end of the afternoon, I started to see little houses for real and then people on sledges and skiddoos; it was Vorkuta. We were now 100 miles north of the Arctic Circle and 1,200 miles north of Moscow. It was a pretty desolate place anyway, but without the railway there would be just nothing here except, of course, vast quantities of coal that were discovered here in 1930. They would have had no way of moving the goods without the freight line. There were no roads. Nothing.

At their peak, Vorkuta mines were producing one-twelfth of the coal supply for the whole of the Soviet Union but, as with so many mines around the world, the supply slowly dwindled and with it went the population. It dropped from perhaps 250,000 in the 1930s to less than 50,000 today. In addition, Vorkuta has a dark history known to all Russians. Originally, it was one of Stalin's gulags, his notoriously brutal system of prison camps. More than two million people came through Vorkuta to work the coal mines and hundreds of thousands of them perished

It was here that I met a lovely guy called Viktor, an ex-miner who agreed to show me the now abandoned mining area where he lived and worked for many years. He took me up the sheer incline to the mines on a skidoo, doing what macho men love doing all round the world, trying to terrify the visiting Englishman by driving as fast as he could and then doing violent turns, grinning and shouting a lot.

Just to let him know that nothing frightened me, I just screamed

I got the chance to test-drive one of the trains at the Kotlas depot.

a lot each time he turned. When we got to the area around the old mineshafts, it was all terribly sad. There was row upon row of dilapidated old houses, the old accommodation blocks for Viktor and his workmates. They had been miners long after Stalin had died and Viktor was able to look back on his many years working down the mine as the best period of his life. But he said the mines were very frightening; they were very dangerous and a lot of them collapsed but he had been proud to be a miner and was very well-paid.

Vorkuta was once a wonderful place, he said, but now it was not so great. They have very limited daylight during the winter and it only improves from February to April and everyone now is desperately poor.

STALIN'S RAILWAY OF DEATH

Vorkuta's coal had been at its most needed in WWII while the next line we travelled was built after 1945 in the cold war between

Russia and America. We joined Stalin's transpolar railway to take us up and over the urals and via the splendid-sounding Labytnangi and on a few miles to Salekhard.

This leg of our journey had been just a short section of what Stalin called 'the great plan for the transformation of nature'. It was to be a 3,000-mile railway connecting the vast mineral deposits of northern Siberia with the Bering Sea. It was to have made the Soviet Union the most wealthy industrial power in the world but thousands of the gulag prisoners who were sent to build it perished in temperatures as low as minus 60 degrees Celsius in the pitch darkness of the Siberian winter.

It became known as Stalin's death railway.

Our own journey was only going to be a little hop, the 170-mile run to Salekhard, but it took 13 hours. We seemed to be stopping every ten minutes, although most of the time nobody got on or off. However, they did all get off at a place called Yeletsky where, again, there seemed to be absolutely nothing except a tiny little station. It was obviously the halfway point where everybody gets off for a ciggy – there were frozen dog-ends everywhere.

Almost everyone on my train was a gas worker, making their way up to the mineral fields in the extreme north. The weather outside the train was sunny but very cold with a bitter wind and yet the locals clearly didn't think anything of the temperature. They were wandering about in T-shirts as they smoked and one guy just walked past our camera in a pair of pants – all very macho, but I am pretty sure he got just round the corner out of sight and then screamed.

We got back on the train and I think we must have been bored because we decided to film the lavatory. It was actually a wonderful thing because you could see from where you sit on the toilet an absurd sign that read: 'Beware: a policeman may be watching'. Why would a policeman be watching? And there was more... the actual lavatory bowl was a great marble creation but I couldn't flush the toilet at all at first. Eventually, I found an ancient foot-pedal that did the trick and then – best of all – the loo seats had a series of studs on both sides that apparently are cleverly designed to stop the cheeks of your backside from slipping off the loo. A magnificent thing and only in Siberia.

Once we'd crossed the Urals, having crawled uphill for most of the day, we definitely felt the train going downhill – this was probably why they had the studs on the loo seat to stop cheeks slipping at this moment. We were now dropping down into western Siberia.

Of course, Siberia is large – in fact, it's huge, but I had no idea just how huge. I looked at the great journey that we were planning, to the most northerly railway station on Earth but, set against the map of the whole of Siberia, I realised that in fact our journey was just a tiny little blip. Siberia is bigger than the land masses of Europe, Canada and the USA put together. Now, that's big.

When we got to Labytnangi the railway line just stopped and we had no choice but to try and grab some sort of taxi on the only road for thousands of miles. So, somehow, at 12.20 am on a pitch-black Siberian night, we found a cabby, who jabbered away in an incomprehensible dialect that might have been Russian, about the price to Salekhard. We nodded our heads even though we had actually not a clue what we were agreeing to. He did manage to communicate to us that we were going over a frozen river that sometimes had weak spots and from there people had fallen through the ice and drowned! I really didn't need to be told that but he just grinned at me idiotically and drove on. Luckily, the frozen river stayed frozen, we made it across and we eventually crawled into Salekhard in our taxi. I don't quite know what the bill was in conversion to sterling from roubles but I think we bought the driver a new house.

Just a few shacks along the course of the river are all that remains of one of the biggest camps of the transpolar railway. Tens of thousands of prisoners were sent to this camp and used as forced labour to work on the railway as it made its way from here eastwards across Siberia. Conditions for the workers were shocking – bitter cold, malnutrition and, surprisingly, disease. I wouldn't have thought any germs could have lived in temperatures as low as minus-60 but clearly they could and hundreds of thousands of the workers never went home.

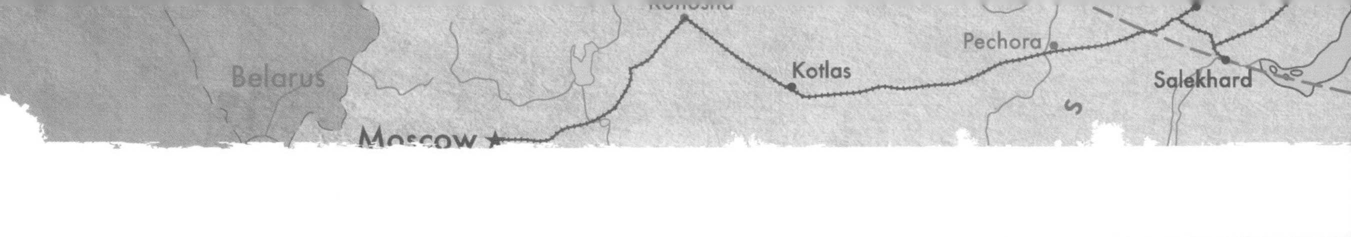

The Nenets' life revolves around reindeer, and their nomadic existence was made much more difficult in the Soviet era.

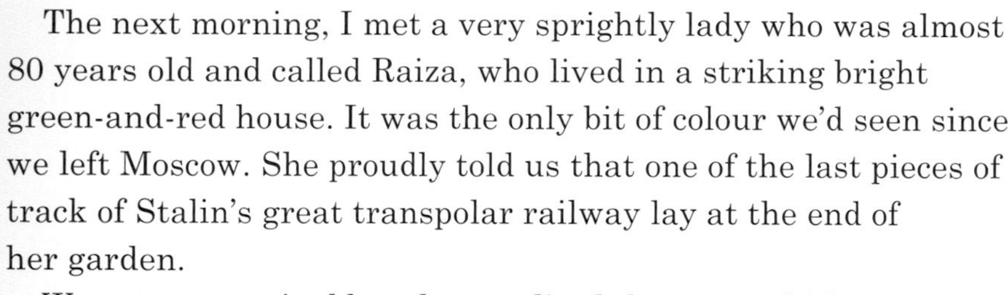

The next morning, I met a very sprightly lady who was almost 80 years old and called Raiza, who lived in a striking bright green-and-red house. It was the only bit of colour we'd seen since we left Moscow. She proudly told us that one of the last pieces of track of Stalin's great transpolar railway lay at the end of her garden.

We got very excited but then realised there was thick snow everywhere and if we wanted to see a piece of this track, we would have to dig. With a shovel borrowed from Raiza, we dug and dug. Until, thrillingly, my shovel clanged into what was unmistakably a piece of railway line. And it would have been one of the very last pieces to be laid because the railway virtually finished at this point in 1953, the year of Stalin's death. Absurdly, with his passing, the whole great plan for the Siberian railway was abandoned. Hundreds of thousands of men had died and all in vain. Raiza said she remembered the men working here on the railway when she was a young girl.

'It was very hard for them and so many died. They tried to escape but were caught later and almost certainly executed. Many of them, desperate to get away, tried to cross the river. In the parts where the ice was very thin, lots of workers drowned. I used to use the railway myself as a young girl; everybody used to use the railway. It's very sad that they closed it down because there are many towns in Siberia that none of us can reach any more; they are just cut off.'

ENTERING THE ARTIC CIRCLE

Salekhard itself was a revelation. It was a very shiny, modern city with lots of hotels, although I'm not quite sure who comes here to use them. It was a bustling place with a magnificent cathedral. There was a beautiful monument – in Russia there's always a beautiful monument and nearly always it's an image of Stalin or Karl Marx.

However, this one, surprisingly, wasn't of Stalin or Marx or even Lenin; for once, it was an architect's abstract creation, celebrating the fact that we were right on the Arctic Circle, the 67th parallel.

We were now in the Arctic and before I caught my next train up to the Yamal Peninsula, up to the very north, I met local inhabitants who'd been living in this area long before the railways came. They were Alexei and Elena from the Nenets people, traditional, nomadic reindeer herders who have lived in this part of Siberia for thousands of years. They follow the reindeer, live in a tent made, of course, from reindeer hide and they dress in reindeer skins. Guess what they were having for lunch when I called? Yes, spaghetti bolognese. OK, sorry, I lied – it was a huge vat of reindeer stew.

They live high up in the Urals, following the herds through the summer months. In the autumn and winter, they come down to the lower ground, as do the reindeer.

The couple were incredibly welcoming themselves, although they had some alarming-looking dogs around the tent. The dogs were, mercifully, pleased to see me, mainly because Alexi handed me a bag of biscuits. I was quite sparing with them because I was pretty sure that, if I ran out of biscuits, the dogs would probably eat me. We also drank tea from ancient drinking vessels but I was disappointed to see that it wasn't reindeer tea, noticing a Tetley teabag in my cup.

The Nenets own a lot of the land in this enormous part of the world, even though it is mainly snow-covered for a lot of the year. The deal for decades has been that the railways use their land to travel through and in return they get free passes to travel on the trains anywhere they want in Siberia. Whether they are allowed to bring their dogs on board wasn't clear and, if they have to stay with the reindeer at all times, doesn't that mean the herd of reindeer would also have to get on the trains too? I never found out but I suspect that in reality Nenets don't use their free railway passes very often.

We now came to the most important part of the whole journey. The Yamal Peninsula contains one of the richest oil and gas

The Nenets survive in what would for many be incredibly inhospitable conditions.

reserves on earth. Russian gas corporation giant Gazprom control it and built a railway line to get the men and equipment to the most northerly station in the world. For us it was to be a full 24-hour journey by rail with no roads to fall back on and no other people except for those on the train.

If anything did go wrong, perhaps my little one-man survival tent might not be as daft and as pointless as I thought. We were in the middle of the Arctic, at least 300 miles from the next station and any sort of help.

There were no phone signals and the temperature dropped to about minus-20 outside. We crawled up the Yamal Peninsula line. '*Yamal*' is a Nenets word that means 'the end of the Earth' and, yes, it certainly was. There were no houses now, nothing. No mountains – not even a little hump; absolutely flat snow for the next 24 hours.

Everybody on the train was a miner or somehow connected to Gazprom and all the passengers, without exception, frowned at us. I think it's a Russian thing; because, when we tentatively asked if we could talk to them about where they work and the jobs they do I was, frankly, amazed when to a man they said, 'Yes, of course.' They were going to repair bridges and gas pipelines near the Bovanenkovo gas field. This vast resource was the reason for the railway; in fact, the reason for everything out here. Twenty-two per cent of the world's gas reserves are from the Bovanenkovo gas field; enough gas to heat every home in Europe for years to come.

These guys stay on the peninsula for two or three months at a time, away from their families and, in the winter months, working in bitter cold and total 24-hour darkness. But that didn't seem to faze them at all. One guy I spoke to, who I think was called Alexander, said, 'The cold does not bother us. We are very used to it living in this part of the world. We are not in Africa – this weather is fine for us.' Many of the guys worked a long way down, deep in the actual mines, which were always bitterly cold. But they all seemed to think that they had great jobs. Employment security in any part of Russia was a problem and if they didn't do this work, many who lived in places like Salekhard would have found it impossible to get anything else to do. They were also, by their own standards, very well-paid. They spend very little of their wages while they were up there; most of it goes back to their families – and, in any case, there was very little to spend it on.

I had expected the air in the carriage to be filled with the sweet smell of vodka, but it was made very clear that this was strictly a no-alcohol train. Three-hundred-and-fifty-five miles across a wilderness of snow for over 24 hours with absolutely nothing to drink seemed a daunting prospect, particularly for Russians, but they accepted this Gazprom workers' diktat. The company did not want miners to arrive drunk to work with dangerous and expensive materials. We, too, had to promise that we would not drink alcohol in our sleeper carriages overnight. Of course, we went along with it; we had no choice and we had to sign an agreement to that effect. There were horrible rumours doing the rounds about me, the camera crew and hip flasks hidden inside cheese sandwiches, but I couldn't possibly comment.

WHITE IS THE NEW BLACK

This line was completed in 2010, having taken 24 years to complete and costing £10 billion – probably paid in cash! I had judged construction by the standards of the almost impossible terrain that we'd seen conquered by railway engineers in places like the Congo and the Andes. By contrast, I thought it would be pretty straightforward building a railway across hundreds of miles of flat, frozen land but apparently it was very hard. The biggest problem, strangely enough, was not the bitter winter, but rather the summer, when temperatures rise from minus-50 to plus-25 or more and all the snow melts. The whole area becomes a massive series of raging rivers and flood plains.

In the middle of absolutely nowhere is, at 2.4 miles in length, the longest bridge above the Arctic Circle. It's called the Yuribey river bridge and it weighs 30,000 tonnes. Rising out of nowhere in this vast snow desert it is an amazing sight.

There was one little heated shack, home to the guys whose job it is to keep this bridge clear of snow. The idea of living here 12 months of the year would be most people's idea of hell – certainly mine. They had to clear the bridge of snow at least three times every day because the railway must get through. There was too much money at stake. Somewhere there is a Mr Gazprom, a very rich gentleman who likely buys yachts and football clubs.

Extraordinarily, I met a family who'd come to this completely desolate place, would you believe it, on their family holiday. They were Austrian – of course they were – and they seemed to be rather enjoying it. They spent 24 hours on the train with nothing to drink and only cabbage to eat and, after arriving at Bovanenkovo, they

Extensive testing showed that, yes, Siberia is rather chilly.

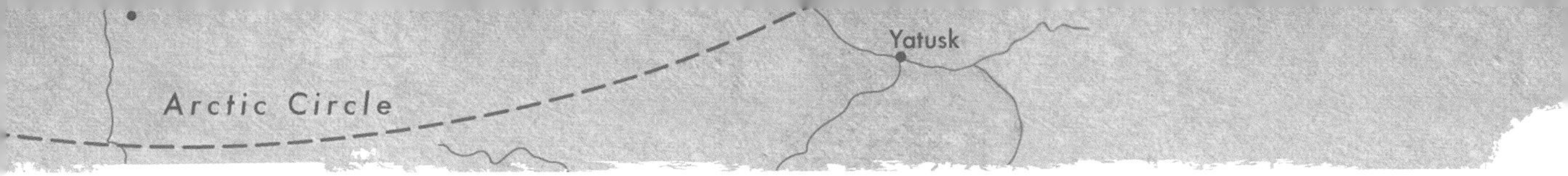

were going to turn round and go back down again. I did suggest to them that it might be more fun if the family went to the south of France or the Maldives but they looked at me like I'd come from the planet Zogg. Each to their own, but I have to say that if I said to my kids, 'This summer we're going up to the northernmost gas field on Earth', I don't think they'd be terribly excited.

As the train crawled on through the relentlessly unchanging snowy landscape, I think I began to lose it. At one point when we stopped (which the train did quite a lot, for no reason at all that we ever learnt, in the middle of absolutely nowhere because there wasn't a single station for 355 miles), I decided to get off and run about in my bare feet. It was very exhilarating but when I got back in the train, all the miners clapped at me, wearing an expression that said, 'Let's all applaud the English madman, he clearly has not long to live.' Indeed, I think I would have settled for going to meet my maker rather than another 12 hours looking out at the snow and eating the fine Russian railway cuisine (endless cabbage).

We had cabbage soup, we had cabbage with potato, we had a salad made of cabbage and, for a change, we had cabbage with cabbage. It didn't help that I wasn't a great lover of cabbage in the first place. I couldn't remember when I'd last eaten cabbage but if I hadn't been prepared to eat cabbage in Russia, I would definitely have starved.

Between meals, the other passengers seemed to be constantly munching on black bread and cabbage sandwiches. I began to become convinced that we would surely soon pass a takeaway curry house or a KFC, or a friendly little Chinese man would come running along the side of the train with a bag of sweet-and-sour pork, but it was to no avail. Back to the black-bread-and-cabbage sandwich.

We'd spent a night and a whole day on the train and I was beginning to feel like I'd been on this train for at least the whole of my life but then we started to see some lights; the first we'd seen for 24 hours! Maybe we were coming into a town or, perhaps more likely, a very small city.

But it was a city, a very big, noisy, brightly lit city. We had

Impressions from Siberia.

Arctic Circle

Yatusk

travelled non-stop across this ice wilderness and now we suddenly came into a place that looked like Las Vegas. We'd emerged from the most desolate, remote area of the world and here we were in a town that was absolutely heaving. Bovanenkovo is one of the richest places on the planet. More than 10,000 people work here in absolutely freezing conditions but, as we got off the train, there were expensive four-by-four cars coming in to pick the guys up and several long Mercedes with blacked-out windows. This was real, mega-wealthy, modern Russia.

There is the most tremendous amount of minerals under the ice desert and all over Russia there are many very rich gentlemen who possess the know-how to get it to the surface and make themselves and a few of their friends even richer. However, it does provide very well-paid employment to those who are tough enough to handle it, in an area of the planet where there really is absolutely no other way of making money.

I was quite amazed at what I saw. I did not expect Bovanenkovo to be anything like the brightly lit, chaotic place that it was, particularly reaching it after we'd finished probably the most arduous trip of all those we'd undertaken. It had been incredibly wearing, in the sense that the view never changed for day after day, night after night. We'd spent a lot of nights sleeping on trains because there weren't any hotels – or even towns – along most of the routes we'd travelled, but we had finally arrived.

The crew and I were exhilarated. We were at the most northerly train station on the planet! But, guess what, you know what was the only way back to Moscow and a plane home? Simple! Turn off the cameras and do it all over again in reverse on yet more trains. Oh, goody, goody...

3

CANADA

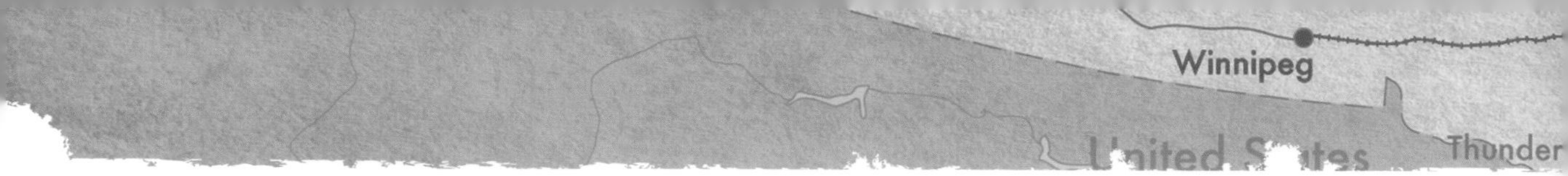

Canada

Beaufort Sea
Baffin Bay
Davis Strait
Labrador Sea
Hudson Bay
Greenland (Denmark)
Inuvik
Cambridge Bay
Kangiqcliniq (Rankin Inlet)
Iqaluit (Frobisher Bay)
Ivujivik
Chisasibi (Fort George)
Schefferville
Happy Valley Goose Bay
Sept-Iles
Chibougamau
Quebec
Sherbrooke
Montreal
Fredericton
Saint John
Charlottetown
Ottawa
Toronto
Lake Ontario
Lake Erie
Lake Huron
Lake Michigan
Lake Superior
Sudbury
Hornepayne
White River
Thunder Bay
Moosonee
Churchill
Lake Winnipeg
Winnipeg
Flin Flon
Regina
Saskatoon
Yellowknife
Edmonton
Calgary
Banff
Lethbridge
The Rockies
Fort Nelson
Watson Lake
Dawson
Whitehorse
Juneau
Prince Rupert
Prince George
Kamloops
Mission City
Vancouver
United States
U.S.
Rail
Road
0 200 400 Kilometers
0 200 400 Miles
N

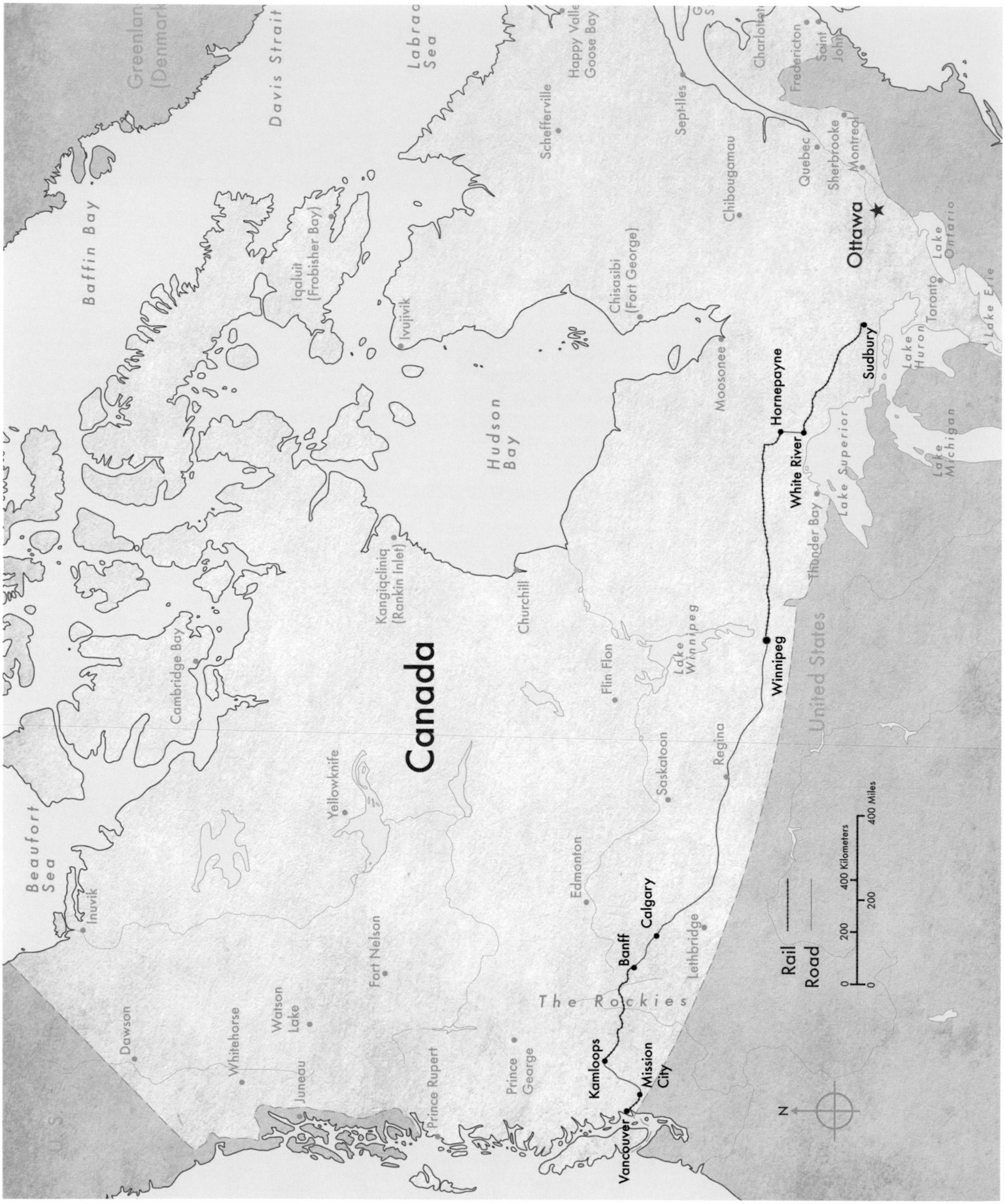

Canada

I love Canada, I love the country and I love its people. Whenever they do one of those surveys about best places to live in the world, with best quality of life, Canada nearly always seems to win. I've been going out to Canada at least once a year for the last 20 odd years.

It has some of the best fishing on the planet and I've fished from Novia Scotia in the east to Queen Charlotte island in the west. I've fished right up in the north on the Alaskan border and across on the Hudson Bay. It's a beautiful place and there are tens of thousands of square miles of water, most of which is hardly every fished. I've driven thousands of miles all over the country, usually in a great, big, hired truck, playing country music, eating giant steaks and drinking Molson beer while exploring the lakes and rivers of this vast land.

But in all that time, I'd never once been on a train, which is ridiculous because Canada has some truly great railway systems and it was these that opened up the country to make it the great economic nation that it is today. For centuries it was just a vast wilderness with not a lot of people apart from the natives living there, but then they built a 2,500-mile, transcontinental railway and Canada became one of the most powerful countries in the world. There are not that many passenger services because freight is the major concern.

Our plan was to travel with our cameras along the whole of the length of Canada. We joined the mighty Canadian Pacific Railway north of Toronto, at the mining city of Sudbury. It was here almost 150 years ago that the construction of the railway began.

Canada has masses of natural resources and they rely almost entirely on rail to reach the sea and the export markets. We

The Canadian Pacific network opened up the country with a vast network of rail for goods transportation.

travelled from Sudbury to a place called White River, an eight-hour journey through an enormous wilderness. It was springtime sunny but still with lots of snow around. Just beautiful.

The first train was something of a puzzle, it was what they call a Budd railcar, it dated back to the 1950s and looked more like a bus than a train. And it stopped off just about everywhere.

The original line was built in 1871 when, to the east there were European settlers and in the west there were more than 600 different groups of indigenous tribes. The only real port of any significance was Vancouver, but there were no real roads or communications to get from east to west. The prime minister, John MacDonald, saw a railway as a real chance to link up the massive country. Before that, Canada didn't really work. He announced, as all politicians do, something completely impossible: 'I'm going to build a 2,500 mile railway in just ten years.' A nice idea and a good plan, but it didn't work.

As we travelled in our Budd car along the first leg of our journey, we could see immediately how difficult it would be to build a railway through this wild country. There are lakes absolutely everywhere and miles of really fast-flowing rivers – that's why we fishermen love it, but railway engineers hated it. There was thick forest everywhere, deep snow in the winter and, when the ice began to break up in the spring, there was a massive snow melt that would bring flooding. Railway building became impossible and many existing tracks were washed away. It took them a very long time to build just this one section of the railway alone.

I asked one of the Budd-car guards what sort of goods they carried. He said, 'It's really crazy the stuff we take on board – a lot of four-wheel drives come on, all sorts of transport, skidoos, dumper trucks and, if the hunters kill a big moose or a bear, we'll take that on board as well.' He showed me racks across the back of a huge baggage car where they hang the carcasses. I couldn't imagine getting on a train and finding a moose hanging up beside me but, apparently, in the hunting season that's the way it is. They shoot

On the bridge at Hell's Gate in British Columbia.

The passenger trains take second place to freight – you just have to sit back and wait.

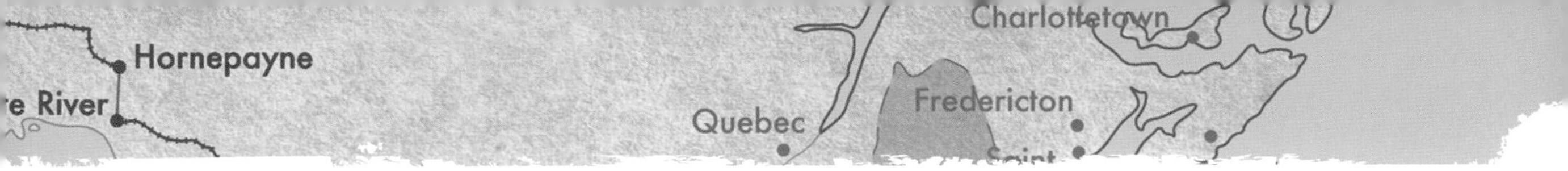

the bears in the summer and the moose in the autumn. He did admit that some of the passengers getting on did 'double takes' as they got on – well, of course they would!

It was before the hunting season and we saw one guy loading up everything he needed for his sporting lodge in the summer months. He packed everything on the train – a big truck, giant spare tyres, snow shovels, guns, cartridges, a crossbow and a ton of food. Once he was loaded up we got going again although, soon afterwards, had to stop once more because a massive freight train was due to come through.

From my experience of railways all over the world, freight trains usually have to wait for passenger services. In Canada, it's the other way around. Freight is very much king here and, when you see the size of them, you're not going to argue. The freight trains running across Canada are truly enormous. Even bigger than the monsters we'd filmed in Australia. The train we were waiting for was two-and-a-half miles long and each of its dozens and dozens of trucks carried the equivalent load of three big lorries. They just kept rolling past our camera. It must have taken more than half an hour to pass and, apparently, they need at least a mile to stop. But most of the time they don't; they pound on through and people like us in our little Budd bus wait and sensibly stay out of the way.

POOH-POOHING WINNIE

After eleven hours – and scheduled for eight – we got to White River, supposedly the first place of any significance on the route, but I have to say that it was a nothing sort of stop. The only thing that White River is famous for – and even this is rather tenuous – is Winnie the Pooh. In August 1914, a Canadian vet, Captain Harry Colebourn, journeyed to White River on the same line and came across a hunter who wanted to sell him a cuddly little bear cub. Harry bought it from him for $20 and named it Winnie, after his own home town of Winnipeg. He took it to London Zoo, where

AA Milne and his son Christopher Robin fell madly in love with the little bear and he was immortalised as Winnie the Pooh.

I was told this tale excitedly by one of the inhabitants of White River and I did manage a quick game of pooh sticks under a river bridge before I left. I didn't like to tell the nice man, but as a kid I always hated Winnie the Pooh; I always thought he was a silly little bear and I had no time for him. I always wanted to tell Christopher Robin where to stick his pooh sticks! And when I grew up I never saw any reason to change my mind.

The next leg of our journey was a bit less straightforward. We had to hire a massive four-by-four to drive away from the Canadian Pacific, which became freight-only for the next thousand miles or so. It was a gruelling drive but finally we pulled our truck into a little place called Hornepayne and were told that this piece of dirt that we'd parked on, by the tracks, was actually a request stop.

I felt vaguely ridiculous standing there next to a completely deserted railway line, waiting to stick my little hand out. I was pretty sure that not much would come along between now and midnight and, if anything did appear, it would probably go thundering straight past. After we had been there three hours or so, at about five o'clock in the afternoon, a massive express train appeared out of nowhere. I tentatively stuck my arm out and to my amazement it pulled up beside me and the driver stuck his head out and said, 'Hey, man, you wanna go to Winnipeg?'

'Yes,' I said in amazement, 'I really would.'

So I scrambled aboard and got on *The Canadian* for another 700 miles to re-join the Canadian Pacific at Winnipeg.

The Canadian is a beautiful luxury train from the 1950s; really classy with leather seats and dark wood furnishings. It was magnificent and as I was going to be stuck on it for quite a long time, sleeping overnight, I was very pleased when a man called Peter came and showed me a button on the wall of my cabin that I could press and, lo and behold, a large, double bed came out of the wall.

Hailing down the express to Winnipeg – astonishingly, it worked.

I had a superbly comfortable journey, with excellent food in the dining car and a really good night's sleep on the run to Winnipeg, but I was aware that this particular section of the railway had been one of the toughest to build. After all the promises, progress with the transcontinental railway was really slow. Everybody began to see that there was a real need for a unifying railway for the future of Canada, but nobody had anticipated how hard construction would be. Predictably, because a lot of money was involved, millions of dollars were squandered by corrupt politicians and railway bosses.

And then a guy appeared with the splendid name of William Cornelius Van Horne, a very bright, far-sighted American who had been working on railways since he was 14 and claimed he could lay 500 miles of track, however difficult the terrain, in a single year. Frankly, it was an over-ambitious statement, but the Canadian authorities were getting desperate and decided to give him a go, starting with Winnipeg.

Our journey into Winnipeg was beautiful, we slowly moved out of the thick forest with the snow melting in the early morning spring sunshine and began to get into the prairies – thousands and thousands of acres of some of the most fertile farmland in the world. This rich landscape surrounds the great city of Winnipeg, but 150 years ago there was virtually nothing here, just a few farms, with a few settlers struggling to make ends meet. Most of the land was owned by the indigenous tribes.

On arrival, we found that Winnipeg has the most wonderful station, mosaic ceilings beautifully designed and constantly re-painted, it's the pride of the Pacific Railway. It was based on the Grand Central Station in New York and dates back to 1911.

Across the city, we had an appointment with a lovely old guy called Bill, resplendent in waistcoat and bowler hat, who runs an old railway line just outside Winnipeg, called the Prairie Dog Central Railway. The Prairie Dog was actually built in Glasgow, Scotland, in 1882 and was shipped across to New York and then to Winnipeg. It actually played an instrumental part in building the Canadian Pacific; she took hundreds of tons of steel rails and timber sleepers for Van Horne's construction teams out of

Winnipeg as they built mile after mile of railway out into the prairies. Every single day they were able to go that bit further and, by the end of year one, although he hadn't quite achieved his promised 500 miles, Van Horne was pretty close. The problem was he was now running out of money.

Then Van Horne had another brilliant idea – he created thousands of customers for the railway before it was even finished by marketing to… farmers. Canadian Pacific offered an amazing deal to any European settlers who wanted to go out to western Canada and try to set up a successful farm. They paid for a ticket on the transatlantic line and then transferred them from the coast to the middle of the prairies and provided a large acreage of farmland with a farmhouse already set up on their new land. It was quite ingenious and it worked.

THE BLACKFOOT AND THE RAILWAY

In the first 30 years, more than three million settlers arrived from Europe. They called it the largest peace-time migration in history and every single one of the newcomers was totally dependent on the railway. I met a lovely guy called Jim Beachell, whose family came over in 1889. He was fourth-generation and he now had several sons working with him on what is now a massive farm. They have been here for 126 years, having made the journey from Yorkshire in England. His great-grandfather and great-grandmother arrived with 11 kids, having been on a boat for 11 days, at one point getting stuck in Atlantic ice.

The train goes right by the family farm and made it possible for them to establish the massive cattle and arable ranch that they own now. Jim admitted that, without the Canadian Pacific, his family would probably still be in Yorkshire.

Van Horne's other problem was gently placating the people who'd been here for hundreds of years, particularly the Blackfoot Indians, but it was badly handled and probably deliberately deceitful. He needed permission to access Blackfoot land. The huge herds of bison that the Blackfoot had lived on had been virtually wiped out by white hunters and by the end of the 19th century they were all but extinct.

Van Horne convinced the leader of the Blackfoot tribe, Chief Crowfoot, that the railway could bring vital food supplies for his people if he agreed to give the trains access. On 20 June 1883, Chief Crowfoot signed a vital piece of land away to the Canadian Pacific owners, who were able to lay track through the land in exchange for a lifetime pass for the chief and his tribe on the Canadian pacific railways.

It turned out to be a disaster.

The railway builders were very careless about which parcels of land they actually built the railway on. Sparks from the trains wheels started wild fires that burned most of the Blackfoot's land. Crowfoot realised his mistake too late, the Blackfoot people never really forgave Van Horne and there is still resentment towards the Canadian Pacific Railway owners to this day.

From Winnipeg, again, there were only freight trains on the next western leg of my journey. So we got back in the four-by-four and made our way by road some 700 miles towards Banff, one of the most beautiful towns in Canada.

Banff is right in the middle of the rocky mountains and, once more, Van Horne had to come up with a cunning plan to make a railway viable. Quite apart from the problem of building a railway over the jagged, snow-capped peaks of the rockies, there would also be no demand for land from settlers because there was nothing to farm.

On a bitterly cold day in the 1880s, three Canadian Pacific Railway workers went exploring just outside Banff and discovered a hot spring. Then another and another. Van Horne saw yet another marketing opportunity; for people to come and take the hot spring waters. Banff became the first Canadian national park and people flocked from all over the world for the medicinal properties and when they came, they travelled – of course – on the railway.

The Banff Springs Hotel became one of the most famous in the whole of north America and, with thousands coming to the area every year, it was the beginning of Canadian tourism. We

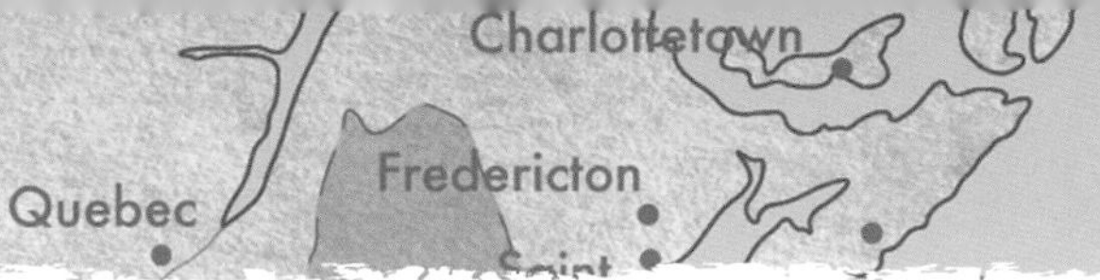

stayed for a couple of nights while filming in the area and found the Springs hotel to be a great one. It's very much like a Scottish hunting lodge, but it also has something of a great French chateau about it. Its guest list has included Winston Churchill, Queen Elizabeth II, King George VI and Marilyn Monroe.

Money was coming in for Van Horne and lots of people were dependent now on his railway line. But the problems of building right through these mountains still had to be faced. The next guy I met treated me to one of the most terrifying mornings of my life.

Greg was one of the coolest guys I've ever met; he's also very lucky to be alive and have all his fingers and toes still attached, but perhaps that's because he is very good at his job. His job is tackling avalanches, one of the biggest problems for lines that, like the Canadian Pacific, go through snow-covered mountains. In Canada, the snowfall in winter is massive and avalanches can bring whole sides of mountains and tons of rock thundering down, taking everything before them, including giant pine trees, boulders – and railway lines; even locomotives and carriages.

This has been a big problem for the Canadian Pacific ever since it was created. Greg takes a helicopter to the highest peaks of the rockies, hunting snow formations that look as if they might funnel and pack into a potential avalanche. Greg hovers over the snow pile and, dropping dynamite, he blows the avalanche apart while it's small, before it can become a big danger.

I trotted along happily to interview him and I thought we were just going to have a nice chat on the ground. I didn't realise that he had plans to take me up with him. He opened a large metal storage container, which, he proudly showed me, was full of dynamite. 'Here, Chris,' he said nonchalantly, 'hold these,' and handed me sticks of dynamite.

Now, I have only ever seen dynamite in comics, but it seemed to me pretty scary stuff. I certainly never expected to handle any and I was convinced we were all going to be blown sky high any minute. Each stick was like a giant candle, with a fuse sticking out of the end. Greg assured me that, unless the fuse was detonated, the stuff wouldn't go off, but I have to say I was far from convinced. So were

Preparing to board a helicopter loaded with dynamite and go hunting avalanches to blow up.

my crew, helpfully all hiding behind the four-by-four. I thought, If this lot goes up, there won't be a four-by-four to hide behind.

All went quietly enough until he announced we were going up with him in his helicopter. 'I've had 408 bombing missions', he said proudly, 'and I haven't been killed yet.'

'How many can you take?' I asked, hoping he would take the whole crew with him and perhaps I could stay on the ground.

'Only two,' Greg said. 'That will just be you and the cameraman.'

The soundman whimpered a happy sigh of relief, deposited some recording equipment in the helicopter and disappeared out of sight, followed by the director and the rest of my lily-livered former chums. So Mike the cameraman, who by now was as white as a sheet, and myself, who was even whiter, went up with Greg over the incredible peaks of the Rockies. They were sharp and jagged even at 6,000 feet and still covered in snow.

DYNAMITE, AVALANCHES, POINTY PEAKS AND STORMS

Greg turned and showed me the bombs he was going to use. He put what he described as 'safety fuse assemblies' into the side of a batch of dynamite sticks, made a hole in one side and another hole right through the stick and then fitted each one with a detonator to make a bomb. So, we were in a helicopter, which I don't like, over the Rocky Mountains that I was beginning to like less and less, with a whole box full of homemade bombs. I didn't feel great. Greg kept enthusing about the whole thing, but Mike and I were finding it very hard to share his excitement.

'How can you not enjoy throwing explosives out of helicopters and bombing the snow?' he said.

'I don't know,' I said. 'Not enjoying it seems to be coming very easily to me.'

He spotted a heavy fall of packed snow on a peak, told me where to throw the bombs and then he'd back off, because they would blow in 15 seconds. I just hoped that his timings weren't 14 seconds out, otherwise it would be, 'Night-night, Banff,' and my widow back in England would be doing a posthumous tribute, saying something like, 'I'm sure Chris would like you all to see this film, even though sadly at the end the silly old fool died.'

So we threw the bombs out as instructed, closed the door shut and pulled only a few yards away from the area. According to Greg, it was quite important that we stayed reasonably close so we could see that they worked.

I had this vision of the dynamite going off on time after 15 seconds but the explosion being so savage that the helicopter would be thrown up into the air out of control. Mercifully, I was wrong, there were two big bangs but the helicopter stayed steady as a rock.

It was at this point, while he was discussing the potential requirement for a second pair of bombs to be dropped a bit farther along the mountains, that he suddenly looked a bit concerned and said, 'It's getting a bit wild up here. We maybe want to get back down.' I had been so focused on the bombs I hadn't really realised that, although we'd come up and over the Rockies on a bright, sunny morning, it had now clouded over and we were in the middle of a driving blizzard with no visibility at all and no radar. We were in a total whiteout.

I was also acutely aware how sharp and savage-looking had been those peaks that we climbed up and above only minutes before.

I had been frightened by the dynamite, I had been frightened by the bombs, but now I was really terrified by our situation. In a helicopter, in a blizzard, way above some seriously dangerous looking rocks with no visibility was no great place to be. And then, to compound my fear, a red light starting flashing and something in the helicopter started making a dreadful 'Whoop! Whoop! Whoop!' noise.

'What the hell is that?' I said.

'That's an alarm,' Greg said. 'It means we're going down too fast.'

'Too fast,' I said, throwing a scared look at Mike. 'Isn't that a bit like crashing?'

'Yeah – it could be,' said Greg, 'but I never have yet.' The word 'yet' held no reassurance in it whatsoever.

As suddenly as the snowstorm had risen, it calmed. The spring sunshine shone again on the mountain tops and lit up the valley below. We made our way down to the crew waiting on the ground who didn't look remotely anxious. I think they had just been wondering why we were late.

'Everything OK?' asked the director. 'Get some nice pictures?' 'Yes, probably,' I said, 'but then again, possibly not.'

And we went to dinner to try and explain.

After a few stiff drinks in the bar I seemed to sleep remarkably well, with hardly any nightmares at all. The next morning, we were going to explore the Rocky Mountains in much more comfort and safety.

The *Rocky Mountaineer* took us on one of the most spectacular train journeys on Earth. It's the only passenger train that takes men, women and lots of children over the Rocky Mountains and we had more than 300 miles of the journey ahead of us, over some of the tallest and toughest mountains in the world, all still covered in snow in the early morning sunshine.

Van Horne by now was getting near to the completion of his dream, but his engineers and surveyors at this point said, 'These mountains are completely impassable by a train, it just won't work. You will never be able to get a train to go up any inclines as steep as these anywhere.' 'Never' is the last thing you should say to a man like Van Horne. He was so completely determined and single-minded that he would find a way through. His team of engineers had to crisscross the railway line back and forth across the valleys as they got steeper and climbed higher.

They built hundreds of bridges and tunnels and slowly made their way onwards and upwards, but there was one construction that almost proved too much even for William Cornelius Van Horne – it was a giant escarpment that was given the obvious but precise name of Big Hill. With double or even treble locomotives, trains could make it up the very steep, rugged rock-face, but coming down was fraught with danger.

The very first time they tried it in the construction of the new railway line, down the hill in 1884, the train went completely out of control and came off the rails. They were lucky in that only three workers were killed, but over the next few years many more trains crashed and the Big Hill at this point is littered with crosses.

They made it safe with a series of spiral tunnels, in which the trains follow a three-quarters circle and each carriage comes out below the rest of the train – the spiral technique. As we were coming out of Kicking Horse Pass, we saw the rear of our train still on its way in.

By 1885, the whole Canadian Pacific structure was all but finished and they drove in the last spike – attaching the final rail to the last sleeper – on the line at Craigellachie on 7 November 1885. In just four years, Van Horne had created a railway that ran across almost the whole of Canada. It was an amazing achievement, a vast transcontinental railway, connecting farms, mines and over 800 scattered communities, but they were still more than 300 miles from the west coast.

While they had been building inland from the east coast, the inhabitants of British Colombia in the west had been building their

The *Rocky Mountaineer* conquers the Rockies.

own section to try to meet up with Van Horne's. A Dutch-American contractor with the splendid name of Andrew Onderdonk was in charge of the western end of the great railway system.

The mountain passes, canyons and ravines were a nightmare for a railway engineer. Van Horne promised 500 miles of track per year, while Onderdonk built less than 340 miles in five years, but the building of the western section was probably much tougher than anything even Van Horne had to work his way through.

We came to a place called Fraser Canyon, which looked down on really wild crazy water from our position high above. The rocks all around us were one deep canyon after another of solid granite and at this point Onderdonk's engineering teams said it just wasn't possible to build any more railway. It was too steep and even if they got the tracks laid no train could stand it. So they built a series of massive ledges running along the side of the rocks to carry the railway. Mile after mile of ledges were built all along the canyon.

We took to a boat at this point, the film crew and me bouncing around in an inflatable Zodiac boat over these raging waters. As we filmed along the course of the river, looking up at all the rock faces above, we could clearly see the shattered remains of a recent derailment, with an engine and carriages that must have plunged at least a hundred feet. No one seemed to know the story of this particular ill-fated train or what happened to the passengers, but we were pretty sure it would not have had a happy ending. So many of the early train journeys shared the same fate and hundreds of lives were lost in the first few years of these railway lines.

Onderdonk realised that to construct this great complex of ledges built on sheer rock to carry the railway line through Fraser Canyon, he needed a massive workforce. With funds limited, he

Setting off in a dinghy to catch sight of the railways cut into the rocks above.

was not going to be able to recruit them from British Colombia and so he shipped in 17,000 Chinese immigrants. Chinese labour was very cheap and they arrived with enthusiasm, but were totally unprepared for the very dangerous work that lay ahead. They were ill-equipped and the conditions were horrific. We looked down from the top at the sheer rock face of one cliff alone, where hundreds of Chinese workers had died. They'd been instructed to abseil down the cliff while holding a stick of dynamite. The plan was then to chisel out a hole in the rock, put the dynamite inside, light the fuse and get the hell out as soon as possible.

They were totally dependent on their mates at the other end of the rope, up the top, pulling them out and up really fast, but often it would go completely wrong. Many, many times the dynamite exploded too soon. They estimated that three Chinese labourers died for every mile of track. And in total they laid 338 miles...

The plan, however brutal, worked and the railway was completed, but Onderdonk understandably remains a controversial name in the history of Canadian railways. He was never seen as a great engineering hero like Van Horne.

But west met east and, for me, it meant that 2,500 miles of my journey was almost over. As we came into the great city of Vancouver we had now travelled on all three passenger arms of the Canadian Pacific and this last leg is the one place where the needs of the commuters going in and out of busy Vancouver are given preference over the long line of freight trains stacked up, waiting to unload their cargo to Vancouver harbour. This is the gateway to Asia for Canadian exports.

The end of the line; the epicentre of the harbour, where the trains are unloaded, is not accessible by passenger train, but we reckoned it must be pretty spectacular, so we hired a plane. No helicopter, no dynamite – just a light aircraft with our camera crew over Vancouver harbour and it was wonderfully impressive.

Port Metro – which in 2016 became simply the Port of Vancouver – is one of the busiest ports on Earth and below us we could see one massive freight train after another waiting at the edge of the harbour to be unloaded. None of them was less than a mile long

– many were at least double that – and all their container trucks looked full from the air. They reckon a freight train comes in here every 15 minutes of the day, 365 days a year.

It had been a wonderful journey particularly as I have always loved Canada. It is a beautiful country, their attitude to their environment and nature is unquestionably excellent and I have always rated them for that, but I never really had a chance to witness what makes Canada such a busy and massively profitable industrial nation.

Undoubtedly, as I had clearly seen, the building of the coast to coast railway was the most important single factor. If it had never been created by the great pioneers like Van Horne, then Canada would still be a very beautiful, but mostly empty, wilderness.

The Rockies dwarf even the most impressive man-made bridges and tunnels.

4324
HH

ALASKA

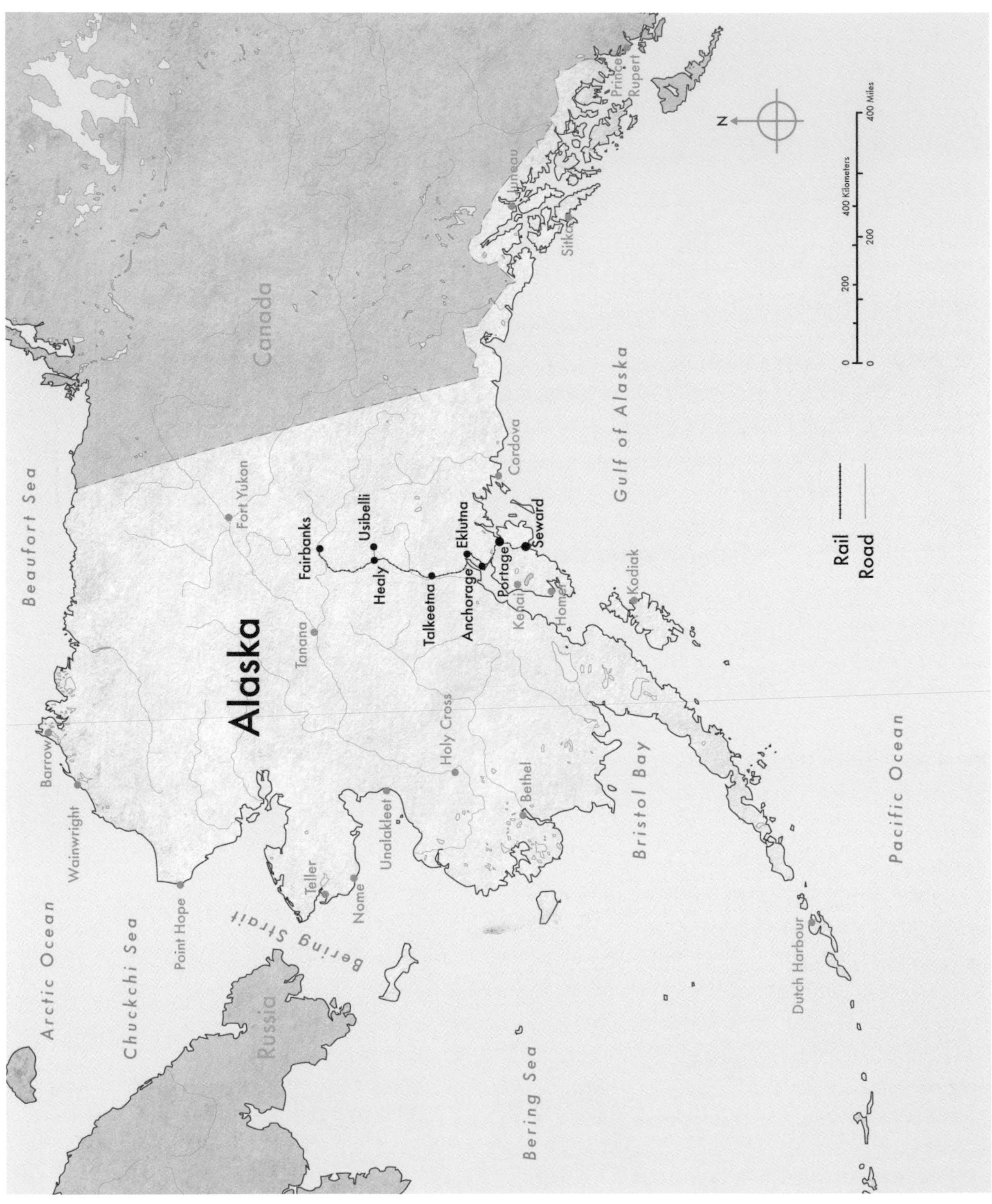
Alaska
Canada
Russia
Beaufort Sea
Arctic Ocean
Chuckchi Sea
Bering Strait
Bering Sea
Bristol Bay
Gulf of Alaska
Pacific Ocean
Barrow
Wainwright
Point Hope
Teller
Nome
Unalakleet
Holy Cross
Bethel
Tanana
Fort Yukon
Fairbanks
Usibelli
Healy
Talkeetna
Anchorage
Eklutna
Portage
Seward
Kenai
Homer
Kodiak
Cordova
Juneau
Sitka
Prince Rupert
Dutch Harbour
Rail
Road
N
0
200
400 Kilometers
0
200
400 Miles

Alaska

I spent a few happy weeks in Alaska several summers ago... It was beautiful, probably one of the last truly wild places on Earth, but my main memories are of a couple of much-too-close encounters with bears.

I will never forget the sight of a grizzly bear running at full speed. It was an awesome thing to watch but also quite terrifying. The speed that these usually amiable, lumbering animals quickly reach and the way they go straight through thick trees, undergrowth and water – as if the obstacles are not even there – is unforgettable.

Ahead of this latest trip, I received a information booklet from the tourist board with the splendid title of *How to be Bear Aware*. One piece of advice that caught my eye was: 'Under no circumstances should you give a bear a biscuit.' Why on earth I would even contemplate trying to hand Mr Bear a chocolate digestive or even a custard cream, I really had no idea. But I filed the helpful note in my memory bank, although we were hoping that when we were there, in March, Mr Bear would still be fast asleep somewhere nice and cosy under the ice.

We flew via the lovely city of Seattle, across the Canadian border and over Vancouver, where only a matter of months earlier we had been filming on the magnificent *Rocky Mountaineer* and then arrived in Alaska at a place called Seward. This is the Alaska Railroad's southern terminus, right next to the Pacific Ocean. It takes its name from a very enterprising American politician, William H Seward, who bought Alaska from the Russians, the original owners, in 1867. Russian missionaries and fur traders had been very busy in this part of the world for over a hundred years when Seward paid $7.2 million for the land. That was a lot of money – in excess of $100 million now, but that was the price for

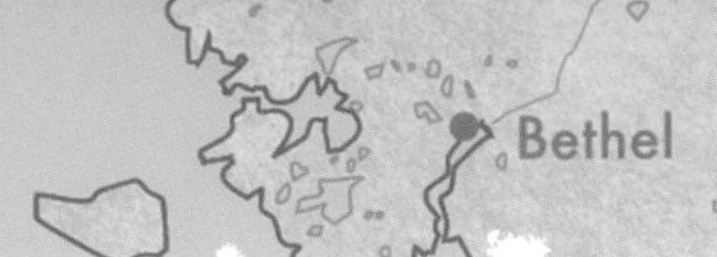

which the Russians agreed to go back across the Bering Straits and leave the country to Uncle Sam.

It always amazes me that the distance between the farthest eastern tip of Siberia and the north-western tip of Alaska is only a matter of four miles, taken from the Diomede Islands in the middle of the Bering Strait, belonging to Russia and Alaska respectively. Alaska has got some of the most inspiring scenery on Earth, some tremendous wildlife and in the Alaska Railroad, one of the most difficult railways ever built anywhere on the planet. Our trip would be a 470-mile summer journey for summer that only a fool would attempt in winter – so, of course, I arrived in early March, still very much a winter month that far north and still very cold.

For a long time, people ridiculed Seward's purchase as sheer madness. Alaska was just a remote frozen wasteland, they said, with very few inhabitants apart from the native Indians. Most of the year it was completely impossible to travel across because everything was thick with snow and solid ice… oh – and it was pitch-black.

It was the discovery of gold in the 1890s that changed everything. Gold Rush fever came to Alaska and, just as they had done in many other parts of the world, smart investors began to see the potential of a railway that would give the prospectors access to the goldfields. Construction began just after the turn of the 20th century, but the bitterly cold weather made building extra-difficult. To find out more, I had to get from Seward to Anchorage – now the capital of Alaska – but the only trains running at this time of the year were freight and even those were few and far between.

I was able to hitch a ride in the cab of a massive freight train, a way of travelling that I've rather come to like over the past few years. The guys driving the train, the engineer and his brakeman, were great – although I'm pretty sure we were a thorough nuisance as we crammed into their cab with our cameras and sound gear while they were trying to do a day's work. We chatted about the problems of running along that stretch of track at this time of year. The biggest problems by far, the driver stressed, were avalanches that could come down at any time and anywhere along the track. Hundreds of tons of rock cascade down the mountain face in a matter of seconds and he told us that, although he had been lucky and had never been hit, he had seen it happen. Several good friends of his had died.

He also talked about the dangers posed from bears and, more often, from Alaska moose, enormous animals that regularly get onto lines, winter and summer, thinking of the track as a nice, easy road for them to travel along. The bull moose is a massive animal and if a driver hits one they have to get out and clear the carnage from the line. This opens them up to further trouble from bears in the summer months and from exposure and frostbite in the winter, when temperatures are down to perhaps minus-40 Celsius. Getting out of the train for even five minutes can be downright dangerous.

It was very clear that the building of the railroad in this wild country had posed even more problems than those that other engineers have had to face around the world. Alongside ice, thick rock, avalanches bear attacks and frostbite, there was another big obstacle. Alaska was totally isolated from the rest of the USA and completely lacked infrastructure. Everything the crews needed – rails, ballast, shovels, pickaxes, sledgehammers; even the timber needed for the sleepers – had to be shipped in at great expense or somehow created by the railway workers themselves in the middle of this cold wilderness. Add to this the fact that most of Alaska is under ice and has only limited daylight for at least five months of every year and you begin to understand why progress on the railroad was agonisingly slow.

COLD FACTS

Construction began in 1903, to capitalise on the Gold Rush but, after five years, the railroad had gone a pathetic 50 miles, which really wasn't enough to keep the project alive. The company that had been set up to build the railroad filed for bankruptcy, and all work stopped. Alaska was still seen by most as Seward's folly.

However, more investors eventually came forward; those who could still see the potential of this enormous country. By 1910, the great Alaskan railway project was back in action. Absurdly, though, they'd learnt nothing and the same old problems remained as they tried to progress the 470 miles to Fairbanks, a major site in the Gold Rush. Progress were agonisingly slow and, after another year of hard work, only 21 more miles of track had been completed.

Enter the US president, Mr Woodrow Wilson, in 1914, who had total belief in the future of this massive state. He got Congress to set aside $35 million to buy up all the track that had been laid so far and get the rest of the line completed. The locals called it the 'Government Railway' but, this time, it was not about investors making a fast buck, it was about Wilson's total belief in Alaska, its importance to the USA and the tremendous potential of its natural resources and mineral wealth. He could see that a road system would be hopeless and totally understood that a railway would take a lot more time than previous investors had anticipated. The long-term rewards could be massive but they would need a lot of patience, belief and, of course, money.

Saying 'Goodbye' to two really nice guys and a lovely warm cab, we left our freight train to see where the whole thing really started. In 1915, the Alaska Engineering Commission decided to locate their headquarters in a tiny fishing village on the Alaskan coast. It was originally called Ship Creek and, not for the first time in my life, I spent a whole day up Ship Creek.

Because this was going to be the head of the railroad, this little village suddenly became massively important. A great tent city sprang up with railway workers and their families; more permanent buildings soon followed and the place became so busy that it quickly became the main harbour for the whole state. The project was no longer up Ship Creek. The locals wanted to call it Alaska City but the name that eventually everybody settled on was Anchorage because the US Post Office department had – arbitrarily – been using the name for a while and it stuck. Anchorage today remains the capital and is easily the biggest city in Alaska; more than 40 per cent of the state's total approximate population of almost 738,000 live here.

It's a great place to visit. We were only there for one night

The Alaskan wilderness presented almost insurmountable challenges to the railway-makers

because we had a big journey ahead, but a lovely guy called Dave Greenhalgh, who was one of the main bosses on the railway system that we were about to join the next morning, invited us over for a barbeque. I have to say he could not have made us more welcome. We drank lots of good dark Alaskan beer and the meal itself was not for the faint-hearted, nor certainly the vegetarian. Luckily, in our crew, there were none... Jennifer – who eats absolutely anything that's not nailed down – and the rest of the boys are all ravenous carnivores. Except Jake Martin, the second unit camera operator.We call him 'Pack Mule' because we load him up with all the crap nobody else wants to carry or deal with. He is prone to fads and this week he'd become a vegan. Well, kind of a wavering vegan though, who floats between lettuce leaf and carrot purée and steak-and-kidney pies... Dave's house was not the place for non-meat eaters because all the food provided – and there were several groaning tables of it – was moose. We had wonderful spiced moose burgers, moose kebabs, moose sausage and enormous moose steaks. Jake seemed to forget whatever oaths vegans swear to each other and got lost deep in Moose Mountain. I liked Dave and his family, I loved spiced moose burgers and I began to get the feeling that this just might be a great trip.

First thing the next morning, having spent the whole night dreaming of spiced moose burger, we made our way to the station and we didn't dare be late. There are only two passenger trains a week out of Anchorage at this time of the year. Ours was the *Aurora Winter Train*, which has a reputation of being one of the nicest passenger trains in the whole of the USA.

When I got to the station I was amazed to see it was already really busy – even this early in the year there were plenty of international takers for this particular train. Many were from much further south in the USA and a large number of others were Japanese, most of whom insisted on wearing masks over their noses and, in some cases, over their eyes. This was something we'd seen all around the world and was a very Japanese thing. There are many splendid things about Japan and its people, as I had discovered, but I never could see the sense of going on a trip to see the world – from behind a face mask! I was in the Maldives a couple of years ago, long after the tsunami and yet several honeymooning Japanese guests wore full, bright-orange lifejackets to breakfast dinner and in the swimming pool! I swear...

The *Aurora* travels all the way from Anchorage to Fairbanks, although we would have to stop off several times en route to catch up with interesting people and places along the line. It was indeed a beautiful, comfortable train, with lovely leather seats and clean – yes, clean – loos. Apart from Japan, I think that's the first time I've said that about any train anywhere in the world for more than three years. But they really were spotless, with blue water and second only in standard to the Japanese trains.

They also had a splendid restaurant car with a really nice waitress who came and asked me if I wanted my breakfast skillet. This, it turned out, was gravy and biscuits with a favourite Alaskan delicacy: ptarmigan (a kind of grouse). Having sampled spicy moose burgers only the night before and loved them, I was in the mood to try anything. I have to say that ptarmigan was pretty nice, too, although probably not that early in the morning. I mean, I love turkey, but I don't think I'd want one for breakfast.

ALASKA COMES OF AGE

Judging by the roaring trade that this train was doing, even on a bitterly cold march morning, the Alaska railroad, after all its early difficulties, was clearly thriving. It was completed in 1923, but Alaska was still very sparsely populated. It is an enormous country, something like twice the size of Texas and yet it had just 60,000 inhabitants then. It certainly wasn't enough to support a railway which, for the next 15 years or so, ran at a loss.

Yet, Alaska was of enormous military significance. The USA feared invasion first from the Japanese and then the Russians. Large quantities of men and materials were shipped up here to protect the US's northernmost borders. Alaska is in the top ten of US states for number of military bases and, although invasion fears were misplaced, they were great for the railroad. Transporting soldiers and their equipment from one end of the state to the other made a tremendous impact on the Alaskan economy. As I sat in the warm, looking out at the snow and enjoyed my ptarmigan and biscuits, it wasn't long before I noticed that we travelled very close to the perimeter fence of an air force base – Elmendorf, just outside Anchorage. Heavily armed fighter planes were just visible through the fir trees from the frosted train windows.

The other great boost to the development of Alaska was a US government scheme to ship in what turned out to be 203 settler families to start farming. The idea of farming in Alaska sounded like madness at first, but the southern half is in fact great agricultural country: the mud flats that were everywhere on the first leg of our journey consisted of glacial silt, which is one of the best substances for growing fruit and vegetables. Alaska gets nearly 20 hours of daylight in the summer months and the farmers duly came in their hundreds to exploit the potential and, of course, they came by rail.

It took a long time but, by the early 1960s, Seward's folly had become a thriving part of the USA. The railroad was the centre of everything and was at last making a big profit. But then there was an enormous setback. On 27 March 1964, at 5.36 pm, the second-biggest earthquake ever recorded rocked southern Alaska. It measured 9.2 on the Richter scale, killed 131 people, most by tsunamis triggered by underwater landslides, and destroyed roads and buildings over a wide area. Anchorage was brought to a standstill and havoc was brought to the Alaska railroad. It was devastated; in some places the track disappeared as much as 20 or 30 feet into the earth. It is a real testament to the hardiness of the Alaskan people and a clear sign of how important the railway had become to this part of the USA that the railroad crews got services running again in just a few days.

The Alaska Railroad was a real pleasure to travel on. All the staff on the train were wonderfully friendly and accommodating and the views were amazing. The country was just beginning to wake up from the bitter cold of the winter. It was still pretty chilly for most of our trip, with temperatures hovering around zero, but the sun shone on the thick snow outside the train window and the ice on the rivers was just beginning to break up. Later in the year, all these rivers would be full of salmon that come here every year from the Pacific to feed the bears and to die. The rivers by August, viewed from the air, are bright red with dying salmon. But for now the streams were just waking up and the snow melt had only just begun.

There were tracks everywhere at the side of the line, mainly of moose, but some of them also of bear. The grizzlies were beginning to wake up too. I've sung the praises of moose burgers, but I don't think I could eat bear. It is a real delicacy up here. although bear hunting is very carefully regulated. Locals will tell you that the black bear is the one to eat; grizzly flesh is pretty grim and is mainly used for pet food.

Long before the Russians or the North Americans came to this part of the world, the locals living on moose and bear meat were not Eskimos (who live much further north) but tribes of hunter-gatherers called the Dena'ina – they dominated central Alaska.

The state was just beginning to waken from its winter deep freeze as we made our journey.

Lee Stephan, of the Dena'ina council, with the spirit houses next to Eklutna's church.

A small handful of their descendants still live in the village of Eklutna, where we stopped. A very impressive-looking figure, Lee Stephan, who is the president of their tribal council, met me off the train. He was very proud of his heritage, although I did get a sense of sadness from him that the village was almost empty. Most of the young members of his tribe had gone away to the big cities and there were now only 35 still living at Eklutna.

They still speak their tribal language and love to keep their traditions. I asked him pointedly if they had been mistreated or betrayed by the Russians or the Americans but, for once, I heard a native inhabitant of a country say, 'No, we were treated well. They were good to us.'

He took me into the village church, built by missionaries in the 1840s and probably one of the oldest buildings in Alaska. To my surprise, it was Russian Orthodox but that was because most of the Dena'ina people had converted to that branch of Christianity by the middle of the 19th century, when the country was still part of Russia.

All around the church were little multi-coloured structures, what the Dena'ina people call spirit houses, designed to shelter the souls of the dead. What was interesting to me was that many of the Dena'ina men had been essential to the building of the railroad. As it came into their land, the tribes had built the tracks and then worked on the railway for many years. Lee still uses the Alaska Railroad a lot and said, 'It has been very good to the Dena'ina people.' He clearly felt a loyalty to it.

I really enjoyed Lee's company; he was good fun and, bizarrely, even asked me to send him a signed photograph, which I duly did when I got home. Apparently, it now sits proudly on the wall of his dwelling, although what the rest of the Dena'ina tribe make of a signed picture of a man with a dreadful, cheesy game-show grin on his face from the set of *Who Wants to be a Millionaire?*, God only knows.

GOING OFF-GRID

As we continued our journey northwards on the next available train, it was clear that the country was becoming more sparsely populated. There are hardly any towns or villages within a 50 mile radius of the railway line. Some people do live in this huge blank area, but they occupy isolated log cabins that don't show up on maps, Alaskans call these people 'off-gridders', precisely because their homes are not anywhere on the map grid. I met a guy called Steve Durr, a musician who's a proud off-gridder and wouldn't want to live any other way. His is the most remote cabin, 232 miles up the Alaska railroad from Anchorage in the middle of absolutely nowhere. It is bitter cold and totally dark for at least one third of his year but he lives there because he loves it. He met me beside the railroad and took me into the forest, still thick with snow, on his skidoo.

I've travelled on skidoos before, particularly in Russia and

Norway, but I've never quite got on with them. I don't like being on the front driving them and I don't really enjoy being a passenger on the back. Even with all the cold-weather clothing, the wind chill cuts into my face like a knife and they are incredibly uncomfortable. Being on board is like riding a bucking bronco with a concrete saddle. It didn't help that Steve had a shotgun wrapped around his neck and the barrels kept banging the side of my head each time we did a sharp corner. It was probably not loaded but there were bears around...

I think Steve was trying to impress me with his technique but, as we came around a particularly vicious bend in the forest, the skidoo went racing straight on, I went flying to the left and Steve went flying to the right. His gun came down in the middle. Of course, the camera crew thought this was very, very funny, but camera crews are like that and it's nothing that a good smack in the ear can't solve.

We got ourselves back on our vehicle, shook the snow off our clothes and out of our mouths and, to my continuing unhappiness, Steve put the gun back around his neck and, at a slightly more sedate pace, made our way to his cabin. I was beginning to regret the detour but, once I got into the cabin, I could see why he loved it. It was incredibly warm, he was never short of firewood, the fire never goes out and the kettle is always on the boil. As a keen musician, there were guitars everywhere and all sorts of Beatles memorabilia, including a range of ties with pictures of the fab four all over them. We even drank our tea from Paul and John mugs.

Steve loves living there and said he has a bird table outside the window that he fills daily to attract all sorts of rare birds who come from miles around. He's right on the shores of a big lake and in the summer it must be pure heaven. I wasn't so sure about the winter though. I asked if bears were a problem and Steve said that they could be, but he was always aware of them and had a gun with him at all times. There were lots of claw marks on the outside of the cabin from bears who had followed the scent of Steve's cooking and tried to get in. Terrifyingly, there was also a very clear set of bear claw-marks on the inside of his door. He'd once come home to find a bear in his cabin and the bear had frantically tried to get out. Luckily for Steve, it did.

Steve also had wolves around the cabin, particularly in the winter, but he said he had no fear of these animals. He loved to see a wolf or the tracks of a bear while he is out walking in the forest and, because he knew how these animals behave, he said he felt perfectly happy living and working around them. He said, 'Cities, with their traffic and their crime problems, are far more scary...' All his kids grew up here and occasionally come to visit. He will sometimes just take himself off for a week and go to New York and walk the streets but, he told me, after a few days he always longs to get back.

I was very impressed by Steve and I could understand the attractions of his chosen lifestyle, but I was also very glad to get the hell out of there before darkness fell.

Back in town we dropped into a place called the Fairview Inn, advertised as the finest bar in the town of Talkeetna (in fact, I think it was the only bar in Talkeetna). It was around teatime although several of the patrons of this fine watering hole had clearly been there for several hours at least – one of them appeared to have been there for several days – but they were all harmless and seemingly very friendly, although I had no idea what most of them were talking about as they came over to us and exchanged slurred pleasantries.

There was a population of just 876 people in the actual town, but with so many people like Steve living in unrecorded cabins dotted around this vast snowy wilderness, nobody really knows how many people live in the whole area at all. In 1915, Talkeetna was chosen as a divisional headquarters for the Seward to Fairbanks government railroad route. Most of the town's buildings, including the general store, the road house and the bar, date from this time. It seemed to be very popular with artists and bohemians and it really was quite a place. At one, time they had a cat as the local mayor and the annual Moose Dropping Festival was a big day in the calendar until 2009, involving tossing varnished moose droppings onto a numbered board to score. Later, numbered moose droppings would be dropped from a crane; nuggets landing closest to target won cash prizes for those holding matching numbered tickets.

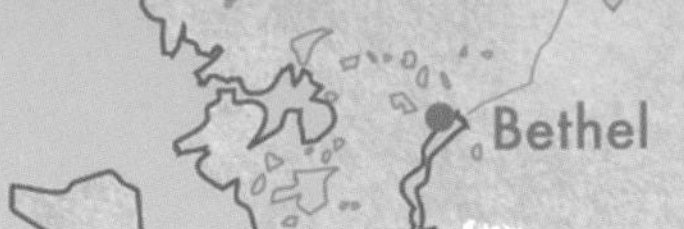

We filmed for a while in the streets and came back into the Fairview Inn to hear live music with Steve on lead vocals. He'd been very sneaky in not telling us about appearing in the bar that night – I think he was a bit nervous about our cameras. Actually, it made a great sequence and he really had a pretty good voice. One of the best songs of his set was a song about the railroad called 'Flag-Stop Train'.

It was a great night, the Fairview Inn was quite a place and does have one other claim to fame. Woodrow Wilson's successor as president of the USA was one Warren G Harding, who ate lunch in the Fairview one day in 1923. I don't think it's a reflection on the fine Fairview cuisine, but Harding died two weeks later. It probably wasn't food poisoning (although they did, apparently, have a new chef…).

However, my accommodation that night was anything but great. I was booked to stay alone in a little cabin on the edge of town called Trapper John's Cabin; there were no street lamps and, as I trudged through the snow with only my little torch to show me the way, I was sure I heard a wolf howling not too far away. The bears were clearly no longer hibernating, because we'd seen several definite tracks, and the last known fatal attack by a wolf in north America happened in Alaska in 2010 – not that long ago. Maybe another was due? The howl was a horrible, eerie sound. I got in Trapper John's Cabin, double-bolted the door and then spent a cosy night in what was a really nice, warm cabin with a bear-skin rug on the bed. They had a black-and-white TV and a record player with a stack of 78-inch records... And I fell into a really deep sleep.

ICE FISHING

For some kinky reason, the crew in the morning insisted on filming me waking up and getting in the bath. I love Mike the cameraman in a manly way, but I don't think he'd ever seen me naked before; it was clearly a bit of a shock. Or maybe a bit of a laugh. There were rumours that the crew tried to sell my bathwater on eBay later the same day but, apparently, there were no takers. I think

'Off-gridders' can easily disappear into the bear-infested wilderness of Alaska.

transportation might have posed a problem or, more likely, nobody in their right mind would want even a drop of it...

A nice guy who worked in the local bar, called Matt Barber, said, 'Hey, Chris, do you want to go fishing?' Now as you may have noticed elsewhere in these rambling pages, I absolutely love fishing; I have fished all over the world and I will jump at any excuse to wet a line anytime, anywhere... well, almost. Because, after all, we were in Alaska, it was March and I had noticed that all the rivers and lakes were frozen solid, so I just knew what he was going to suggest.

'Ice fishing, Chris,' said Matt. 'It's really cool.'

'Matt,' I said, 'I've done ice fishing in Finland and Norway and it's very kind of you, but it is the dullest, most boring form of fishing on Earth. In fact, it's the dullest form of anything on Earth. We all sat around a silly little hole in the ice, freezing our nuts off, catching nothing and I absolutely don't want to ever do it again. Although, of course, thank you very much for your kind offer.'

'Come on, Chris,' he said, 'you'll love it.'

'I won't love it, Matt,' I said, even as he was bundling me into his four-by-four and taking me out towards the edge of what was, apparently, in summer a large lake. 'I really, really won't.'

I was very perturbed by the fact that it was now spring, the ice was beginning to thaw and I didn't fancy disappearing through a hole in the ice. Even as a kid, when we could skate in my local park, I still always had a fear about falling under the ice. I witnessed a guy drown like that in a lake in Middlesex many winters ago and, by the time the divers got down to him, it was too late. I still can see his manic, terrified eyes looking up from below the ice. I've always had a real phobia about that. Yet somehow, Matt got me, with a camera crew, walking very tentatively across the ice on the lake that felt to me like it was becoming distinctly slushy.

He then gave me some kind of large drill thing and sat back with Mike and JT, the idiot Chuckle Brothers, while I started to sweat and drill a hole through what turned out to be mercifully very thick ice. They sat there like a couple of grinning muppets for half an hour while I drilled until eventually I struck not oil or gold but icy water which came squirting back up, making me wet and cold and even more fed up.

'Matt,' I said, 'this is even duller than I remember and there won't be any fish down there anyway.'

'Trust me, Chris,' said Matt, 'they'll be down there.'

'Trust me, Matt,' said Chris, 'they won't.'

And I lowered down some evil-smelling shrimp concoction on a silly little rod, no more than two feet long, through the hole. I was totally cheesed off, I was definitely close to throwing my toys out of my pram and wondering why on earth I agreed to be part of the whole silly business when, within seconds, there was a tug on the line and I pulled up a plump winter trout. To say I was pleased would be an understatement; I was ecstatic, Matt gave me high-fives and we ran around, whooping like a couple of footballers who had just won the FA Cup. In the excitement I even forgot about the dangers of running about on the ice in my giant snow boots. I was thrilled. 'I knew it was a good idea,' I told Matt and, with an almost blasé look on my silly face, I lowered my bait down again and caught another!

What a lovely afternoon… and what a brilliant idea of mine it was to go fishing.

There's no cold like Alaskan cold.

The next leg of this extraordinary journey was to take me from Talkeetna to a town called Healy, a distance of 110 miles. The scenery now was quite epic, thick fir forests and snow covered mountains all around us, lots of bear tracks at the side of the railway. They were quite unmistakable, like the impression of an enormous dustbin lid with razor blades on the top. We hadn't seen any owners of the prints on this trip but several of them were clearly very much up and about.

At one point, Mike the cameraman decided to go and take a nice shot looking up at the railway from down by a frozen river. He was a very happy chappy in his work and he called out, 'Moose tracks everywhere.' We idly looked down at the tracks and realised these weren't moose at all, but a very fresh set of bear paw marks. For a few seconds we thought briefly about not telling him, but decided that was rather irresponsible to say the least, and screamed, 'Mike, Mike! Get the hell back up here! You're going to die...!'

Far from being grateful for us having saved his life, he was positively cheesed off with us for stopping him filming a pretty sequence. The bear never did appear, but it was obviously somewhere close.

A FLAG-STOP LIFE

As we travelled on we realised that this was one of the most remote isolated bits of railway we'd seen anywhere in the world. Hardly anybody lives around here; the nearest highway is about 20 miles away and there are no other roads. Everybody here is dependent on the railway.

There are no stations in this region and they have a very specific way of getting trains to stop. Would-be passengers put a flag out by the side of the track and keep their fingers crossed that the engineer will see and stop the train in time. Bearing in mind that people are sometimes doing this in temperatures of minus-40 Celsius, it must be very alarming if the train is late. By the time it arrives and stops at the flag, the passenger could be a human ice lolly! However, it all seems to run incredibly smoothly.

A really cool guy called Harry Ross was the conductor on our train – he was a very prominent member of staff, who had worked on the railway for years and seemed to know everybody who got

Long-time conductor Harry Ross takes care of everyone who boards the passenger trains.

on board. And sometimes those who didn't. He threw out a bundle of newspapers by the side of the track in the middle of, seemingly, absolutely nowhere and gave a loud whistle. Right on cue, a large dog appeared, picked up the papers in its mouth and went running back, presumably to its master's cabin.

Harry said, 'That's the only way he gets his papers every week and the dog never fails.'

A few miles further on up the track, we then spotted another flag and a wonderful couple got on, Clyde and Mary Lovel. They had the most extraordinary story to tell – they came here in 1961 because Clyde had got a job on the railroad, which wanted people to transfer to this very remote part of the country.

Mary said, 'We just had a kinda hankering for a simple life. For many years things were very tough – we had young kids growing up, we had no heating and no running water. Things came, eventually, but we still had all sorts of problems like most people would never believe. We've had several attacks from bears but, luckily, they always backed off – or at least they have done so far – and we had some medical problems, particularly with my husband. We had real problems getting him to hospital. Without the railway, I'm sure he would have died.

'I'm 79 now and he's 87. I don't know how much longer we'll be able to stay in our cabin but, if we could and the Lord is willing, we'd like to stay here forever. We just love this kind of flag-stop life; our trains are everything.'

They really were the most lovely contented couple and had lived in their remote cabin up here, in this frozen wilderness, for nearly 60 years. They are tough, these Alaskans – you have to be to survive.

As we travelled on, the sheer drops became more sheer on either side of us and we came to the Nenana river canyon. The river Nenana flows through the bottom of this terrifyingly steep valley which, as we passed, was still frozen solid. However, there were huge chunks of ice sticking up in all directions, which indicated the tremendous force of the water underneath. Back in the 1920s, when the railway was being built, it was the climate of this valley and the wild geology of the whole area that gave the railway construction crews all sorts of problems.

The whole area is in the rain shadow of the Alaska mountains, where very low rainfall over millions of years has given the area unusually loose, gravelly soil – and that was the problem in a steep-sided canyon. There was a terrifyingly high risk of rock-fall during the summer and avalanches during the winter when the snow was piled high on the mountains. The railway lines had to be laid high above the Nenana river, on a narrow ledge, because rail-track in the valley would almost certainly have been wiped out by flooding.

We arrived in Healy, which is probably one of the dullest places on Earth, but we could meet up here with the guys whose job it is to maintain the track and keep it running 365 days a year. I met a terrific guy called Matt Morrison and his big Tongan assistant, a huge bear of a man called Tupu. Shaking hands with him was like shaking hands with a bear, but he had an infectious grin and was clearly enjoying the experience of being on the telly.

The crew were on call 24 hours a day and they'd had an alert earlier that morning to say there was a very large pine tree that

The Nenana river road bridge.

looked like it was going to fall across track. We had to put on hard hats and all the protection gear and travelled in a vehicle they use a lot in this part of the world called a hi-rail. It was a really cool vehicle, basically a car that was altered to drive on the railway lines and, when you get to your destination, there was a simple adjustment underneath to get back to driving on a road. It was smooth, obviously very tough – because it needed to be – and there was no need for a map or sat-nav, as the only way to go was straight ahead on the rails.

We were in constant communication with a nice-sounding lady on our radio system, and Matt had to tell her exactly where he was at every moment to make sure that each section of track was closed for the next hour or two while they dealt with the emergency. Only when he radioed in that the track was clear again could trains use the railway. It seemed, initially, rather a tedious process but, in that remote part of the world, it was absolutely essential. The last thing the guys want while they're working to clear an avalanche or in this case a massive tree is a train coming unexpectedly around the bend.

LEAVES ON THE LINE – AND A MASSIVE PINE TREE

So we got the security all-clear and in we went. Sure enough, exactly where the radio operator had reported, there was the most enormous tree, leaning at 45 degrees across the track. On one side there was a great cliff with huge boulders and trees looking as if any one of them could roll down or cause a full avalanche at any moment. On the other side was a sheer drop into the Nenana canyon. It was quite a hairy place to be. Matt made it very clear he wanted to do the job and get out of there as fast as possible.

'Ideally,' he said, 'we'd like to get the tree to bounce on the line and go over the canyon. That way we don't have to clear it up and we can get out much quicker, but it's a very big tree and may well not do what we want it to.'

I have to say, standing there in my safety helmet, it didn't look like it was going to bounce at all. It was massive. Matt talked cheerily about some of the problems they've had with avalanches, of the dangers from bears and wolves (although, so far, bears had purely investigated noise out of curiosity rather than because they were hungry). Matt admitted he'd been lucky over the years and there had been attacks.

When we got to the spot, Matt and Tupu showed Mike the cameraman, JT the soundman and I exactly where we could stand so that he could 'guarantee our safety'. It still seemed to me we were standing horribly close, but he knew all the angles from years of felling trees and promised us that a certain point that he marked out on the track was the closest we could get for the best possible shots.

Isn't it strange how you instinctively trust your life to complete strangers? But guys like Matt just inspire trust. The two of them then went running up the side of this seriously steep incline with a chainsaw in Matt's hand and started making a huge v-cut in the pine tree. It was quite extraordinary that, when it finally started to topple and eventually landed with a tremendous crash, it was exactly where Matt had told us it would. About five feet from Mike the cameraman's left ear.

Sadly for Matt, it didn't bounce but just lay as one massive lump of trunk and branches right across the line. They then set to work with chainsaw and axes and had the whole thing logged up and clear beside the track in a matter of minutes. We told the nice lady on the radio that we were leaving the area and she gave us the all-clear. It had been a great morning and the guys were mega-efficient.

It was so impressive to see how they keep this railway running all year round in this remote, tough wilderness, sometimes in flood, sometimes in thick snow. But you had to wonder, as the gold rush is a long time over, why did they persevere with such keenness and enthusiasm? The answer wasn't yellow gold but it was black gold.

The huge Usibelli coal mine has been working flat out for more than 70 years and thousands of tons of coal are totally reliant on the railway to get to the rest of the USA and the great ports in the south. Every single lump of coal is shipped out of the mine by train.

There are a hundred tons in every single freight car and some of the trains are more than a mile long; you just couldn't handle that sort of bulk by road.

The coal-mining industry everywhere has suffered considerably in recent years with a big fall in prices, but it is still being used for heating all over Alaska. While I was enthusing about the length and sheer power of these coal trains running up to Fairbanks, I then realised that we had missed the second passenger train for that week and the only way to get to the end of our journey was on a coal train. Fortunately, we didn't have to travel in with the coal and instead we got ourselves a lift with the driver and his crew. So our final triumphant arrival in Fairbanks wasn't quite the luxurious arrival that we rather hoped. We arrived in a coal truck.

Before you reach the town you go over an amazing, 700-foot long, steel bridge, one of the longest single-span railway bridges in the whole of north America, the final link in the chain of building this railroad. In 1923 the president came to Alaska and hammered home the traditional golden spike at this point to celebrate the completion of the railroad. Fairbanks is now the second-largest city in Alaska, thanks to this railway and the people who believed in the country and pushed on against all odds. They went bust twice but never stopped believing. Alaska is now a tremendous state – one of the greatest, most spectacular and wildest places in the whole of the USA.

We'd had a tremendous trip; one of the very best. We came all the way from Seward on a mixture of freight trains, hi-rails and the splendid *Aurora* passenger train, all in the depths of winter. We never saw a single bear, although we did see lots of tracks – and you can bet they will have seen us.

The Usabelli coal mine transports its goods by rail.

FERROCARRIL NACIONAL
114
GENERAL ROCA

ARGENTINA

Paraguay
Brazil
Argentina
Uruguay
Chile
San Miguel de Tucuman
Formosa
Corrientes
Andes
San Juan
Cordoba
Santa Fe
Mendoza
Resario
San Rafael
Buenos Aires
Olavarría
Las Pampas
Coronel Suárez
Bahía Blanca
Mar del Plata
South Pacific Ocean
Zapala
Patagonia
Bariloche
Viedma
Perito Moreno
Esquel
Nahuel Pan
Rawson
South Atlantic Ocean
Puerto Deseado
Puerto Santa Cruz
Rio Gallegos
Ushuaia
N
0 100 200 300 Kilometers
0 100 200 300 Miles
Rail
Road

Argentina

My third visit to South America inside eighteen months came after two trips to Bolivia – one good; one disastrous. I was now bound for Argentina, a country that had fascinated me for years but that also might pose a lot of problems for a visiting British film crew.

There were lots of stories of crime in the bigger cities, where the people are usually portrayed as desperately poor. After the war in the Falkland Islands, which the Argentineans still refer to as Las Malvinas, I had a feeling that we might not be very welcome. There remained a large percentage of Argentineans – from their president down – who still thought they should try to repossess the islands. They lost more than 600 servicemen in the brief but bitter conflict, so why would they welcome me or anyone else from the UK? And some of us really irritate them. Just ask Jeremy Clarkson.

Also, whenever we have played the Argentineans at football, it's been a pretty bloody affair. With lots of cheating going on – just ask David Beckham.

But it is a beautiful country and, when I arrived in the capital, Buenos Aires, I was immediately impressed by how very European the city is and how much it looks like Paris. It was so much nicer and cleaner than I expected. It has some of the widest avenues in the world; there are trees everywhere and rows of elegant, well-kept buildings. It is a lovely place. It also produces some of the best red wine in the southern hemisphere and we were offered a range of enormous steaks the size of dustbin lids everywhere we went to eat.

Our main reason for travelling to Argentina was that it once possessed the biggest railway network in the whole of South America. It was British-built, as so many rail systems were more than 100 years ago and people used to come to Argentina specifically

to travel by train across this colourful country. It was railway heaven. Nowadays, however, very few people want to make what was once a classic journey. In fact, only somebody incredibly stupid would even attempt to do so – so that'll be me then.

We wanted to travel from Buenos Aires to Patagonia, a distance of over a thousand miles, and we were aware that in many cases the old railway network simply didn't exist any more or was crumbling towards extinction.

It was a wrench leaving Buenos Aires; although I had been quite apprehensive about being a Brit in the capital, I had no problems at all and was made very welcome. Signs of the great British investment that was made into the country around the end of the 19th century were everywhere. A lot of familiar objects are still in use on the streets of Buenos Aires today, such as red telephone boxes and even bright-red post boxes. UK investment had really begun in the 1850s. We poured money in to create one of the largest and most reliable networks in the world. The system was the envy of all the neighbouring countries although now, like Argentina itself, it has a lot of problems. It's been allowed to run down a lot in recent years with successive governments refusing to prop it up financially and there have also been a large number of petty crimes on stations and in the trains themselves.

Our first scheduled journey was to run from the very typical British-built station at Constitución. It's a beautiful old building, a lot like our London terminals, but it also has a bad reputation. There are homeless people sleeping rough all around the area, there had been several violent crimes in recent months and pickpockets and muggers were known to be a constant problem. I was understandably very wary. I am too large and gangling and obviously English for the average mugger not to be licking his lips. I deliberately took off my watch and didn't carry a wallet, but I still felt a bit of a target.

The awfully nice people from the Argentinean railway system provided me with a funny little chap, whose name is pronounced '*Hayzoos*' but is actually spelt 'Jesús'. He was quite short, but incredibly wide and I realised he was following my every step

Constitución station was built in the 1860s, much added to and rebuilt in the 1920s.

and carrying at least one very large, frightening-looking gun. He certainly did the trick because I walked into the station with the crew filming and got quickly onto the train without any problems. Apparently, there had been a stabbing on the train that we got on only a few days earlier, but I must admit I have been more frightened in England on trains travelling away from football matches than I was on the way to Olavarría. Most of the people on the train were women with children or babies and they didn't look too frightening.

The train itself was bumpy, incredibly dirty (it was impossible to see out of the windows), very smelly and there was no sign of a restaurant or a bar. I had foolishly bought an empanada for the journey. These I'd been told are very popular all over South America. Well, not with me, it wasn't. It was a sort of spicy, meaty pasty but, I have to say, after one mouthful it went straight back into its brown-paper bag and, as far as I know, it's still there, at the bottom of a Latin American bin. It was truly disgusting.

HAVING A BALL ON THE FARM

Once we crawled into Olavarría, we managed to check in to a one-star local hotel but were just glad of a short night's sleep because the next morning we were up early to make our way to the Estancia la Isolina, one of the oldest and largest cattle ranches in Argentina ('*estancia*' is Latin American for 'cattle ranch'). It dates back well over a hundred years and employs a number of gauchos, who, hopefully, would be showing me their skills as horse riders and even how to use the lasso. I couldn't wait.

In reality, I discovered they were showing me skills all right, but not riding horses or lassoing – they were busy castrating a string of young bulls, which, for some reason, they were very insistent that we filmed in gory close up. Strangely, the poor animals didn't seem to make much of a fuss about it at all, although the gauchos went at it with real enthusiasm, snipping away at one set of testicles after the next with an enormous, razor-sharp, bloody-looking set of pliers and then adding indignity by injecting them in the same – by now hugely sensitive – area and daubing paint. I was trying desperately to conduct an interview with the owner of the ranch, Jorge, while all this was going on but I did find myself struggling to concentrate and instinctively wincing as one bollock after another was removed about five yards from my left ear.

Fortunately, things then got a bit more civilised when Jorge took me into his beautiful house for lunch. The original farm had been bought by his great-grandfather in the middle of the 19th century. The old boy had come over from Fance and slowly bought up parcels of land from the locals. He raised cattle from the start and, in those days, it was easy to market them because there was a railway that came on its own private siding right the way into the ranch. The house that Jorge now lives in is a magnificent affair in the centre of the *estancia* and, although they have sold off quite a lot of the land, he still has a very large estate. They bought the original thousands of acres of land for a very small amount and today, by any standards, it must be worth a fortune. They have some 1,300 head of cattle, most of them British varieties – Hereford or Aberdeen Angus – so I was able to ask him, 'Is the bulk of the beef that has made Argentina so famous actually British?'

He looked at me for a while, with a strange frown on his face and then suddenly burst into a huge laugh, shook my hand manically and said, 'Yes, of course.' He was a lovely guy, resplendent in a red beret and he reckoned to know all of his cattle by name. I asked if he still used the railway for moving cattle to market and he said, 'Absolutely not ... when the railways were managed by the British we used them. We loaded them up here and got them to market quickly without problems. When the railway passed into local hands [in 1948], there were long delays. It took four hours to get to market and, on arrival, the calves were starving.'

His father switched to road transport in the 1960s and so did everybody else. The fact that Argentina's railways can no longer be relied upon to get the cattle to market for such a great beef-producing nation as Argentina, is a sad reflection of how far standards have slipped since the glory days of the first half of the 20th century.

Jorge's wife, María, was a lovely, larger than life, woman who'd prepared a barbecue lunch for us all with mounds of steak chicken and burger. However, one plate contained a pile of dark, spherical objects that for some reason just didn't look too clever. Then we were told they were fresh bulls' testicles, snipped off that very morning... Oh, yuck! The gauchos were feasting happily away on this delicacy but only one of our party could find the stomach to eat them. Jake Martin, the vegan, was becoming weirder by the day and this won't have helped. Maria, smiling, insisted I had to drink a cup of *mate* (pronounced '*mahtay*'), before I left. I looked at her blankly, before

The railway network in Argentina is poorly maintained and in many places a shadow of its former glory.

she took me into an old bunkhouse, where the gauchos have slept, eaten their meals and drunk their *mate* since 1880.

Mate is a hot drink made of dried yerba mate leaves, whatever a yerba is. It is made with hot, but not boiling water, María told me, and drunk through a steel straw. It used to be enjoyed solely by gauchos but now it's pretty much a national beverage. They even serve it in expensive tea houses in Buenos Aires, but María said she knew the only way to make it. She advised me to sip carefully and, whatever I did, not to pull a disapproving face or she and the gauchos would be very offended. So I had a swig. I have to say it tasted absolutely dreadful but I did the best I could to pretend I was enjoying it, nod a bit and feign enthusiasm. I then feigned a need to go to the bathroom, where I spat the whole lot out.

I reappeared to find María and the others all laughing manically, saying, 'Of course you hated it! Everybody always hates their first drink of *mate* and we couldn't believe you kept up the pretence for so long.' With their crazed laughter in my ears and the taste of something like the scrapings off the bottom of a budgerigar's cage in my mouth, I made my way away from La Isolina.

After a strange night in a particularly cramped hotel room in somewhere called Coronel Suárez, which was not unlike Bolton in the 1930s, I was dragged out of bed by a loud, screaming alarm clock and an even louder, screaming director, to make my way to what they laughingly call their main station, for 5.30 am.

As has happened so many times over the years of filming this series, it was still pitch-black and there was absolutely nobody at the station but, amazingly, as I sat alone on the platform with only the town dog for company, there was the sound of a train horn coming through the night. There was my train to Bahía Blanca, bang on time, give or take 20 minutes; the same service I had caught the other evening from Constitución in Buenos Aires. It was even more crowded this time, even smellier and getting on a busy train that had travelled all through the night was quite daunting, There were no lights and in my pre-paid seat there was a very large

The Argentine railway system has decayed over the years.

pile of blankets with, I suspected, a very large man underneath. I just sat myself down in the only seat I could find available and waited for daylight to give me some clue as to where I was.

ROCA'S RAILWAY

The line we were travelling on was built in the 1880s. It was known originally as the Buenos Aires Great Southern Railway but, after WWII, it became the state-owned General Roca Railway. Roca is immortalised on all Argentinean hundred-peso notes. He remains a controversial figure. Julio Argentino Roca was twice the president; he's best known as the man behind the conquest of the desert, which was a long military campaign that virtually wiped out all the Indians from a large portion of Argentina, including the area we were travelling through this morning.

Over a thousand Indians were murdered during the campaign and thousands more were either imprisoned for no reason at all or forced to migrate to other areas. Some people hail him as a hero, others – I rather think quite rightly – say he is guilty of genocide. It did open the way, however, for thousands of European immigrants, particularly from Italy and Spain. The land that greeted them wasn't exactly desert but certainly wasn't good farm land. It was just scrub that had never been cultivated and the immigrants got to work at once, planting trees, crops and turning the Pampas into one of the most fertile agricultural regions in the world.

Again, in the early days, most of the region's produce was sent by train when nowadays just about all of it goes by road. Freight trains are a rarity and even passenger trains like the one I was on, covered in graffiti and dilapidated as it was, are few and far between. Their future is very uncertain.

When we got to Bahía Blanca, I was asked to meet a gentleman called Marcello, the station-master. As part of my goodwill towards all South American people I, of course, said, 'Yes,' but only when I'd agreed did they tell me he wanted to show me his model railway. Now, I have to say, I'd been up since about 5.30 am, I'd travelled a couple of hundred miles on a really evil-smelling, pretty unpleasant train and this was the last thing I wanted to see. But as a PR thing I had agreed – God knows how I was blagged into it – but I was astonished to be greeted by the most amazing model railway I have ever seen in my life. It was absolutely enormous, with dozens of little trains racing around everywhere. I was not converted to becoming a model-railway enthusiast but I was very impressed and Marcello himself was impossible to dislike. He came from generations of railwaymen and had a wonderful, infectious enthusiasm for everything he did.

I suggested that maybe this passion for his hobby was a substitute for the excitement of the days at Bahía Blanca when the railway system was really buzzing and trains raced through day and night. He grinned at me and nodded. 'I agree,' he said. 'I love my models but it's nothing like the real thing. I just hope that one day Argentina begins to believe in its railway system again and puts in the time and investment to make it once more one of the great railways systems of the world.' He was a good man but I took my leave of him thinking, Yes, mate, but dream on. Argentinean politics, from what I have seen of them, make it unlikely that they could ever agree on anything. They just can't seem to get their act together.

Bahía Blanca is known for something far more sombre. On 2 May 1982, one month into the Falklands' War, a British Navy submarine fired a torpedo that sank the *General Belgrano*. The ship had sailed from a naval base about 15 miles from Bahía Blanca and most of the men on board came from this town. Three-hundred-and-twenty-three died. The sinking of the *Belgrano* was hugely controversial at the time and the notorious GOTCHA headline in the sun was condemned by many in the UK as well as in Argentina. Some still view the British naval action as a war crime.

So, more than 30 years later, I found myself in a Malvinas' memorial park on the outskirts of Bahía Blanca, where I was scheduled to meet a group of Malvinas – or Falklands – War veterans who were all linked to the loss of the *Belgrano*. They had no reason to be friendly or even polite. Each of them knew people who had died on the *Belgrano* and one had actually been there when the British torpedoes hit.

At the entrance to the park is a beautiful Las Malvinas heroes memorial with a picture of each young man who died on the *Belgrano*, alongside their date of birth. Many were younger than 20 years old, some had been no more than 16 or 17. Underneath each young, smiling face was one date – that of their deaths. It is clearly a very black date here in the consciousness of this town.

I was, for once, apprehensive, and if I'm honest, a bit nervous, ahead of the interview. We exchanged fairly brusque handshakes and I tried to catch their eyes but they were cold and evasive. A big bear of a man called Hector had lost his brother on the stricken ship. It wasn't a great start. They were very patriotic and they were extraordinarily articulate. They were also very reasonable.

The veterans hated the fact that so many of their young friends had died before their eyes. They would never forgive that particular generation of Brits for being instrumental in their friends' deaths. They were adamant that Margaret Thatcher was using the

I met Argentinean veterans of the 1982 Falklands War in Bahía Blanca.

Falklands as a political game, probably to seek re-election, but they also conceded that the Argentine government did exactly the same thing. For their leader, General Galtieri, it had been the ultimate gamble but his troops lost and he lost and, in a strange way, the veterans conceded, it built the future for the Argentina of the 21st century.

I asked them quite pointedly if they hated the British and they equally and quite without pretence, said, 'No, we do not hate you. We hate some of the generation that caused that war, but mainly the politicians. We have no quarrel with the English, we love many of you for what you did for this country but we will want Las Malvinas back one day and it will happen. Geographically, it is so obvious the islands mean nothing to you or the people of Britain. They are right off the coast of Argentina and you are 8,000 miles away – what do you want them for? It is ridiculous. The Malvinas will come back to us one day.'

I asked, 'Would you be prepared to go to war again for your right to these islands? Would you risk the lives of your own sons to get these islands back?'

Without exception, each said, 'Absolutely not; it will be about education and people's understanding that the Malvinas should and will belong to Argentina, but we would be mad to go to war again. We should never go to war again for anything. It is madness, we have been there.'

AN INSPIRING ENCOUNTER

I came away from a quite exhausting interview with these guys, feeling really heartened. Why should they not hate the British? But they were very positive and very reasonable. Patriotic in the extreme and passionate but very sensible and actually very warm towards me with my irritating questions.

I find it hugely refreshing that the more I travel the world, the more I see just ordinary men and women who do not want to kill each other and they do not want to set off suicide bombs to destroy each other. Most people just want to live, bring up beautiful kids and die in their own beds. It is politicians and fanatics who start wars, it is governments who kill young men.

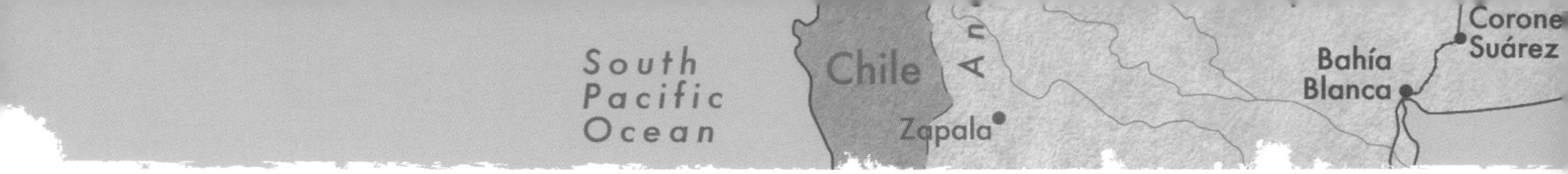

I was fairly exhausted by the time I got back to our hotel in the middle of Bahía Blanca. I was wrecked. It seemed a ridiculously long time since I'd emerged onto the platform at Coronel Suárez that morning and I still had over 800 miles to travel before we got to our destination in Patagonia.

Oh, and, yes, I was then told that the following morning would involve an even earlier alarm clock. Would the fun ever start?

A familiar pattern: I woke up in Bahía Blanca, seemingly minutes after I went to sleep. It was well before daylight and I had a cab waiting to take me to the station, only this time it was a bus station, not a railway station. I hadn't been on a bus for years and I really thought the whole thing was a bit of a cop-out when we're called *Extreme Railways*. Yet there was a 170-mile gap in the railway line and absolutely no other way of getting there – apart from cycling or hitch-hiking in a quite scary region. OK, then, bus it had to be.

The line between Bahía Blanca and Viedma – my next destination – had been suspended in very strange circumstances several years ago. The official reason given was that sand dunes blowing onto the line had made the service hopeless. However, any local Argentinean would tell you that the real culprit was government cutbacks or, more likely, an attempt to tip the balance in favour of the bus operators. The rumour – and I say nothing more – was that cash changed hands, but I was shown no evidence to confirm that except that we travelled for 170 miles and I never saw a single grain of sand...

Well before dawn, we arrived at the bus station and what a revelation – what a building! After the drab and hopelessly rundown facilities that I'd seen so far in Argentinian railway stations, this was something else. It was bright, it was busy, it was spotlessly clean, and it was much more like a modern airport concourse than a station.

We travelled for about three hours on a luxury coach with air-conditioning, colour TV, a coffee machine etc., and I have to say it was absolutely brilliant for an hour or two, until we slowed down on a main road behind a large truck. Then the penny dropped: you never have to put up with this on a train; buses, however modern, just get you from A to B. With a train, you are always on a 'journey'; it's an adventure. I expected that such thoughts would probably come back to bite me over the next few days but I think I knew what I was on about at the time. It's sort of like saying that a train is for life but a bus is just for Christmas... do you understand that? No, nor do I.

When we finally drew into Viedma, known as the gateway to Patagonia, I felt really emotional. Ever since I was a little boy, the word 'Patagonia' had always conjured up a wonderful, mysterious place somewhere at the very end of the world. Now I had finally got there and I realised I had been right – we were now more than 7,000 miles from home. I'd read about Patagonia at school and it had taken me very nearly all of my life to get here.

The thing that many people don't realise about Patagonia is that it's absolutely enormous – over a million square kilometres in all and incredibly diverse in terms of climate and scenery. Hopefully, we were going to make the long trip deep into Patagonia by train. There was a sleeper train called *Tren Patagonico* that only went once a week, but we were assured it would go this evening to Bariloche, a beautiful city by an enormous lake, 500 miles west. We were supposed to be travelling non-stop for more than 18 hours – in reality, it was to be nearer to 24.

At Viedma station I was made very welcome by the guys from the railway and one of them, Hector, turned out to be a real find. With great pride, he showed me some of the extraordinarily well-preserved old carriages that they collected at this station. They were from 14 different countries, some dating back to the 19th century. He excitedly showed me one old freight car where the guys who worked on the railway slept and lived while they were building the line. This was just after WWI, when Germans, Russians and Poles – who had every reason to hate each other – shared these cramped spaces. In the end, they were just men with a job to do and it must have worked because some of them stayed in those carriages for nearly 25 years.

THE FÜHRER ON THE BEACH

Hector joined me on the *Tren Patagonica* to Barlioche and once on board, we talked about the railway's passengers – a mixture of tourists and locals, sportsmen who just wanted to tramp through the wilds of Patagonia and, in the winter months, skiers. They were still not making a large profit on this beautiful line but Hector had great hopes for the future. As we idly chatted about who used the line and any famous faces seen over the years, he dropped a bombshell of a name. 'Adolf Hitler,' he said. Hitler was, apparently, seen on this line and in this area after 1945. I was dumbfounded and certainly sceptical, but Hector, a very rational man, said, 'I've heard the stories many times and I honestly think I believe them.' He produced a small swastika out of his pocket and said, 'My mother found this on the beach here. It's believed to have been dropped by the Führer.'

I was certainly prepared to at least think hard about his theory, but the swastika didn't prove anything about Hitler. It is well-known that many Nazis escaped to South America. Josef Mengele, Martin Bormann and Klaus Barbie were said to have made it to the continent and Adolf Eichmann certainly did. He was dragged back to Israel from South America by Nazi hunters, tried and hanged. All this was pretty much in the public domain – but Hitler? I had never heard anyone suggesting such a theory before. I'd just always taken it for granted, as most of us surely always have, that he committed suicide with Eva Braun in the bunker in Berlin. But then again, it made me think – there was no DNA preserved – the Russians were believed to have kept the burnt bodies but never released details.

I was still pretty sure that Hector's theory was nonsense, but he was a very solid, likeable guy, not seemingly given to wild stories

Mar del Plata

The overnight train that took me into Patagonia.

or exaggeration. Apparently, at the time, there were several locals who claimed to have seen Hitler in this area as late as 1946. A chance chat with Hector on a train somewhere in the deep south of Argentina had completely shaken my views on history.

We went off to our beds and woke up in Bariloche, on the shores of a very large lake with some large mountains, some of them already with snow on the tops, in the distance. The town looked incredibly Swiss – or maybe that should be Austrian because I was beginning to feel the bizarre Germanic connection that Hector talked about the day before quite acutely. It had never crossed my mind to think anything but that the 20th century's most evil human being died in Berlin. But there was an incredibly German feel to this part of the world and there was no doubt it would be a great place to hide.

There were no trains available for the umpteenth time again this morning, so the next part of my journey I had to drive a four-by-four on a series of big old dirt roads, but we made our way to Perito Moreno station and I was very intrigued to meet a man called Abel Basti, a well-known Argentinean journalist who had made quite a career out of exposing Nazis in South America and had some very definite beliefs about the movements of Adolf Hitler. He was an extraordinary man, at once very amiable and credible. I asked him in all seriousness if he believed that Hitler travelled to the Bariloche region in 1945, and he said straight away, 'Yes, of course, I am certain. I believe that he arrived in a submarine somewhere along the shore south of Buenos Aires and was then taken by Nazi sympathisers to a quiet country railway and arrived here at Perito Moreno.'

There was a very wealthy German who owned this whole area and he was a fanatical Nazi. Apparently, this station was the closest one to the landowner's large ranch and they could guarantee Hitler's safety. The son of a woman who had been the aristocrat's cook, among many others, said that the former German dictator arrived in the house at the age of 56, was very low-key and subdued and didn't look the way people knew him. He'd shaved off all his hair and trademark moustache and Argentina was so far away from

Europe that the events of WWII hadn't been of huge significance. He was seen frequently, always in the company of other senior Nazis, although he seemed to have lost none of that arrogance and was not remotely apologetic for any of the things he'd done.'

Nobody, as far as Abel knew, tried to hand Hitler over to the authorities; in fact, it seemed they rather liked having him around. It was a delicious secret. Abel believes he left for Paraguay, where he died in 1971. Basti was amazingly convincing, he had no doubt at all about the veracity of his witnesses and he said that so many people had told him similar stories that it just had to be true. It does seem that most people in Argentina believe the same thing

He said that nobody at the time in Germany ever reported Hitler as dead and Stalin always believed he was alive and was desperate to get him on trial with the others at Nuremberg. Over the years, MI6 and the CIA also admitted they thought Hitler survived the bunker and was almost certainly in South America.

Did Adolf Hitler escape Berlin and arrive somewhere near the station of Perito Moreno? Abel Basti is convinced he did.

Quietly chatting to Abel in that little railway station, in the middle of absolutely nowhere with the remote hills all around, made his account seem very believable. I'm still not at all sure that Hitler came here, but the whole thing made the hairs stand up on the back of my neck.

I drove on, deeply affected by my conversation. We drove towards our next train but it was unlikely that I could catch it until first thing the next morning. We had a long journey ahead, but there was one shot of a steam train that Jeff, our director, was desperate to get. A beautiful old steam locomotive would come under a stunning bridge arch with a raging river in front and snow-capped mountains behind. Trouble was it wasn't due till 5 pm and we just couldn't spare the time. We needed a gesture, we needed a sacrifice – Jake was just such a man, so we left him with the second camera and sandwiches to while away seven hours in the middle of absolutely nowhere… to capture the BAFTA-award-winning shot of a lifetime and then meet us for dinner that evening – oh, and it was pouring with rain...

BUTCH, SUNDANCE, ETTA AND A CABIN

Wrenching ourselves away from Jake (it took us about five seconds), we made our way along yet another seemingly endless dirt road to a second, long-kept secret. This one was the supposed hiding place of Butch Cassidy and the Sundance Kid. We pulled into some strange cabins tucked away at the back of an old ranch near Esquel, and one of the local guys proudly showed me a picture of three people sitting sombrely at the front of these very same cabins. They had been confirmed apparently as definitely Butch Cassidy (real name Robert Parker), the Sundance Kid (Harry Longabaugh) and his girlfriend, Etta Place. They had all come to Argentina on board a steamship from New York to get away from US lawmen who were chasing them for a whole string of violent train and bank robberies. They arrived here in 1901 and posed as innocent ranchers, while planning more robberies.

Inside the cabins it was wonderful to think they really had been here. It was also quite cramped. Harry and Etta apparently slept in one room while Robert slept next door. He must have been a bit of a gooseberry. I very much doubted whether they enjoyed the kind of happy-go-lucky, existence that Paul Newman and Robert Redford enjoyed with Katherine Ross in the magnificent 1969 movie, but the photograph taken outside the cabin did make it clear that they were very much at home and, for a long time, out of reach of the law.

In 1905, men from the Pinkerton agency caught up with them and they fled yet again, first to Chile and then onto Bolivia. What happened next is a bit of a mystery. Some say that Butch and Sundance died in a gunfight just like at the end of the film, others, though, believe they survived and got away and no one has a clue what happened to Etta Place.

This wild, beautiful part of the world does seem to have all sorts of secrets. It had been a great day and the valley between Bariloche and Esquel was one of the most beautiful I've ever travelled. Massive rivers and lakes running either side of the dirt road, mountains everywhere and mile upon mile of grazing cattle and sheep. It is a beautiful part of the world, but also you begin to realise just how enormous Patagonia is.

We got to Esquel, parked up the four-by-four and shared a bottle or two of Malbec and went to bed, hoping to be getting on yet another train. Early the next morning, I drove to a tiny little place called Nahuel Pan with just about the most remote and unloved station I've seen anywhere in the world, but although it only has one single track, it does regularly host a brilliant train.

This runs on a narrow gauge, it's a steam train and the Argentineans call it *La Trochita*, which means the 'Little Gauge'. It's also well-known as the Old Patagonian Express, which was written about famously in the 1970s by Paul Theroux (the travel writer and Louis's dad). In those days, it was the epitome of the beauty and elegance of rail travel, Argentinean-style and it is actually still a great little train. Really nice, old-style but very smart wooden carriages and warm inside – each carriage has a wood burning stove. We also had live entertainment from a guy called Eduardo Paillacán. He's a Mapuche and his people dominated this part of Patagonia until the 1880s, when thousands of them were killed by the savage General Roca.

Understandably, the Mapuche who survived campaigned for years to get the name of this railway line changed. They didn't really see why they should travel on a section of the General Roca Railway. Common sense prevailed and the name was dropped, which seems fair enough. It's now called the Old Patagonian Express line.

Eduardo sang Indian folk songs and twanged his guitar as we travelled. He was hardly Eric Clapton, but it did seem to give our journey a nice local flavour. The other people who shared this part of the world with the Mapuche, bizarrely, weren't the large number of Italians, French or Germans who arrived in their thousands in most other parts of Patagonia, but rather the Welsh.

Some 153 of them came here, mainly Welsh-speaking non-conformists who were very badly treated back home in 1865. Far from clashing with the Mapuche, many of them bred with local families but it is still quite commonplace to hear someone say '*Iechyd da*' (pronounced '*Yacki daa*') as you call into one of the little shops. There was a lovely little teashop in the main city centre and there was also a Welsh non-conformist chapel at the end of the line.

This was a thriving line in the 1930s and 1940s and a vital lifeline for the people of this region, particularly the sheep and cattle farmers, but now it's strictly once a week for tourists. It was still one of the greatest little trains I've ever travelled on and the view, as we steamed through a huge winding valley with the smoke running past the windows of our old wooden carriages, was wonderful.

Sadly, at Esquel, we reached the end of the line and the end of my journey. We were pretty much in the centre of Patagonia. I suppose I've learned that the country itself is absolutely beautiful and far bigger than I'd imagined; the people don't seem to hate us at all, considering so many of them died fighting for the Falklands – on the contrary, they were very friendly and welcoming; and that, somewhere in the quiet little villages and valleys tucked away in the mountains of this remote corner of South America, Adolf Hitler,

The team and I find a hideout – the cabin used by Butch Cassidy and the Sundance Kid. Back row, from left: Jon 'JT' Thomas, soundman; a contributor to the programme, fixer Gloria Beretervide, me, and Jeff Morgan, the director. Front row, from left: Valeria Appel, co-producer and cameraman Mike Harrison.

with shaven head and no moustache, may, just may, have quietly moved among the locals. It had been one of the best of all the rail journeys of these last three years and certainly gave me the most food for thought – come to think of it, it also gave the most food…

PS: Oh, yes, you're right – I almost forgot. Did Jake wait until 5 pm, alone by the old railway line in the pouring rain, then come back tired but elated, having got the award-winning shot of a life time? Well, er, not exactly… well, in fact, not at all. At 4.55 pm, the train duly arrived in the station, whooping its whistle about 400 yards away, and Jake raced to his tripod, ready to capture a beautifully composed shot of the beautifully polished, classic locomotive, framed as it came steaming under the ancient stone bridge with snow-topped mountains as the stunning backdrop.

That was the plan.

But the wretched train, having picked up its passengers from the station, did a magnificent toot-toot of its whistle as it picked up power and then… broke down on the spot some three hundred yards from Jake. As far as we know, that train never worked again… And Jake? He arrived at our hotel about eleven o'clock at night – and he was really fed up.

CRAGHO

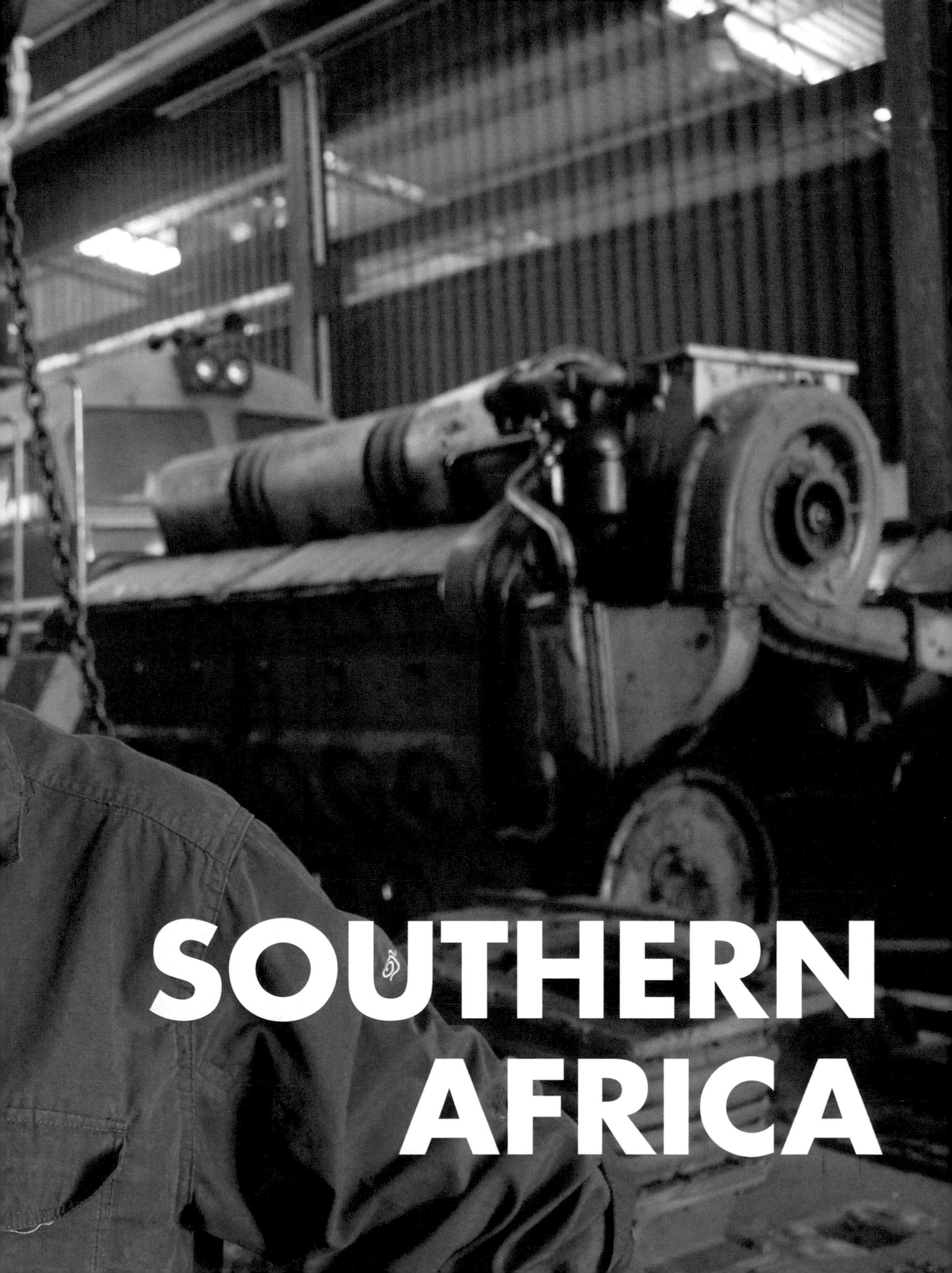

SOUTHERN AFRICA

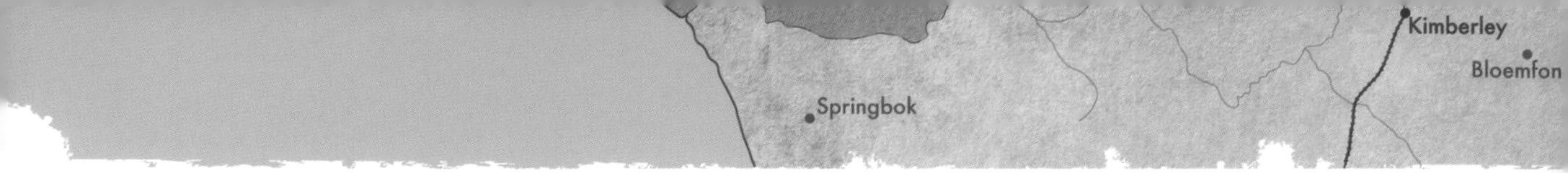

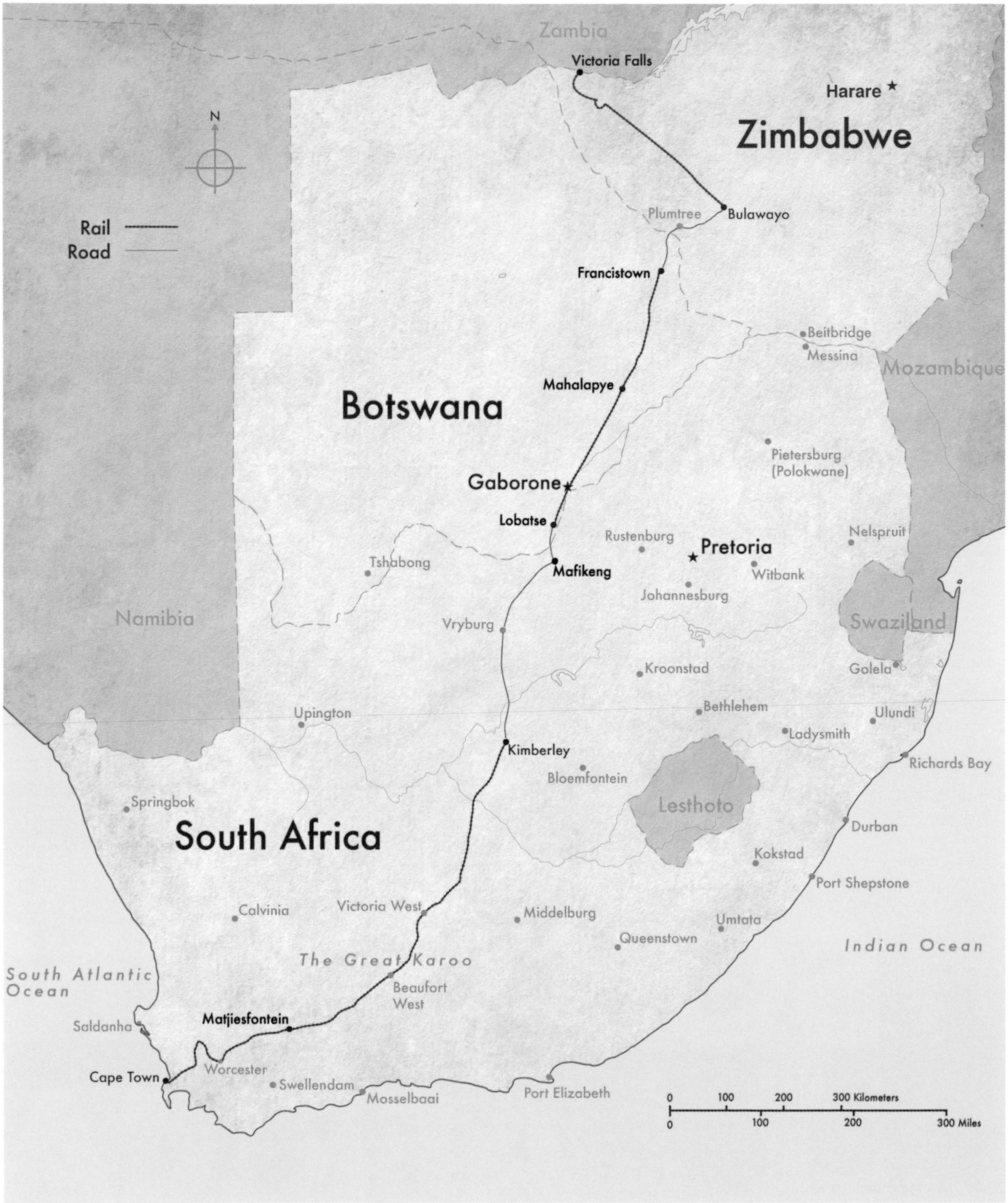

Zambia
Victoria Falls
Harare
Zimbabwe
N
Rail
Road
Plumtree
Bulawayo
Francistown
Beitbridge
Messina
Mozambique
Mahalapye
Botswana
Pietersburg (Polokwane)
Gaborone
Lobatse
Rustenburg
Pretoria
Nelspruit
Tshabong
Mafikeng
Witbank
Johannesburg
Namibia
Vryburg
Swaziland
Kroonstad
Golela
Upington
Bethlehem
Ulundi
Ladysmith
Kimberley
Richards Bay
Bloemfontein
Springbok
Lesthoto
South Africa
Durban
Kokstad
Port Shepstone
Calvinia
Victoria West
Middelburg
Umtata
Queenstown
Indian Ocean
The Great Karoo
South Atlantic Ocean
Beaufort West
Saldanha
Matjiesfontein
Worcester
Cape Town
Swellendam
Mosselbaai
Port Elizabeth
0 100 200 300 Kilometers
0 100 200 300 Miles

Southern Africa

I love Cape Town. I was there at New Year's Eve 2015; it is just a wonderful place to come at any time of the year, but particularly during our winter months. It is warm, clean and ridiculously cheap. We spent a lot of time eating and drinking in the huge choice of restaurants and bars, all around the Victoria and Alfred harbour and were lucky enough to watch one of the greatest matches of cricket of all time between England and South Africa, when both teams scored over 600 and Ben Stokes scored more than 250. We then went on a safari further north, near Johannesburg, a blissful way to start 2016.

When the *Extreme Railways* production company rang and asked me if I'd like to go back to South Africa, filming in August of the same year, I was, of course, absolutely delighted. I wasn't quite so delighted, however, when they told me we were travelling north, following Cecil Rhodes, on up through Botswana, which I knew to be a lovely place, and then Zimbabwe, which I knew to be not at all a lovely place – downright scary, in fact.

We were trying to find Rhodes's original railway line from Cape Town to Victoria Falls. The rails were still there but we weren't at all sure if there were trains all the way. Our journey began on the famous Blue Train which has been delighting wealthy passengers from all over the world since the 1920s. It is one of the most luxurious trains in the world – you are greeted like a celebrity at an airport, there's a magnificent VIP lounge where the champagne flows and the service carries on like that for the whole journey. I was met by a wonderful, immaculately uniformed African steward with a huge smile, who was called Thank You. He attended to me non-stop throughout my all-too-brief journey.

Kimberley
Bloemfon
Springbok

Inevitably, the air rang with 'Thank you, Thank You', which he appeared to love, although he must have heard it a thousand times… well, you try not to keep repeating his name when you're being waited on by a bloke called Thank You.

People seemed to be drinking champagne from half-past eight in the morning to the very small hours at night. The food was magnificent and the staff worked on the smallest detail to make the traveller comfortable and positively pampered. It was great, but I was very much aware that this, sadly, was not to be the way I was to travel for the full fortnight and that we would have to get out of the Blue Train in the small hours of the morning. But we enjoyed it while we could.

We left Cape Town in bright sunshine, it was 24 degrees Celsius even in what they call their winter, with the city set, as always, against the beautiful backdrop of Table Mountain. The Victoria and Alfred harbour was built by the British more than 150 years ago as a stopping off point for ships on their way from Europe to Asia. We had 1,500 miles to travel through three countries, hopefully getting on whatever trains we could find.

Cecil Rhodes's railway was built with blood, sweat and diamonds. We were getting off the train at Kimberley, where the line swings up towards Botswana and then crosses the border of Zimbabwe – or Southern Rhodesia as it used to be known – and makes its way on up to Victoria Falls. Whether any railway was going to work at all in Zimbabwe seemed a little unlikely and the prospect of driving through the country also didn't fill me with great excitement. When our team went out to recce the film the driver ended up in handcuffs! However… I'm getting ahead of myself.

The Blue Train had a wonderful, friendly atmosphere – I think the early champagnes helped, but everybody enjoyed the five-star chill-out, including several honeymoon couples. There were South Africans, Brits, Americans, Dutch, Japanese and Chinese and the only ones I didn't seem to hit if off with were in a party of Korean ladies who wore splendid hats. I tried to get on friendly terms with

Richards Bay

Durban

We took the luxury option when we left Cape Town.

them, by saying, 'Hasn't Kim Jong-un got a lovely haircut?' but apparently, they were all from Seoul and seemed a bit huffy.

The train manager was the most lovely guy – his name was Herbert Prinsloo and he'd been working on the Blue Train for over 25 years. He said the proudest day of his life was when Nelson Mandela came on the train and Herbert was chosen to be his butler. He also talked to me about much darker times, about how, in Apartheid days, a black man like himself wasn't allowed to serve anyone drinks at the bar or at the dining table. It seems unthinkable now, but blacks were only allowed to work in the kitchens or to clean the rooms. Even if black passengers got on, from the USA or the UK, black men were not allowed to serve them. It was amazing and wonderful to see how much things have changed.

I met a very attractive woman called Nicole, who described herself as 'coloured': she grew up in the middle of Apartheid and said that as a little girl she didn't really notice things were wrong because she didn't know any different. She wasn't allowed on a bus with white people, nor into a public swimming pool and certainly not a restaurant or a bar with her parents. Both her mother and father would also be described as 'coloured' and she still remembers vividly when, as a little girl, she was thrown off a public beach because of the colour of her father's skin. It remains a bitter memory.

I suppose it would be fair to say that in many ways it was the success of Cecil Rhodes that led to Apartheid. The discovery of diamonds at Kimberley was what made Cecil Rhodes his fortune, but his large and almost entirely black workforce laboured in his mines in appalling conditions for hardly any money at all while Rhodes and other whites made more money than they could ever dream of. You can certainly say Rhodes was a white supremacist and very definitely racist – for example, he is quoted as saying of the English, 'I contend that we are the finest race in the world and that the more of the world we inhabit the better it is for the human race.' It probably didn't sound more than mildly contentious when he wrote that in the late 1800s but, only a few decades later, it would have been perfectly in place at a Hitler rally.

He became prime minster of what was then the Cape colony, passed legislation taking away the rights of black Africans in favour of the ruling white minority and laid the groundwork for Apartheid.

HOME SWEET HOME

Meanwhile, we continued along his route to the north. One of the highlights of travelling on the Blue Train was a strange town called Matjiesfontein, built by the British as a railway town in the 19th century. It was a real slice of little England: spotlessly clean, with a bar, post office, small hotel and a tea-room – there was even a red London bus that seemed to be a source of great excitement for all the other passengers. The Koreans in particular couldn't wait to get on it, almost knocking each other over to climb up the stairs.

As the train was only due to stop for ten minutes, the bus was quickly driven up the road, did a small circle, parped its little horn a couple of times like Noddy and Big Ears in their car and came back again to the station. In the meantime, an incredibly irritating man in a silly bowler hat kept playing the army call 'Come to the Cookhouse Door, Boys' on his trumpet and putting his hand out for a tip; my tip would have been 'Don't play your trumpet anywhere near me or I'm going to stick it up your rectum.' He really was the most unpleasant, sweaty man. He only had the one totally irrelevant and annoying tune and had one of those faces you could never tire of hitting. Even more aggravating was the fact that all the Koreans seemed to love him.

After this excitement, we got back on the blue train where Thank You was waiting with hot towels. The Koreans were smiling and saying 'how much they enjoyed London'. You couldn't make it up.

We were to leave the deep luxury of the Blue Train behind at Kimberley, our next stopping point on the original Rhodes route. We weren't in great spirits because we were due to get off in the small hours; we set our alarms for half-past two, got up feeling distinctly shabby and then the train started to do all sorts of

Getting off the train to sample the bus.

strange shunting manoeuvres to let a huge freight train go past and we didn't actually get off until three in the morning.

Our mood wasn't helped either by the fact that our GoPro camera on the front engine had disappeared during the middle of the night – they changed locomotives but forgot to tell us. Somehow we got it back but we were all pretty grumpy and, frankly, exhausted. We cheered up a little though because we were staying overnight in Cecil Rhodes's own private club, the Kimberley, which was all cigars and fine wine, wonderful staircases and oak panels, with paintings and busts of Cecil Rhodes everywhere we looked. There were pictures of King George VI and Elizabeth the Queen Consort over the bar and Elizabeth II and Prince Philip had signed the register. I even stayed in Rhodes's own suite – more pictures of him all around the walls, but also wonderful huge pillows and a really deep bath.

For reasons that are too boring to go into, Jake the camera operator and some of the others were travelling up to meet us by car and staying in another hotel a few miles away. Jake the Vegan, it was reported to me, had an enormous lamb pie for his dinner and, the next morning, he had bacon for breakfast… his devout veganism seemed to be just a little bit shaky.

We arrived in Kimberley in the small hours of the morning, after several days in the glorious sunshine of the Cape, and we should have known that things were going downhill. We were greeted with a violent thunderstorm and huge electric flashes lit up the night sky. The Kimberley club was a splendid place to hide but it didn't really reflect the rest of Kimberley which, to be honest, was a bit of a shambles, but it has to be said that what happened here – the first great discovery of diamonds in the mid-19th century – completely changed the future face of South Africa.

There remains a tremendous example of excavation in the middle of Kimberley, complete with a viewing platform that enables you to hang at the very lip. It's known to everyone as The Big Hole – 'cos that's what it is. It is a mine that was over 200 metres deep, where, at one point, Rhodes had 50,000 men working. As a result, by 1880, Rhodes was a very rich man and one of his first Acts of Parliament was to support the development of the railway from Cape Town to Kimberley. He knew that was his best bet for transporting diamonds, but he clearly had even grander ambitions. I was allowed to see the very map that he drew up in Kimberley to impress potential backers and politicians when he was trying to get them to agree to the railway extension. He wanted to span the entire continent of Africa, from Cape Town to Cairo. The map still had Rhodes's own pencil marks all over it.

Kimberley was very much the centre of the whole diamond industry and even when Rhodes became prime minister of the Cape, it was still the place that he used as his base. The following morning, I had a soak in his own personal bath, using a bar of soap that the chambermaid insisted was one of his own, although,

A big hole called The Big Hole.

bearing in mind he died in 1902, I was understandably sceptical. Smelling delightful, I moved on towards Botswana.

BOTSWANA-BOUND

There was no passenger train on this section of the railway and we could not get permission to join a freight train, so we had to drive. I'm never very happy driving in Africa and, with Botswana and Zimbabwe ahead of me, I wasn't keen on driving at all. However, by driving particularly slowly and carefully, we got into Mafikeng. It is a town, of course, steeped in history and when the railway line arrived here first in 1894, it turned what was a small town into a place of real strategic importance. However, something very strange had happened. Cecil Rhodes, normally a very cool, calculating businessman, supported an attack on Johannesburg in 1895 that went badly wrong, left a lot of casualties and upset just about everybody, particularly the Dutch.

Four years later, in 1899, the Boers retaliated and attacked British-owned territories. This was the start of the second Anglo-

Boer war that lasted three years and left tens of thousands of casualties. The most bitter fighting happened around the town of Mafeking; it lasted for seven cruel months. The Boers had thousands of troops all around the outskirts of the city, but the British had only 500 inside and were trapped inside Mafeking.

One British commander held out magnificently and, after more British troops arrived at the turn of the century and finally defeated the Boers, he was celebrated throughout the British empire. His name was Robert Baden-Powell and, six years later, he would go on to create the Boy Scout movement. This was inspired by the young cadet force he had used in the siege of Mafikeng to help maintain courier services between British outposts and the town. We met a number of young scouts, all black, at the historic Mafeking scout hut and it was great to see that Baden-Powell's movement was as strong as ever in this part of the world. Many of these young people were from really tough backgrounds and were clearly loving everything to do with scouting – camping, learning to tie knots, cooking, providing first-aid and fending for themselves in the outdoors. One of the guys in charge said that if they weren't Scouts many of these young kids would probably end up in prison.

The scouting tradition, alive and well in South Africa today.

Springbok
Kimberley
Bloemfon

The Scouts remains a great movement and there are still 308,000 members in South Africa alone.

All of this history of Mafikeng was fascinating, but the reality is that the town itself today is pretty grim; in fact *very* grim… in fact, it was a tip. After the magnificent start that we'd had in the Victoria and Alfred harbour in the sunshine in Cape Town and on the Blue Train, things had definitely started to deteriorate. It's not the sort of place that you'd want to take your family on holiday; it really is a sprawling mess of a city and, heroic though he may have been, you do wonder why when the Boers first turned up, Baden-Powell didn't just say, 'Oh, go on, then… you can have it!'

One of the unmistakable things in Mafikeng was were posters advertising Dr Mountain and his surgery specialising in penis enlargement. They were absolutely everywhere. It's not something that I've ever seen advertised before, anywhere, and I never ever thought penis envy was an African problem but, clearly, Dr Mountain had the market cornered in Mafikeng. I tried to see if there was any way to spot one of the good doctor's proud patients but it was a big crowded city so I only got as far as eliminating all men wearing shorts before it was time to move on.

From Mafikeng we travelled just 18 miles and then crossed the border into Botswana. I've been to Botswana several times on safari and it is one of the nicest countries in Africa, with a tremendous head of wildlife. It's very different to South Africa and Zimbabwe, not having been colonised by the British in the same way and, when we were there in 2016, it was celebrating 50 years of being a fully independent country. They were taking this anniversary very seriously; the whole nation seemed to have got behind it. They proudly wore blue and black, the national colours of Botswana (every Friday the whole nation tries its best to put on something blue to celebrate). At first it seemed a bit silly but, actually, I loved it. I've never seen any young nation so proud of their achievements. The feeling is that they are very much a young country and they've very much achieved everything for themselves.

Cecil Rhodes wanted but was not given the control of what was then Bechuanaland and, although he did some good elsewhere in lots of ways, Botswana – as it became – was having none of it. They were and remain a fiercely independent people. Rhodes wanted to move his railway north through both Bechuanaland and an area that was known as Northern Rhodesia and Southern Rhodesia (later Zambia and Zimbabwe); having made a fortune from diamonds, now he wanted to mine these countries for gold. But everything Rhodes ever did was in the cause of furthering the power and influence of white British men and the black population of Botswana always resisted that. It's not perfect in many ways but it's a shining example to the rest of Africa.

We were treated to a new passenger service that had only been running a few weeks from Gaborone, the capital, up to Francistown in northern Botswana. It was clearly the country's pride and joy. OK, it was not quite Blue Train standard but it was pretty impressive; absolutely spotless, very comfortable, modern, clean and air-conditioned. It's mainly a night service, and is incredibly popular. The train we joined was full of families, including women with young babies and it travelled mainly overnight as Botswana's roads are notoriously dangerous at night. Both drunken drivers and animals on the road pose a threat. Not so much the elephants or big cats that I associated with Botswana but, rather more mundanely, cows and goats. They are everywhere and they are a real problem.

DEPOT STOP

As always with these journeys, things were not to be as simple and cosy as I had hoped. Yes, I was on a nice sleeper train but, once again, as a nod to 'extreme railways', I had to get off at one o'clock in the morning at a place called Mahalapye station. I say 'station' but, actually, there was no station, I just got off onto a bit of flat sand into which a Mahalapye sign had been stuck on a lamp-post and trudged grumpily towards yet another hotel, leaving everybody else on the train nice and warm and fast asleep; there was a pattern developing here and I didn't think I liked it much.

The reason for getting off at Mahalapye was that it is the centre

Damage to trains by livestock and from human error is all too common.

of the Botswana railway network and it is here that all the trains are repaired. There is a lot of damage to fix, particularly caused by livestock. They reckon some four trains a week hit cows and have to be taken out of commission as result. The trains can't stop and – without being too graphic – great chunks of mangled cow or goat go under the train and get into the hydraulic piping. The cows can't really help it; they're just a bit simple and, tragically, they've got too used to trains in recent years and have no fear of them.

Human negligence is far more of a problem. Botswana's roads are incredibly dangerous and that is one of the reasons why they've invested heavily in the bigger and better passenger train service. One of the locomotives in the maintenance sheds, a huge diesel engine, had been smashed to pieces at the front. We were told that it crashed into a lorry a few days earlier when the driver ignored the warnings at a railway crossing and went straight through, giving the train driver no chance of stopping. The foolish lorry driver was killed instantly and the engine didn't look too clever either. In fact, it would be a miracle if they did get it back into service.

I liked Botswana and I liked its people but, just as I was getting comfy once again and enjoying what now was fierce sunshine and temperatures of more than 30 degrees Celsius during what was still only the end of winter, I had to make my way towards Francistown, close to the border with Zimbabwe.

I was too late for the passenger train – that would not travel again until the next night – so I managed to cadge a lift in a freight train. The freight side of Botswana's railway is bigger than the passenger portion. The main commodities are coal, grain, concrete and salt; not particularly sexy, but very valuable. One of the reasons why Botswana is doing so well is that it's managed to retain a lot of the diamonds and other minerals discovered under its soil.

My train was driven by a really splendid young woman, Aone Keokgale, one of only eight female train drivers in the country. Botswana railways are very proud of their new intake, as in many parts of Africa female drivers would still be totally unacceptable. We sat cramped and sweating in the cab with Aone and her trusty overseer, a lovely old train driver since way back when, called Johnson. He watched her every move and was clearly very proud of her. She was a young engineer who had just wanted a change and decided that train driving was an interesting job. She said that although initially some of her male colleagues were very sniffy about the idea of a woman driver, they have now accepted her and she is given respect everywhere she goes. Also, her family are absolutely bursting with pride – her mother and brothers are just so excited by the idea of little Aone driving a massive freight train.

She talked about the problems about the animals on the line and, as she talked, a large, pregnant cow wandered incredibly stupidly across the track, as if to emphasise her point. She repeatedly tooted her horn but the animal continued to move at the speed of a snail – fortunately, we somehow missed the silly creature by about a foot.

Aone ran us up towards Francistown and, although she was brand-new to being interviewed and having a camera stuck up her nose, she chatted away happily and continued to be in total control of the train. She was in many ways a real symbol of the new, young Botswana where everything is possible and it made me think that if Cecil Rhodes could see a woman, particularly a young, black woman, driving a train on his beloved railway he would be

From left, Wamorena Maruapula and Sereo Thabeng, our young Botswana Railways chaperones. They took care of us all the way from Lobatse to Francistown – and even dropped us off at the Zimbabwean border to make sure we got over OK!

absolutely horrified. She was terrific and I loved the thought of how appalled Cecil would be. The next morning we left Francistown by road for the Zimbabwean border – there are no passenger trains effectively working cross-border and we couldn't get on any of the freight trains. We drove with some trepidation out of Botswana, where they had been so friendly, into Robert Mugabe's Zimbabwe.

Botswana's side of the border was the site of what was probably the only fun immigration-control point I have ever been through in my life; the women were all laughing amongst themselves and smiling – yes, smiling – at us and giving each other high-fives. However, I did suspect that the next bit would not be quite like that.

Getting our Zimbabwe visas took for ever, in what was a long, grey, tedious building with large pictures of Robert Mugabe at both ends. One thing that amused us was that there was a large box at the end by the door with a slot in it for 'Any suggestions to defeat corruption'! I wonder if anybody dared to put a suggestion like, 'A change of government would be a good idea,' with his or her name and address on the bottom. I suspect not.

WELCOME TO ZIMBABWE

We crawled out of Zimbabwe immigration with our precious visas after almost four hours and we were finally in the former Southern Rhodesia. We were genuinely all a bit nervous and not quite sure what to expect. Jennifer Perelli, the producer and my constant helper, and I were paranoid about leaving any references at all to Robert Mugabwe in the script, so we went around frantically tearing them out and destroying them. I think dedicated Jen may even have eaten them just in case anybody read a script by chance and we ended up in a Zimbabwe prison. We really were that paranoid. We did know that roadblocks were likely to be a big problem.

Zamo, our cool young African driver and second fixer had come out with Neil Ferguson, the director, on a recce a month before our arrival and they reported back that they were stopped all over the place, quite unnecessarily and usually given a fine to be paid on the spot in dollars. Zamo actually ended up in handcuffs. Eventually, after several hours, he was able to talk his way out of what could have been a really frightening situation but, of course, yet another fine was levied against him.

We only had about 60 miles to travel to Bulawayo, the second-largest city in Zimbabwe, but within seven miles we encountered the first roadblock. We knew it was going to happen, but it was actually quite scary. There must have been seven or eight large Zimbabwean policemen with what were very serious-looking guns and, most shameless of all, they had a box in the middle of the road containing a great mountain of dollars that one of the officers was busily counting.

They went round and round the car looking at everything, went through the inside looking at cameras, all our sound equipment, etc; we had to show all our papers, permits passports, explain what we were doing, etc. It was a little bit frightening, of course, but mainly just unnecessary and tedious and, to their disappointment, they had to let us go, having paid them nothing at all.

Over the next 50 miles to Bulawayo, we were stopped three more times. Apparently, Zimbabweans just get used to it but, of course, when the people are as poor as they are, it is an extra unnecessary expense that drivers just can't afford and in recent months there have been a lot of protests.

We finally got to Bulawayo; it is an extraordinary city. Clearly, when it was part of Rhodesia, up to about 1980, the white minority who ruled the country lived really rather well. The suburbs of

Kimberley
Bloemfont
Springbok

Bulawayo were beautiful, with lovely, tree-lined avenues and some great-looking houses, where a mixture of blacks and whites now live. Everywhere there were signs of splendid old colonial houses and architecture, but clearly the whites lived rather too well; they all had nice houses, nice weather, nice railway trains and nice golf clubs. But, for the black majority, things were not so good. Predictably, with the coming of independence and the Mugabe government there was an uprising and in the years that followed, most white landowners, particularly the white farmers, were forcibly and frequently violently kicked out. Several were murdered.

Zimbabwe's economy is a disaster. The dollar was devalued over and over again. I was given a five-billion-dollar note, which looked great but was worth marginally less than nothing. At one point you could get a trillion-dollar note and that was worth three American cents. The Zimbabwean dollar was abandoned in favour of foreign currency in 2015. The bottom has clearly fallen out of Zimbabwe, the people are very poor, among the poorest in Africa and, inevitably, there is a lot of crime. It was very obvious in the city centre where every single shop – and I do mean every single one – had thick metal bars across their windows. Looting and smash and grab are rife.

What we did find – and, perhaps, if I am truthful, I didn't really expect it – was that the people were incredibly nice and welcoming. I thought they would be rather antagonistic towards us Brits and understandably feeling down on their luck and aggressive but, everywhere we went, people made us feel very welcome.

This was the final resting place for Cecil Rhodes, who went up to a beautiful area outside Bulawayo called the Matapos Hills. Here there are the most stunning, 360-degree views of the beautiful African countryside. Rhodes was so taken with the place that he decided when he did pass away that this is where he wanted to be buried. It was a magnificent setting for a memorial. What I did find a bit odd – in fact, downright weird – was learning that he frequently used to go up to the place chosen for his funeral plot, lie down full-length, close his eyes and have a little practice. Now that's bizarre.

When he did eventually die, this extraordinary, controversial figure was only 48 years old. He had achieved so much; he created huge wealth for South Africa – but mainly for himself and a few of his white contemporaries. He had also clearly laid the foundation for a lot of the troubles ahead.

When we got to Bulawayo station we were more than a little bit alarmed to be told that the Bulawayo to Victoria Falls service hadn't been running for the last six months because nobody had been paid. However, we were promised that it had been working for the last few days and 'it should be all right'.

FINDING THE FALLS

There was a wonderful timetable featuring all sorts of railway services to Harare and Francistown, with 'No service', 'No service', 'No service' written over them. But on the main passenger information blackboard in the station, written clearly in chalk was a notice: 'Bulawayo to Victoria Falls tonight at 7.30 pm'. We could only go along, stand on the enormous platform – at over 700 metres long it was the longest in the world for some time – and wait with our fingers crossed for the night train.

It didn't look too clever; there were all sorts of signs everywhere, saying: 'We can only apologise for the lack of service on this line'. But there were quite a few people, including men carrying potatoes and carrots on their heads and a group of young girls carrying babies on their backs, making their way onto the platform, so I thought there was an outside chance.

There was a huge picture of Robert Mugabe over the ticket office – well, of course there was. I didn't quite know if I should bow, curtsey or, '*Sieg Heil*!' You never get pictures of our prime ministers at the Kings Cross booking office but, as everybody seemed to be ignoring him up there, I did the same. People were queuing for tickets to go somewhere, so I hung in there.

I got to the front, and a lady said, 'Yes, there is a service tonight that will go to Victoria Falls.' It was leaving at half-past seven, it would be a 14-hour journey but, yes, it was a sleeper and, yes, there would be a pillow. She didn't mention whether or not there would be a bed but at least there would be a pillow... so, proudly clutching my ticket, I walked onto the enormous platform and spent about 20 minutes in pitch-darkness trying to work out where there was a train that looked like it was going to go anywhere.

Eventually, having walked the full 700 metres down one side and very nearly the same along the opposite side, I found a train with a light on and people who seemed to be getting on. 'Victoria Falls?' I said to one man.

'No,' he said, as if I was an idiot. 'Bulawayo.'

'Yes, I know I'm in Bulawayo,' I said, 'but is the train going to Victoria Falls?'

'Probably...' came the reply. Well – that was helpful, wasn't it?

One or two other people confirmed that it was indeed going in the right direction, so I got on and, actually, my cabin wasn't too bad at all. It had a bed, a splendid red pillow, a sweet little 1930s' basin with real water running out of the tap – presumably pumped fresh from the Zambezi river. A few minutes later we were off.

I took an exploratory walk along most of the rest of the train and found a restaurant area with a bar, but I have to say that it was pretty grim. From the looks of things several of the men in the bar had been drinking for some time. The main carriages further down the train were absolutely rammed, with women breastfeeding babies, quite scary-looking men giving me a hard stare and others giving me big smiles and high-fives. It was incredibly over-packed. I went back gratefully to my nice little cabin and settled down to what I thought might be a decent night's sleep.

Well, it certainly wasn't; the train was so noisy – there was this clattering noise from the rails all through the night. I suppose in the 1950s that was just how it was and I found it almost impossible to sleep. I had discovered another terrifying thing on my walk along the train – several of the doors leading off the train kept swinging wide open and just wouldn't shut. Health and safety doesn't seem to have arrived on Zimbabwe's railways. What with the doors banging all through the night and the clattering of the rails, it was the noisiest night I have ever spent. I kept hearing strange muffled yells and I was convinced somebody had fallen out.

In addition, every 20 minutes all through the night the train would stop. Each time I was convinced it had broken down, as my train had in a tunnel in the Congo, but it seemed as if people were just getting on and off all through the small hours. The only thing that kept me vaguely sane was the thought that in the morning, when the sun came up, I should be looking out at Victoria Falls.

Eventually, the beautiful African sunrise arrived, even though I had no idea where I was. The countryside around was really wild and uncultivated. In most other African countries you'd expect to see herds of zebra, elephant, wildebeest and maybe even a lion from the train window. Certainly in Kenya, Tanzania and the Kruger national park in South Africa, that is exactly what you would see, but on the long haul up towards Victoria Falls we saw no wildlife at all.

This is almost certainly because the people of Zimbabwe are desperately poor, it is a pretty lawless country and poaching is rife. If any wild animals had not been shot for their ivory, they probably have been killed to feed starving families. It's all so sad.

As the sun rose higher we continued rattling northwards along Cecil Rhodes' railway. The doors in the next carriage were still swinging back and forth, wide open onto the track and I was puzzled for a while why the letters RR appeared on our carriage windows.

Jake Martin, second unit cameraman, showing how he got his nickname 'The Pack Mule'.

Roy of the Rovers? Roy Rogers? Ronald Reagan? The penny suddenly dropped: this, of course, was a carriage that dated back to the 1950s, the era of Rhodesia Railways.

At almost exactly 9.30 am, having left Bulawayo at 7.30 pm – a 14-hour journey, as promised – with almost Japanese efficiency, we were at Victoria Falls station. At first we started seeing spray in the distance, coming out of thick jungle and realised that it must be coming from the waterfalls. It was an incredible feeling; we pulled into a beautifully kept station with a magnificent garden alongside it, apparently the grounds of the hotel that we were staying in. It was a perfect way to complete our 1,500-mile journey. There was even a red carpet on the platform to welcome us.

THE BRIDGE FROM BRITAIN

The Victoria Falls hotel is one of the great hotels of the world and I walked through the main foyer and out onto the perfectly manicured back lawn, where there is a magnificent view of the gorge of the river Zambezi below the gardens. I looked across at a massive bridge that spans the great river at this point. It is 200 metres long and was actually built in Darlington in the north of England of all places and assembled here in 1905. The two ends of the bridge were joined at night as the metal cooled after the baking daytime African temperatures. As the metal contracted the two lined-up ends met perfectly as planned.

Beyond the bridge there are the Falls themselves. They are just magnificent, over 100 metres deep and nearly 2,000 metres wide – just enormous – and you cannot begin to imagine the power of the water. No one would last ten seconds if they fell in – and yet people rock-climb and bungee jump all round it?

There was the constant drone of helicopters throughout the morning, with visitors looking down at the falls and taking photographs from the air. They are one of the seven wonders of the natural world.

So it was the end of our journey. Rhodes's original dream was to build a railway from Cape Town to Cairo but Victoria Falls was about as far as it got. Other railways in Africa were built, but they had different gauges so they couldn't match the locomotives on Rhodes's early railways. When Rhodes died – exactly like Stalin after him – the driving force for the great railway project died with him and the dream was allowed to quietly fade away.

Three countries, five very different trains – it had been one of the most demanding but worthwhile railway journeys of all. We had come from Victoria and Alfred harbour in Cape Town via a string of trains, good and bad, overnight and daylight, passenger and freight and ended up in one of the most beautiful settings on earth.

What is extraordinary to realise is that this amazing place, with the falls pounding down all around us, with spray and wonderful rainbows everywhere and the rocks above full of carefree tourists from all around the world, is actually still Zimbabwe. It feels like a totally different country, but you are still in Robert Mugabe's Zimbabwe.

The hotel was magnificent and I was delighted to see that I didn't have a huge portrait of Robert Mugabe over my bath or, worse still, looking down at me from my bedroom ceiling.

The tragedy is that Zimbabwe could and should be one of the most beautiful and richest countries in the whole of Africa.

Meet the crew: from left, Mike Harrison, cameraman; Rick Matthews, fixer; Jon 'JT' Thomas, soundman; Zamo Shadrack Nala, fixer and driver; me; Neil Ferguson, director; Jennifer Perelli, producer and Jake Martin. Mike, JT, Jennifer and Jake are also grizzled veterans of no less than five other of our extreme railway journeys – Cuba, Japan, Siberia, Canada and Alaska.

ЧС11-09

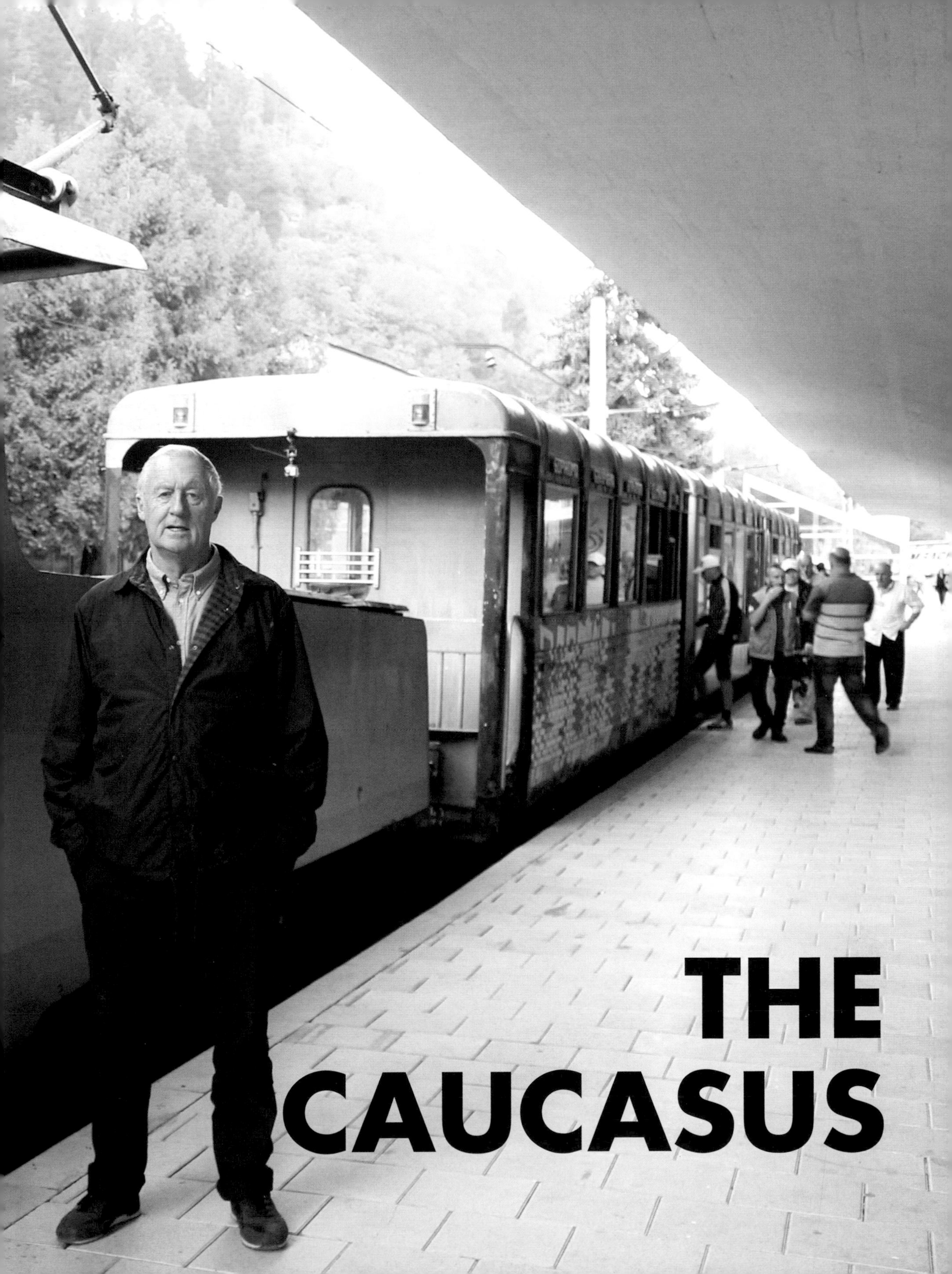

THE CAUCASUS

Black Sea
Poti
Samtredia
Kutaisi
Tskhinvali
Tsipa
Ureki
Borjomi
Likhi
Gori

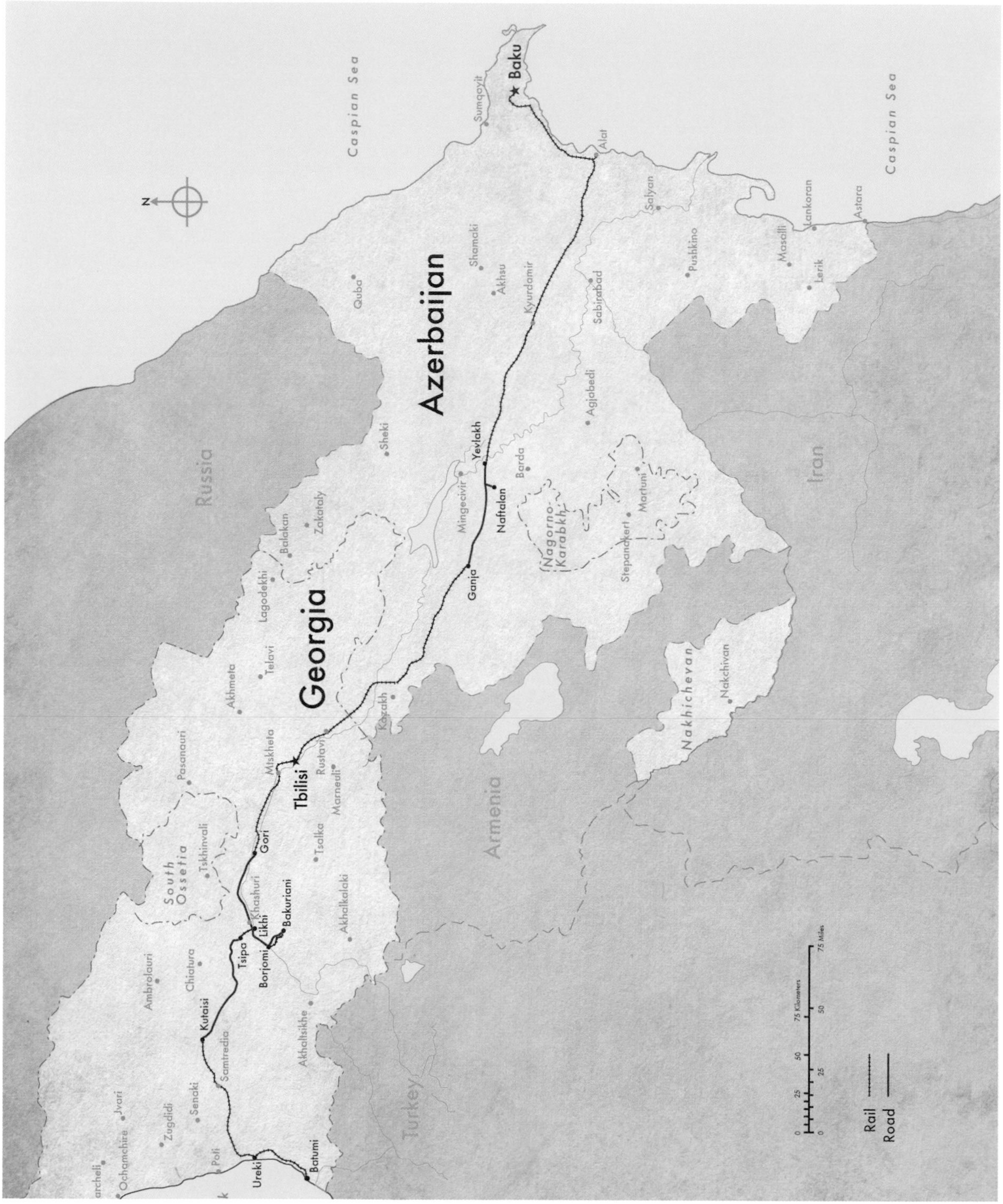

The Caucasus

It's 3.45 am and I'm tip-toeing out of the house. My partner, Jane, says to me without even opening her eyes, 'Never go anywhere you can't spell.' With that gem of information lodged in my brain, I make my way to Heathrow on a pitch-black September morning.

I'm flying to Baku, the capital of Azerbaijan, and I must say I have a certain amount of trepidation about the city, the country and Azerbaijan Airlines. I needn't have worried: the plane was spotlessly clean with splendid hostesses in bright shiny uniforms. Coming in, over the mountains and down to the Caspian Sea, the city was a great sight and I was ashamed of my misgivings. The airport was the cleanest I've ever seen, with nice carpets and all the escalators actually worked.

At the baggage conveyor, all seemed to be going well, as we waited under a giant picture of Wayne Rooney advertising Azerbaijani mobile phones – until the belt came to a shuddering halt. Neither Jake nor I had got our suitcases. We then spent a very frustrating hour with a particularly unhelpful man from Azerbaijan Airlines, who promised the lost cases would be on the next flight. Well, they weren't on the next flight – or the one after that. With the one set of clothes that I was standing up in, there seemed to be every chance that, by the end of a week's filming, I would look as if I had been run over by a truck and smell like a dead donkey. There are those who, rather unkindly, suggest that this is what I look and smell like anyway, but enough about my kids.

Baku was a complete revelation; the place was absolutely buzzing. It had magnificent, tree-lined avenues on a par with Paris or Buenos Aires and everywhere oozed wealth. Baku makes Monte Carlo look like Barking – there were Bentleys, Rolls-Royces and

Ferraris on every street and all the shops seemed to be top-end brand names.

They struck black gold in the Baku region in 1846 and, by the end of the 19th century, more than half the world's oil supply came from Azerbaijan. For most of the 20th century the proceeds helped to prop up the whole of the Soviet Union. However, when communism collapsed in 1991 and Azerbaijan declared itself independent, it was at last able to hold onto its own minerals and the discovery of vast offshore oil fields in recent years has assured the country's future as one of the world's leading oil-producing nations.

The streets of Baku are busy day and night with hundreds of black London cabs (spelt '*taksi*') picking up mega-rich passengers from all over town. There were Iranians and Iraqis everywhere, apparently coming here for their holidays by the shores of the beautiful Caspian Sea and, due to the recent drop in oil prices, Azerbaijan is a reasonably cheap place to shop.

We passed through a place called Yanar Dag ('the flaming mountain'), which was full of tourists and, as I turned a corner, a giant gas fire greeted me. The heat as I got close-up was savage, the result of natural gas bubbling up out of the ground. There's a vast pocket of it under the earth in Yanar Dag and, apparently, if there are cracks or fissures in the rock, any spark will set the gas alight. This particular fire was started by a careless shepherd dropping a match back in the 1950s and it's been burning merrily away ever since.

We boarded the overnight train from Baku Central to a place called Yevlakh. The train was on time, busy and reasonably comfortable. Before we left we had a massive meal of kebabs, washed down with Caspian-brand lager, which would have been much more in place in somewhere like Istanbul than a former Soviet country, but Baku is full of contradictions.

I wanted to see whether the massive wealth of the city was shared around the rest of the country. Azerbaijan is sandwiched between Russia in the north and Turkey, Armenia and Iran to the south and it straddles the divide between Europe and Asia. It is a very mountainous country, although our railway was travelling mainly across the flat central plain, heading south along the shores of the Caspian.

The Transcaucasus Railway was built in the 1880s with a view to carrying oil rather than people, although nowadays it's more half and half. As we travelled through the night, we could clearly see the bright lights of the Sangachal oil terminal, one of the biggest in the world. Thousands of gallons a day come from rigs way out in the Caspian. Some is pumped via a pipeline into Turkey, but a large amount is still loaded onto freight trains which go up to Batumi, way over the Georgian border, a distance of more than 500 miles – sometimes very tough miles. And that, of course, was where we were headed...

Our first stop was Yevlakh, which couldn't have been more different to the wealth and sheer bling we encountered in Baku. One lonely old Lada with, as always, '*taksi*' on the roof came to collect me from the station. There was not a Bentley or a Ferrari in sight.

Although it was early in the morning there was enough light for me to be able to see quite clearly what a dump Yevlakh was. After just a few hours on the railway we'd gone into another world. In the middle of a great mountain of brambles, nettles, and appalling

A former oil-pumping station in Yevlakh.

piles of litter, was a large derelict building with virtually no roof, with the date 1904 written on the front in large numerals. It was obviously once a massive structure and clearly the ruins of what was once a magnificent oil-pumping station, but as I walked inside I couldn't believe how much it had been left to ruin – there's disrepair and disrepair, but this was disgusting. Director Jeff Morgan, Mike Harrison, JT and I stepped gingerly over tons of dog shit; there were flies buzzing all over the place and it was hard not to gag. There were also soiled nappies dumped randomly all over the once-beautiful floors. Apart from when I was once filming in the slums of Sierra Leone, where cholera, yellow fever and dysentery are rife, I do not remember anywhere that was in such a dreadful state. It was shocking and certainly disease-ridden and yet it was very close to a main road and women and their children walk through the area every day.

PIPELINE OF A TSAR

We had got off our nice, cosy train especially to go and see that building as it had been a place of great significance, part of an amazing scheme; the construction of the world's first long-distance petroleum pipeline. It was built on the orders of Tsar Nicholas II and was hailed as a wonder of the world when it was completed in 1907. It ran all the way to the Black Sea and it had the capacity to transport 800,000 tons of oil a year from the Baku oil fields to Georgia.

Eventually, the old pipeline fell into disuse and virtually all of Azerbaijan's oil was then transported for many years by rail. However, in the last 20 years, two new pipelines have been built. They go underground so they are invisible, but you can see the pumping stations that are owned by a very wealthy international consortium and guarded by heavily armed security. We came to one of those stations on the road to Naftalan, still in my trusty Lada. My driver, a lovely man with the most perfect set of gold teeth I have ever seen outside a James Bond movie, took me to a spot that he said was 'as close as we can safely go'. There were cameras everywhere and men with very serious-looking guns. As I didn't fancy being shot that particular morning or even lingering for 20 years or so in a former Soviet prison, we didn't go an inch further than suggested.

We drove on into the centre of Naftalan, a town with a series of health spas that people flock to, just as the English used to flock to Bath or Harrogate in the 19th century. The story goes that hundreds of years ago a group of herdsman were driving through Naftalan when one of their camels became too sick to travel. The camel's owner, with some sadness, left the animal to die and moved on with his reduced caravan. When they passed through the same area again several months later they discovered, to their amazement, that not only was their old camel not dead, it was very much alive and well and bursting with health. There was something, it seemed, coming up out of the ground at Naftalan with extraordinary healing properties. It was the oil under the soil that caused it, which became known as the miracle of Naftalan.

Intrigued or, perhaps, plain stupid, I decided to try out the healing oils for myself. Rather than immersing my body in lovely bubbling natural spring water, I had to sink into a bath full of the most disgusting-looking brown slurry. I slipped and slid as I

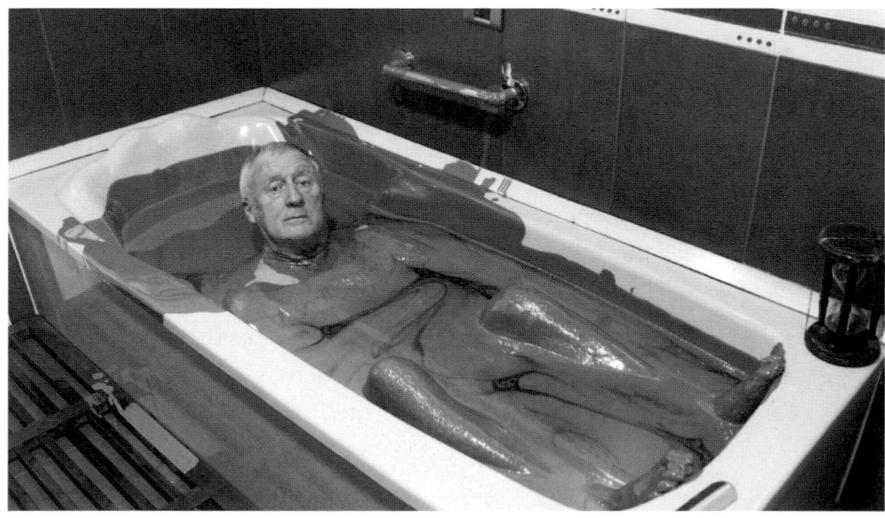

Oil be seeing you… What, you thought these looks were natural?

climbed in and it reached my neck, which, of course, the crew found very funny. I found it deeply unpleasant, if not ludicrous. I lay there, looking like a giant toffee apple for a full ten minutes, while the wonder oils took their course. I even had to have a full medical and ECG before they'd even allow me into the dreadful goo.

Apparently, it is a cure for all sorts of skin diseases – none of which I had (at least, not before I got into the gunge tank) and aching joints – which I certainly do have, after years of abuse and sleeping on river banks. It is supposed to create a feeling of great well-being. Instead, I felt plain daft and, despite several showers, I didn't seem able to stop the oil seeping out of my pores. This, combined with the fact that for three days, thanks to the airline, I'd been wearing the same clothes, meant that I was to become extremely pungent; not a problem for me, but certainly one for everyone else.

I might have been the only one out of step here, because hundreds of people come to the spa every week and swear it does wonders for their bodies. It's a very specialised oil, the Naftalan product, nothing like engine oil, so one of the crew threatening to drop his lighted cigarette end in the bath didn't phase me. It's so precious that when you get out, they gather up every single drop and recycle it so, basically, I was in somebody else's bath water and some other poor soul would be getting mine. It reminded me of a particularly silly children's television programme in the 1970s – whatever happened to its presenters?

Feeling distinctly oily, I climbed back into the trusty Lada, with my driver with the gold teeth smirking and making a point of keeping all the car windows open as we drove to catch the train for Georgia.

We came to the town of Ganja, which in Jamaica is a word meaning 'marijuana'. I didn't find myself hallucinating or wanting to play Bob Marley, but it was nicely charming. It is the second-biggest city in Azerbaijan and was clean, with lovely open squares. It was Sunday evening and there were couples walking hand-in-hand everywhere and kids playing in the parks in the setting sun. Sadly, we only had a few hours there. The next morning at 3.45 am

My friend with the gold teeth and I swallowing up the miles in his cosy Lada.

– yes, that's 3.45 in the morning – still smelling strongly of oil and wearing the same clothes, I boarded the overnight train from Baku, which stopped at Ganja on its way over the Georgian border.

GEORGIA ON MY MIND

The train was unexpectedly comfy and we were able to grab a few hours' kip in a sleeper before the border. There was a rather tedious process of leaving Azerbaijan, filling in lots of forms before going back to sleep with our passports and visas on our pillows beside us. The customs officials were extraordinarily friendly. A terrifying-looking dominatrix came into my cabin, in full peaked hat and black outfit, demanding my passport and forms, but when I handed them rather sheepishly over, she broke into a huge grin and said, 'Welcome to Georgia' and went smiling happily on her way. I still think that if I had dared to cross her, she would have bunged me into a Soviet-era cell and done something dreadful to me with a hosepipe. Tbilisi, the capital of Georgia, is no Baku but that was rather nice. Baku was a bit too like Dubai for me. Tbilisi is charming. There's a splendid funicular railway, built in 1905, that runs to the top of the hills overlooking the city. We went up with the information

The train to Georgia was very clean, very modern and they obviously took safety very seriously, judging by this sign above the window of my compartment. I was in very safe hands…?

that it was the railway nobody ever actually needed and that, in 2000, a cable holding the car on the way up snapped. The car, with people screaming inside, smashed down to the bottom. Somehow, and I really don't know how, nobody was killed and staff were at pains to assure us that it had been repaired meticulously. As the crew and I made our way up the hill, at quite a decent speed, our eyes were riveted to the cable, grinding away in front of us. Mercifully, it was fine, but I think it was a piece of news that we hadn't needed just before embarking.

The view from the top was stunning, looking down on the city that's been here since the fifth century AD, having survived so many volatile times and invasions and always come out smiling. The funicular railway had been commissioned to serve a suburb that was planned to take an overflow in population at the top of the hills high above the city. The genius planners hadn't thought that maybe the population at the top might need water, which doesn't actually run uphill. The suburb was shelved and the railway now largely serves the tourist market – the 1.15 million population of Tbilisi more or less doubles in the summer months.

I absolutely loved the city; we sat down at night, sharing huge bowls of local stew, plates of assorted meats and all sorts of vegetables – including thorn salad, which I became very fond of – and lashings of crisp white wine and a wonderful red called Pheasant's Tears, which we all became far too fond of. There was live music everywhere; we found the most wonderful, smoky jazz bar to complete what had been a very long but very splendid day.

By now I had been wearing the same clothes for four days and nights. The latest news was that my suitcase had been found in Paris, France, at Charles de Gaulle airport. It turned out that it had been there with Air France for four days, since Friday morning. It had made it off the Air France plane but somehow didn't get on the Azerbaijan Airlines flight for the second leg. Now there was no longer any point sending the luggage to Baku because we were hundreds of miles west and going further all the time. I went out and bought a few new clothes and went to bed thoroughly fed-up.

On Tuesday morning, we had a bit of a lie-in; my alarm didn't ring until quarter-to-six that morning – it felt like teatime... We got on the morning train from Tbilisi up towards Gori and, as we went out into the country, there were mountains everywhere and the sun came up on a truly gorgeous morning. Georgian Railways are probably the cheapest on Earth. My ticket to travel a distance of about fifty miles – was one lari (about 30p); Network Southeast, Virgin and co., I hope you're reading this. Now, *that's* value.

I thought we should do a nice, gentle piece to camera saying how nice it was to be in Georgia. I was halfway through this fairly innocuous opener when a large bucket lid missed my head by about three inches, followed by a string of abuse from an unknown gentleman at the far end of the compartment. For reasons that we never really understood, he was clearly incensed and I suspect he was also alcohol-fuelled as he had breath like a blowtorch. Security men, to Georgian Railway's credit, came from everywhere and grabbed him but he carried on ranting in our general direction. Several women started shouting at him: 'Leave

Jake having a terrifying dream.

them alone, they're just doing their job – they're saying nice things about Georgia.' He then started to scream a lot of abuse at the women with words that even we understood – 'cow' and 'bitch' – he really was a piece of work.

We moved off to another carriage with our cameras. He and I had an eyeball-to-eyeball as I passed and I explained in rather guttural English what I thought of him. He didn't speak English but I think he got my gist. Sometimes, it does help being six-foot-two-inches tall.

GORI'S GORY SON

Gori is an interesting station – there's a big statue tucked away behind glass doors that are mainly locked. It is of a local man who would certainly be their most famous – no, make that infamous – citizen, not just in Gori but in neighbouring Russia. He was the supreme leader of the Soviet Union from 1929 until his death in 1953 and he's generally accepted as having been responsible for the deaths of something in excess of 20 million people. Historically, he's always been judged as a monster, but not necessarily by the people from his birthplace. He was born in Gori, his whole life was gory and he was, of course, Joseph Stalin. There are statues of him all over town but, interestingly the one in the station is behind locked glass doors with a notice in Russian and English: 'For strangers entry is prohibited' – which means, I suppose, 'Go away, foreigners, and leave cuddly Uncle Joe alone.'

We made our way across town in a taxi to the Gori Stalin museum, but on the way there we spotted an extraordinary sight, a supermarket with a huge picture of Stalin. It seemed unreal, like having massive billboards of Adolf Hitler advertising Tesco. And there were all sorts of Stalin memorabilia for sale inside, as there was in the museum: T-shirts, giant carpets, key-rings, mugs and hipflasks, the lot…

People from all over the world packed out what was in some ways a magnificent museum with the most enormous range of pictures of Stalin as a child and as a young man. Ailsa Fereday – the new, young producer on our team – said to me, bewilderingly, 'He was a bit of a hotty, wasn't he?' I really couldn't see it myself. There were also hundreds of paintings, photographs, statues and busts of Stalin in the scary, overweight moustachioed persona he was later known for and lots of oil paintings of him holding up children. It very much perpetuated the myth of 'Uncle Joe'. The fact that he was a mass-murdering psychopath didn't appear to deter people from admission and it was almost like some sort of fan club. I personally found it revolting.

We walked through his personal railway carriage, which weighed 83 tons, most of it armour plating – fear of any enemies for Uncle Joe? Surely not! I walked through the bodyguard quarters, communication centres, saw his private bath tub and the conference room at the end of the train where he must have sat with his sycophantic followers, fearful for their own lives while he plotted the deaths of thousands of his own people. Increasingly, the realisation that I was actually in the same room where this monstrous man once moved and plotted murders made me feel positively queasy. I was very glad to get out into the fresh air, as were the crew. We were all stunned and very quiet for a while about the whole thing. Presumably, the local council allow it because it brings in the tourist dollar, which it clearly did, but also because at least some of the people of Gori feel a real pride that 'Uncle Joe' was one of theirs. Personally, I would love to see the place razed to the ground.

Someone who would agree with me is a wonderful lady called Lela Serebryakova, who came very begrudgingly to sit outside the museum and talk to me about Stalin's influence on her family. Her great-

Ever got the feeling that someone's watching you? Looked down on by one Josef Vissarionovich Djugashvili (aka Joseph Stalin) in Gori.

He may have been adored as Dear Comrade Stalin, but he still made sure his personal train was very heavily armoured.

grandfather was a quiet, intelligent literary professor without a political bone in his body but Stalin hated and feared intelligence. He was suddenly arrested and whisked away in 1938 and was never seen again. Lela's grandmother was just seven at the time and she and her mother hung on to the hope that he was alive year after year. He had been executed, shot in the head only three days after his completely spurious arrest on charges of plotting against the Soviet Union, but they only discovered 60 years later, in some archive documentation that showed he was registered as 'Dead by shooting'.

Lela's grandmother, though just a young child when her father disappeared, was, shockingly, for years made to stand up every morning at school assembly and be pointed out by the teachers and the other children as 'the child of an enemy of the state'. She did sound the most wonderful woman and had been brave and very tough. And there were hundreds of thousands like her...

Lela thought the Stalin museum was a disgrace and that Georgia should be ashamed of Stalin. They have 'so many other great heroes', she said, 'he does not deserve to be mentioned in the same breath as any of them.'

We went back to our hotel that evening in a very sombre mood, although we had yet another wonderful Georgian feast awaiting us. I did find the people of Georgia – with the exception of that morning's phantom bucket-flinger – to be some of the kindest we've met in all of our travels. The country is beautiful, with long raging rivers everywhere and deep forests that climb almost to the peak of some of the mountains. The valleys that the trains travelled through were just stunning.

CLIMBING THE MOUNTAINS WITH A PEPPER POT

The next day dawned after rather a heavy night on the Pheasant's Tears – and a great mountain of assorted meats for all. Except, of course, for devout vegan Jake, who piddled around with some silly vegetables – before wolfing down black pudding stuffed with meat! – the cooking in Georgia really was excellent; some of the very best in all of our world travels. To be fair, Jake had been doing reasonably well apart from the occasional lapse, like a great mountain of cheese that apparently was not very vegan and a brief flirtation with a plate of beef stroganoff that was not vegan at all. Oh, and then there was the pork kebab…

I got to the platform in Borjomi just as the sun was coming up; it's a lovely low-lying town right next to the river in the valley of the Kura and I was looking forward to a trip up the mountains.

However, what greeted me when I arrived at the station was a bit of a shock. Of all the trains we've used around the world, this had to be the most unlikely locomotive yet. It was ridiculous. It looked like a pepper pot between two butter dishes and was about as aerodynamic, with the driver's cab in the middle. It was wonderful, but in equal proportions it was absurd and daft. It was built in Czechoslovakia back in 1966, when there were lots of these unlikely little locomotives all across the Soviet Union and they were doing serious work like hauling long trains of coal and iron ore. My little locomotive and I had quite a climb ahead of us, with him doing all the work; we were going up to Bakuriani – which sounds like something you have with poppadums and mango chutney but is actually the little town at the top of the mountain that looms over Borjomi. It was a 25-mile journey but quite a roundabout crawl up the mountain that was estimated to take about two and a half hours. With us jumping on and off to film, it took an extra hour, but none of the passengers seemed to mind, which was rather refreshing after the events of the previous morning.

The views were magnificent and, as we climbed higher, instead of fading away, the wonderful fir trees on the sides of the mountains just seemed to get thicker and. if anything, greener. The only area not thickly forested was high on the peaks where, apparently, when the Russians invaded Georgia in 2008, they dropped fire bombs to make it easier for their troops to march in. They almost made Tbilisi before an uneasy peace was sorted out. In the meantime, the beautiful mountains have thousands of acres of completely burnt-out ground and leafless, lifeless trees.

After an hour or so, we came to a sharp bend, where the very accommodating driver let us stop and get off to look at a very

The mountain train that resembled a pepper pot between two butter dishes.

famous bridge. It spans the Tsemistskali river, which is more than 200 feet down at the bottom of the gorge. It must have been really tough to build, but it was completed on time, apparently, in 1902, and was designed and built by none other than Gustave Eiffel, who built both the Eiffel Tower in Paris and the Statue of Liberty in New York. The rivets on the Tsemistskali bridge are apparently very special and personalised and were also used on the Eiffel Tower. I have to say, although I absolutely love his more famous work, this particular bridge was a bit of a let-down. Not very impressive at all and some of the bars at the side were distinctly weak and wobbly.

As we got higher, I realised why it took four years to complete what is quite a short bit of railway line. The terrain is really tough, with very hard rock – mainly volcanic with a lot of very steep terrifying looking ravines – and it is a tribute to the builders and engineers that nobody was killed in its construction.

When we got to Bakuriani, I had to get straight into a four-by-four and drive down some pretty savage mountain dirt tracks for my next appointment, about 30 miles away, with a very bright young lady called Sophio Khidesheli. She is a senior engineer with Georgian Railways, who promised to show me a very significant tunnel that, apparently, was a big part of the early Transcaucasian railway.

We met at the side of yet another strangely shaped locomotive, except this was purely for mountain maintenance: a large, bright yellow, very Soviet-looking machine that had been used for rescuing trains in trouble throughout the seasons for many years. We climbed on, the driver gave me a friendly Georgian grunt and we made our way into the tunnel.

The Tsipa tunnel is approximately three miles long and was built between 1886 and 1890, when it was the longest tunnel in the Russian Empire. It took only four years and is a mighty construction. Considering they only had shovels, picks and dynamite, the fact this it's still standing now almost 130 years later and is able to handle the heavy traffic of a modern railway system is impressive, particularly when you consider that cement hadn't been invented and the rocks at the side and roof of this great tunnel were glued together with egg yolk, I swear. And however many chickens were required?

I followed Sophio and her torch into the tunnel; it became increasingly cold, but she became very excited, because there was something on one of the walls she wanted to show me. When we got to the spot, she positively squealed and, flashing her torch up at the wall, she revealed a big, square stone covered in Russian words, symbols and numbers. 'Great,' I said. 'It's a safe, there's five million lari in there; we can go halves and never need to work again.'

Looking at me as if I was clearly mad, which does tend to happen a lot, she said, 'No, this is the point where the two teams working end to end came together.' Considering one team came from the west and one team came from the east and that they must have been working through different degrees of rock, problems with flowing springs, landslides etc., it's amazing that, when they finally made the breakthrough, both crews were almost exactly the same distance from daylight.

Russia
Akhmeta
Lagodekhi

Above left: The Tsipa tunnel cost a hundred lives but is still in daily use.

Above right: Georgian Railways engineer Sophio Khidesheli showed me how the Tsipa tunnel was made.

END OF THE LINE

The tunnel was great, but the drive back to our hotel was horrendous. It must have been the most relentless and scary dirt track I had ever driven on: for about an hour and a half, we were squealing around the corners in the four-by-four and looking down sheer drops on either side. We got into our hotel in a town called Kutaisi and the 'Pheasant' started weeping again…

So, our last morning and, for Jeff, Mike, JT, Jake and I, it was all a bit strange. It hadn't been the same crew for all of the shoots, but we had done most of them together and we'd certainly come through a lot. We were demob happy and looking forward to finishing, having a good drink, a mountain of Georgian food and going home, but we were all rather sad that we probably wouldn't be doing it again. Jeff even treated us to a rare lie-in and we didn't get to the platform that morning till 8.15 am – practically sunset. We were riding from Kutaisi to Ureki and from there to my final destination: the Black Sea port of Batumi.

We boarded a freight train and it was a little bit tricky at first, as I wasn't really feeling the love from the driver and crew. I suspect nobody warned them that a big, gangling fool from England with a film crew was going to turn up and then there was the problem that they spoke absolutely no English and I spoke even less Georgian. Our train was around half a mile long and, eventually, I somehow winkled out of them that the large number of very big containers that we were dragging came from Baku. I've been in longer trains but not one with an entire cargo of crude oil. We had two locomotives pulling a huge weight that was almost certainly worth millions of dollars.

The braking distance was more than a mile because, if the train did have to stop suddenly, the sloshing of the oil would throw a huge extra tonnage forwards… The load was hugely flammable and while nobody smoked I was still very aware that we were towing a potential fireball. I was told that, statistically, if a train carrying this much oil exploded, it would be much more powerful than the atomic bomb that vaporised Hiroshima – how scary is that?

We didn't seem to be getting very far at all after the first mile or so and we stood in the very cramped cabin, getting in each other's way and, I suspect, getting on the Georgians' nerves. It turned out we had been diverted into a siding so that a more important train could go past on the main line. Most of the Transcaucasian railway has been double-tracked now for quite a while apart from, just our luck, this last section down to Batumi. It was the opposite to many other countries, like Canada, where freight is absolutely the number-one priority. It was a false economy as well, because freight, particularly Azerbaijani oil, provides the bulk of Georgian Railways' income and it's the reason why their fares are so wonderfully cheap.

We eventually moved off but we still needed to get to Batumi to get our flight home. I certainly didn't want to miss my plane after my recent aggro with the airline, although I suppose the only plus-point was that I would be flying home with only hand baggage.

We got into Ureki just in time and I was glad to get out of the rather cramped cabin and spread myself out in a nice passenger compartment. It was even nicer than I had dared hope. Our final train was one of four Swiss double-decker trains that Georgia had recently purchased. They looked great and inside they were magnificent; upstairs and downstairs were both wonderfully really quiet and absolutely spotless and they are the pride of Georgia's railways. They are a regular sight as they power through the Tsipa tunnel – how amazing, how forward-thinking were the tunnels engineers to have created something that would easily accommodate the height of a double-decker train 130 years later? And with a tunnel held together by egg yolk! In the words of Socrates, '*Mange tout*, Rodney, *mange tout*.'

And then, all too soon, it was over. We came into the seaside town of Batumi along the coastline with the sea calming and the sky clearing after a storm. It was a great journey and a fitting end to my first-ever experience of the Caucasus railways. We'd gone from the Caspian Sea to the Black Sea – a distance of more than 500 miles, of the most wildly differing terrain and a real mix of people. We'd had very few setbacks and it was a nice end to everything that we'd experienced over the past four years. It seemed a very long time since we'd waited patiently for the best part of a week for that very first train in the Congo.

We've had some brilliant times over the years and we also have had some really tough ones. In many of the more remote villages and stations that we got to, I expect they hadn't seen a white, European face for many years. But – give or take the odd flying bucket lid – the locals in most parts of the world had been pretty friendly.

We've seen some good railways, we've seen some great ones; we've seen some bad railways, we've seen some dreadful ones. Each was part of a quite incredible experience that I had been privileged to share with an exceptional bunch of men and women great at their jobs but, more importantly, really good mates.

In all our travels, we've covered 168,212 miles – that's nearly six times around the Earth. I've loved it, but no wonder I look absolutely knackered.

Tarrant's Top 20

Which country has the most impressive train?
It's got to be the bullet train in Japan.

What is the best train to travel on?
The Blue Train in South Africa – although Canada's *Rocky Mountaineer* and Australia's *Ghan* both provide wonderfully luxurious journeys.

What was the most dangerous journey?
The night train in Zimbabwe – the doors kept flying open, out onto the track. Not only that, but the doors that swung open the most seemed to be next to the bar, where several gentlemen were feeling no pain.

Where can you get the best on-board food?
Massive steaks, anywhere in Argentina – but also huge bowls of meat stew and giant meat platters in the Caucasus.

Which is the best drink?
Argentinean Malbec, but I also loved the Stellenbosch wines on the Blue Train in South Africa. Pheasant's Tears red wine in Tbilisi, Georgia, and ice-cold Siberian vodka. There was also delicious – and very strong – vodka jelly in Siberia.

Where did you have the worst food?
Cuba, without a doubt – although the Japanese Bento box was pretty grim, as was India's liver dhansak. Normally, I love curry but not that one. Yuk – God knows whose liver it was.

Where are the most punctual trains?
Easy – Japan.

...and the least punctual?
Even easier – Congo... their delay of five days, one hour and 55 minutes was never beaten.

Where was the best hotel?

The Victoria Falls hotel in Zimbabwe. It was so unexpectedly superb in such a poor country. I also loved the Banff hotel high in the Rocky Mountains and the Hilton Batumi, which had wonderful views of the Black Sea.

What was the worst hotel?

The Atahualpa, the one covered in tarpaulin that we thought was a building site in Ollagüe, Bolivia.

What was the scariest situation you found yourself in?

There were quite a few of those to choose from! I might go for the overnight train in Zimbabwe or maybe the terrifying drive down the mountain passes in Bolivia... and then there was breaking down in the pitch-dark in a tunnel in the Congo. No – none of those. Easily the most frightening moments were spent in a helicopter full of dynamite, caught in a raging blizzard in the Rocky Mountains.

Where was the coldest place you filmed?

In Bovanenkovo, Siberia. One night it dropped to minus-26 degrees Celsius. In deep midwinter, in the coal mines, the temperature can drop to minus-60 degrees Celsius. I can't even begin to imagine working in those conditions...

...and the hottest?

The Atacama desert in Bolivia. It was 40-plus degrees Celsius – and a really dry heat. The beer there was actually awful but, in that temperature, God, it tasted good.

What was your lowest moment?

Having the whole film of the first Bolivian trip stolen in São Paolo airport… that was just the blackest day.

Who has the cleanest trains?

The Japanese, of course. They were spotless – they even smelt nice, with lavender coming through the air-conditioning system.

...and the smelliest?

Cuba has the most disgusting toilets. Not only that, but our seats were next to them.

What place would you least want to go back to?

After reading this far, you might guess it would be Cuba; I love the Caribbean but it was just awful. Also, São Paolo – for obvious reasons.

Then there was the disgusting ruins of the old pumping station in Yevlakh, Azerbaijan. I'd never seen so much unhygienic rubbish in one confined space: piles of soiled nappies, mounds of dog and human faeces – the disease must be rampant. And Alice Springs, come to think of it, was such a letdown, and Mafikeng – what a dump!

...and the place you'd most love to visit again?

So many! Buenos Aires; in fact, the whole of Patagonia, Banff in Canada, Adelaide and Cape Town, South Africa. Sucre in Bolivia was such a beautiful city and then there was Tbilisi for its wonderful food, nightlife and music, and everywhere in Myanmar.

Which railway line was the worst?

The one through the middle of Burma; we all bounced so much we kept banging our heads on the carriage roof. Can you imagine commuting on that route twice a day, six days a week?

Where was the most beautiful setting?

Sorry, just too many to pick one… spring sunshine over the Rocky Mountains... the Matobo Hills, where they buried Cecil Rhodes, at sunset… and the salt flats at Uyuni in Bolivia. Seeing the sunrise over Victoria Falls, Zimbabwe, was probably the most beautiful sight I'll ever witness. We've been made welcome by so many people all around the world, who had never seen a European. We've been so very lucky to have experienced so much.